CSE

Statistics for GCSE

Helen Wright MA PhD

Pitman

PITMAN PUBLISHING
128 Long Acre, London WC2E 9AN

First published in Great Britain 1988

British Library Cataloguing in Publication Data

Wright, Helen
Statistics.
1. Mathematical statistics
I. Title
519.5 QA276.12

ISBN 0 273 02865 0

Printed and bound in Great Britain at The Bath Press, Avon

To my family

Contents

Preface

With the arrival of the GCSE examinations, the subject of Statistics has taken on greater importance. Firstly, every examining board now offers Statistics at GCSE level. Secondly, with the increased emphasis on practical investigations in many subjects, such as Geography and Biology, most pupils need to have some familiarity with statistical methods even though they may not be taking an examination in Statistics. This book aims to cover the topics in the Statistics syllabuses of the GCSE boards and at the same time provide a useful statistical reference book for all GCSE pupils and their teachers.

The subject material is broken down into 19 main topic areas. Within each of these chapters, there are further sub-divisions and plenty of exercises. Answers to the exercises are available to teachers and lecturers in a separate booklet obtainable from the publishers free of charge. Some pupils may need to study only the earlier sections of each chapter but those entering for the higher levels will usually need to complete the chapters. Teachers can decide whether they want to cover all the sections in a chapter in sequence or whether they wish to take just the early parts of some chapters before returning later in the course to the more advanced sections.

Chapter 19, Sources of statistics, is essentially a reference section and most of the practical exercises in that chapter can be undertaken once the basic ideas of charts and diagrams have been mastered in Chapter 6. Some teachers may wish to study some of Chapter 17, Probability, much earlier in the course. In fact, several of the practical exercises from Chapter 6 onwards are introducing the fundamental ideas of probability ready for the more formal approach in Chapter 17.

As well as exercises to give practice in the types of question that will appear on the final examination papers, suggestions for practical work have been included in every chapter. These practical exercises are an essential part of the course and are intended to be carried out alongside a study of the chapter. One aim is to develop the skills that pupils need in order to undertake investigations independently. Some practicals, therefore, involve surveys or experiments and students are encouraged to plan investigations thoroughly and to try to foresee any possible difficulties. Class discussion is to be welcomed as an important part of this process. A major emphasis in GCSE Statistics is to encourage pupils to look critically at statistical presentations in the press and on television, so other practicals concentrate on these areas.

I am grateful to the Controller of Her Majesty's Stationery Office for permission to use extracts from the Crown copyright publications: *Employ-*

ment Gazette, Monthly Digest of Statistics, Annual Abstract of Statistics, Social Trends, OPCS People in Britain Wall Chart No. 1.

Special thanks are due to my husband, Humphrey, who spent many hours word-processing the manuscript and without whose assistance the book would not have been completed to schedule. My son, Andrew, did some word-processing in the initial stages and my daughter, Elizabeth, helped with checking the typescript. Thanks must also go to my brother, John Reed, for useful discussions on betting odds.

Lastly, I acknowledge with gratitude my students over the past 20 years. Their reactions to practicals and lesson material have been extremely valuable in shaping the contents of this book.

1 Introduction

What is statistics?

You have been finding out about the world around you and the people in it since the day you were born. You have gained knowledge. You have stored it away in your brain and recalled it when needed. You have organised it and told others about it. You have used it to make decisions and to give opinions. In short, you have been doing what a statistician does. The knowledge and the facts that you have gathered are termed data.

Statistics as a subject deals with the collection of data and their analysis, presentation and interpretation. We want to use the best ways to go about these tasks so that we obtain information as quickly, cheaply and effectively as possible. Information is the name given to data that have been organised in some way.

Governments, local authorities, companies and other organisations, as well as individuals, need to collect and use data. Political parties want to know the results of electoral opinion polls, television authorities want to know how many people watch their programmes, HM Treasury wants to know the state of the economy, companies want to know their trading positions, trade unions want to know how much prices have risen before submitting wage claims, the Department of Health and Social Security wants to know numbers of people suffering from particular illnesses, local authorities want to know the risks of failure of essential power and water supplies, manufacturers and consumers want to know whether goods are of the desired quality and how long they are likely to last, drug manufacturers want to test new products to see whether they are effective and safe, ... the list is endless. All need to have facts available so that they have records of past performance and present positions. These can be used to forecast future happenings or to help in making decisions about different options.

Exercise 1.1

For one week keep a notebook with you and record briefly any reference to statistics on television or radio and in any newspapers, magazines or journals that you read.

Terminology

Statistical investigations can be classified either as **surveys** or as **experiments**. In a survey we find out about objects and people as they are, without trying to alter or control them in any way. In an experiment we deliberately set up a controlled situation concentrating on those relationships and changes that we feel are important.

If we collect all the data about a particular situation, we have complete information and we know all about a **population**. Population is the word used by statisticians to denote the set of all possible measurements or observations that might be of interest. (You will find in your study of statistics that many terms used have different meanings in everyday life.) If we gather data for a whole population, we are conducting a **census**.

Often we collect data only from part of a population. This is called **sampling** and we obtain partial knowledge of the population. Probability theory helps us to state how reliable are the conclusions or **inferences** that we make about the population from the sample. Sampling is fundamental to statistical methods.

The word 'statistics' originally meant facts about the state but it now refers to data on any topic. In the singular a **statistic** refers to a single numerical fact found from a sample. The corresponding value for a population is called a **parameter** of the population. Suppose, for example, that there are 741 boys in a school of 1500 pupils. In a sample of 10 pupils from this school, it was noted that there were 4 boys. We can work out:

$$\text{proportion of boys in the population (the school)} = \frac{741}{1500} = 0.494 \quad \text{(a parameter)}$$

$$\text{proportion of boys in the sample} = \frac{4}{10} = 0.4 \quad \text{(a statistic)}$$

If we take many different samples of 10 pupils, the value of the statistic will change from sample to sample, as we are unlikely to have exactly 4 boys in every sample.

Exercise 1.2

Put 50 red tiddleywinks and 30 yellow tiddleywinks into a brown paper bag. What is the proportion of yellow tiddleywinks in this population? Mix the tiddleywinks well and take a sample of 10 tiddleywinks from the bag. Count the number of yellow ones. What is the proportion of yellow ones in this sample? Return the tiddleywinks to the bag and repeat this sampling procedure until you have results from 20 samples in all. What is the smallest value you found for the sample proportion? What is the largest value you found for the sample proportion? What are the largest and smallest values that it is possible for this sample statistic to be? What is the most common value you found for the sample statistic? Is this close to the population parameter?

More about sampling

You might think that a census is always the best way of collecting data. This is not true for several reasons:

(a) it can be too expensive or take too much time, particularly if the population to be covered is large or scattered;

(b) it may be impossible—for example, a manufacturer of torch batteries cannot test all his production to see how long they last because he would have none left to sell;

(c) a more thorough and carefully controlled investigation can be made if data have to be gathered from only a relatively small number of people or objects.

Provided the sample is chosen in a suitable way, we can estimate an unknown parameter of the population to any desired precision, provided the sample is large enough. To do this the sample must be a **random** sample. Random does not mean haphazard. A random sample of a given size is one where every subset of that size has the same chance of being selected. In Exercise 1.2, every group of ten tiddleywinks in the bag must have the same chance of being the sample if we are making a random selection. Assuming we mixed up the tiddleywinks well, we should get random samples but it can be difficult to set up a random sampling procedure.

If you want to take a random sample of five people from a group of 50, you can use what is called the 'lottery' method. Get 50 pieces of paper of the same size and put one name on each piece. Mix up the pieces of paper and choose five. The people whose names are on these papers are the sample. In this example and in Exercise 1.2, we sampled without replacement, i.e. we did not allow any item in the population to appear more than once in the same sample. This is often the way that sampling of human populations is carried out in practice.

To sample with replacement, mix up the 50 pieces of paper and take out just one, note down the name on it and then return it to the others. Repeat this procedure another four times. The five names this time might not all be different. The theory of sampling with replacement is easier to work out. ERNIE, the equipment that selects Premium Bond winners each month, samples with replacement so, in theory, a single bond could win more than one prize in the same month.

Exercise 1.3

1 Repeat Exercise 1.2 but this time sample with replacement. Did you obtain similar values for the sample proportions?

2 Choose a random sample of five different BBC1 television programmes from today's schedule. In what ways do you think your sample is (a) representative, (b) unrepresentative, of all today's BBC1 programmes?

About your course

When you have collected data, you need to sort them out, look at them, summarise them and then make decisions or give judgements. This course will show you efficient ways of doing all these tasks.

You will need to construct tables, graphs and charts, make calculations and summarise your findings in words. Most of the calculations involve addition, subtraction, multiplication or division. For more advanced work, you will need to be able to find squares and square roots. It is convenient to use algebraic formulae to summarise more complicated procedures.

As well as processing your own data, you will need to be able to understand the tables and diagrams that accompany articles in the press or discussions on television. In particular, you need to recognise when they are misleading.

When you are working with statistics, always have a calculator, squared paper and a ruler to hand. For some charts, a pair of compasses and a protractor are also needed. Access to a microcomputer may be useful in your course, especially if you undertake a large-scale project.

Get into the habit of setting work out in a neat and orderly way. It is a good idea to put dates and headings on all your work so that you can refer to it easily. Try to check your work at every stage. Use your common sense to alert you when results seem odd or unusual. You might have made a new discovery but it is more likely that you have made some mistake in your calculations or reasoning.

Exercise 1.4

Keep a scrapbook for one term. Collect graphs, charts and tables of numerical data from newspapers and magazines. Comment by each one whether you think it is well constructed and easy to understand.

2 Preliminaries to data collection

Definition of the problem

As you start a statistical investigation, there are several important points to consider. Careful planning can save much time and effort.

Often you have just a vague idea of what you want to know, for example, you might have been asked to find out attitudes to the possible introduction of continental-day timetabling at your school. Before you can collect the data, you must decide exactly what you want to know. You might want to discover whether people are definitely in favour, definitely against or not bothered. You might want to find out whether people are uncertain in their views. Attitudes might depend, for example, on

- the proposed length of the school day;
- whether the school is to be used for community purposes at the end of the school day;
- whether school lunches will be provided;
- whether all schools in the area adopt the same hours.

You must decide at the outset what is the main objective of the investigation. It is a good idea to list all the factors that you think might have an influence and then you decide which of them you are able to consider.

Scope of the investigation

You have to decide also how wide your investigation is going to be. In our example, concerning the possible change to continental days, will the survey cover just schoolchildren and staff? Are parents' views to be considered? Are there any other opinions that might be important, such as those of the bus company that provides transport to and from school? You must try to ensure that your investigation is complete and that no important aspects are neglected.

Types of variable

When we record data from the different elements making up a sample or population, we are classifying or measuring each element in some way. The data we collect are either **qualitative** or **quantitative**. Qualitative variables are defined by some name or description in words, whereas quantitative variables are measured on a numerical scale.

Some of the ways we could characterise an adult, for example, are

country of birth	*qualitative*
first language	*qualitative*
smoker or non-smoker	*qualitative*
voting intention at next general election	*qualitative*
number of brothers and sisters	*quantitative*
UK shoe size	*quantitative*
height	*quantitative*
weight	*quantitative*
body temperature	*quantitative*

Quantitative data can be considered as either **discrete** or **continuous**. A discrete variable is restricted to taking only certain specific values, whereas a continuous variable can take any value within a given range. 'Number of brothers and sisters' is a discrete variable because it can take only whole number values 0, 1, 2 ... 'UK shoe size' is also discrete as it is restricted to values such as ... 5, $5\frac{1}{2}$, 6, $6\frac{1}{2}$, 7, $7\frac{1}{2}$, 8 ... There is a distinct gap between one value a discrete variable takes and the next.

The remaining quantitative variables listed above are continuous. A person's height is not restricted to being a whole number of centimetres. In theory, we can measure height to any desired degree of precision but, in practice, we are limited by our measuring apparatus. Thus, we might choose to record someone's height to the nearest centimetre. That is our choice but we are not implying that the true value of the height is an exact whole number of centimetres.

Exercise 2.1

1 Which of the following are qualitative variables and which are quantitative variables:
   (a) favourite song of a teenager;
   (b) height of a sunflower;
   (c) number of prickles on a holly leaf;
   (d) area of a piece of carpet;
   (e) price of a share on the Stock Exchange;
   (f) marital status of an adult;
   (g) type of material from which a street-lamp standard is made?

2 State which of the following are discrete variables and which are continuous variables:
(a) number of petals on a flower;
(b) number of pupils in attendance at a school each day;
(c) shirt collar size as given on the label;
(d) weight of a chicken;
(e) volume of fruit juice in a carton;
(f) amount of wool needed to knit a sweater;
(g) population of Wales.

Scales of measurement

Once you know which variables are of interest, you need to decide what type of measurement is possible. There are several different scales of measurement and they are distinguished by the way in which the unit of measurement and the zero of the scale can be defined.

Integer scale

An integer scale is associated with counting. A variable such as 'number of brothers and sisters' would be measured on an integer scale. The zero and the unit are automatically fixed by the nature of counting. In our example, zero corresponds to no brothers and sisters and each unit added corresponds to one extra brother and sister.

Ratio scale

The integer scale is a special case of a ratio scale. Physical measurements such as lengths and weights are measured on a ratio scale. The zero of a ratio scale is an inherent characteristic, for example, a line of no length corresponds to zero on the scale whatever the actual units of measurement. The unit of measurement is defined by reference to some standard length. It could be an inch or a centimetre, for example, but any measurements in one unit can be converted to measurements in another unit by multiplying by a constant amount. To convert from inches to centimetres we multiply by 2.54.

A length of 66 cm is twice as long as a length of 33 cm so we can compare the ratio of two lengths whatever the units and we will obtain the same answer. A unit increase in length from 66 cm to 67 cm is exactly the same physical amount as an increase in length from 70 cm to 71 cm and we say that a ratio scale has the property that equal intervals are equivalent.

Interval scale

There are scales where equal intervals are equivalent but where the zero of the scale can be arbitrarily defined. This means that the measurements using one set of units are not constant multiples of measurements using a different unit. In this case we have an interval scale. A familiar example of interval scales is temperature measurement in degrees Celsius and degrees Fahrenheit. Although both scales are defined in terms of the freezing point and boiling point of water under standard conditions, the zeros as well as the units are different. We cannot say that a temperature of 30°C is twice as hot as 15°C but it is correct to say that a temperature of 30°C is 5°C hotter than 25°C, which in turn is 5°C hotter than 20°C.

Rank scale

On occasions it may be possible only to put observations in some order. A consumer may be asked to taste eight spreads to put on bread. The consumer has to rank them in order of preference giving rank 1 to that liked most, rank 2 to that liked second best and continuing so that the one liked least is ranked 8. The results might be:

Spread	A	B	C	D	E	F	G	H
Ranking	3	2	4	1	7	6	5	8

There is an order in this scale ranging from 1 for that liked most, to 8 for that liked least but there is no unit of measurement, so equal intervals are not equivalent. The consumer might have had great difficulty in deciding a preference between D and B, which are given ranks 1 and 2, but might have had no doubts at all that B was much preferable to A, which was ranked 3. Thus the difference between ranks 1 and 2 does not measure the same degree of difference as between ranks 2 and 3. A rank scale is sometimes called an **ordinal** scale. It does not have a zero. Any situation where we can assign observations to categories that have some natural order is capable of being measured on a rank scale.

Nominal scale

If we assign observations to categories that have no natural order, we are using a nominal scale of measurement. The variable 'country of birth' would be measured on this type of scale. It is not numerical in any way and has no unit and no zero.

Choice of scale

It may be possible to measure a variable using more than one type of measurement scale. You must decide what is appropriate for your investigation. A multiple choice examination containing 50 questions could be marked on an integer scale $0, 1, 2 \ldots 50$ questions correct. Alternatively the results could be listed on a rank scale from grade A, the highest, through grades B, C, D and E to the lowest grade F. In some situations the simple scale 'pass' or 'fail' might be used. In general we get least information from a nominal scale and most from an interval or a ratio scale.

Exercise 2.2

1 What type of scale would you use for each of the following measurements?
(a) daily number of absentees from your school;
(b) times taken for 15-year olds to run 100m;
(c) annual salaries of 2000 employees, worldwide, in a multinational company;
(d) goals scored in a football match;
(e) 'beauty' for entrants in a beauty queen contest;
(f) marital status of an adult;
(g) intelligence of a schoolchild;
(h) wind strength.

2 Convert the following measurements to the units stated, using the information that

1 inch = 2.54 cm   1 kg = 2.2 lbs   £1 = \$1.60   £1 = 2.45 Swiss francs
Water boils at 100°C and 212°F.   Water freezes at 0°C and 32°F.

(a) 11 inches to centimetres;
(b) 84 cm^2 to square inches;
(c) 92 kg to pounds weight;
(d) \$1500 to pounds sterling;
(e) £250 to Swiss francs;
(f) 40°F to degrees Celsius.

3 Consider ten sports or games. What types of scale of measurements are used to measure performance in each of them? (More than one scale may be used at different stages, e.g. at tennis you should consider game, set and match.)

Definitions of terms and units

Some variables can be measured in different ways. The output of a bakery could be measured by weight, by the number of loaves and cakes produced or by value. Any terms used must be clearly defined. This is not always easy. In official statistics, for example, great care is taken to define terms such as 'unemployed' and 'a household', but the definitions can be changed from time to time by legislation or at the wish of the government.

You should specify what units of measurements are to be used for variables such as lengths and weights. You can convert from one set of units to another but it is much easier if the units are the same from the outset. Although metric units such as centimetres and kilograms are generally preferred nowadays, there are instances where imperial units, such as inches and pounds weight, are used, even for official purposes.

You should decide what degree of precision is appropriate for your measurements. For example, state if you want a person's age in years and months or just years. The precision you can achieve may depend on the apparatus you are to use. With a ruler, for example, you can only measure to the nearest millimetre.

Resources

At an early stage you must consider what resources are available to you. Time, money and labour are the three main restrictions and they are interdependent. Their availability may affect whether you use a census or a sampling method, how large a sample you choose, what apparatus you can use. Is anyone going to help you collect and process the data? Are you going to have access to photocopying or typing facilities and, if so, at what cost? Can you make use of standard computer programs to process your data? Does this affect the way you plan to collect the data?

If you use a census method, you will obtain complete information, in theory. If you use a sampling approach, you must also decide what **precision** you want in your final estimate. Do you want to know the percentage in favour of a proposal to within 5% or to within 1%? To obtain a more precise estimate you have to take a larger sample. This problem will be considered further in Chapter 13.

If you are unable to collect all your data in a reasonable length of time, circumstances may change and comparisons will not be valid. Always try to ensure **uniformity** of your data. Wages data, for example, should be collected within a month at most, otherwise, pay increases may affect the later data you collect.

Try to ensure that you are going to be able to make valid comparisons. You may need to divide your investigation into comparable or **homogeneous** parts. If you wanted to compare the weights of 15-year olds at one co-educational school with those at another, it would be better to split the pupils into boys and girls and consider each group separately. This is because it seems likely that there will be more weight difference between the sexes than between the schools. If you wanted to compare the distances these 15-year olds travel to school, however, there would seem to be no need to consider the sexes separately.

It is a good idea to plan out a timetable for any investigation to make sure it is possible to achieve all you want with the resources available. First put general headings such as preliminary planning, data collection, data analysis, writing-up the results, and then detail the resources you think you will require at each stage.

Class exercise 2.3

You have decided to conduct a survey to try to find out about the ages of cars in the staff car park at your school or college.

Discuss how best to organise this survey. You should consider the following points:

(a) Which cars are to be included in the survey?
(b) When are you going to conduct the survey?
(c) How are you going to find out the age of each car?
(d) What units of measurement are you going to use?
(e) With what precision are you going to record the ages?
(f) Can you do this survey on your own or are several people needed?
(g) How are you going to record your findings?
(h) Are there any difficulties you foresee?

How would you modify your planning if you wanted to carry out similar surveys to find out about the ages of cars in (i) the car park of a large factory near your school and (ii) the car park of a local supermarket?

3 Methods of data collection

Personal investigation and delegated personal investigation

There are several ways of collecting data in a statistical investigation. It is important to select a method that is efficient. It is necessary to ensure that all the information that we require can be obtained from the data and that we keep within any time and cost restrictions. If an investigation takes too long, conditions may have changed. If we plan too large or too detailed an investigation, we may run out of funds and time halfway through the project.

If a small-scale project is to be undertaken, one person may be able to collect all the data. Such **personal investigation** has the advantages that

(a) the researcher knows the purpose of the survey and is keen to obtain full results in a suitable form for later analysis;

(b) the data will be likely to be collected in the same way throughout the investigation.

The disadvantages are that

(a) the personal bias of the investigator may influence the way questions are asked or measurements made, particularly if the investigator has strong ideas on what the results might be;

(b) the investigator can be in only one place at any one time so this is a limitation on the types of project that can be undertaken.

In a **delegated personal investigation**, one person is in charge of the overall planning, design and analysis of the investigation but the collection of data is delegated to a group of people.

The advantages are that

(a) data can be collected more quickly and hence larger-scale investigations are possible;

(b) data can be collected at the same time in different places.

The disadvantages are that

(a) the personal bias of each member of the team may affect the data he/she collects;

(b) the leader cannot be certain that the data have been collected in the desired way and it is harder to control the data collection;

(c) the team may not be as interested in the project as the leader and so may not be as keen to complete the data collection;

(d) if the investigators have to be paid, this will be more expensive than a personal investigation.

The disadvantages can be minimised by

(a) full briefing of the team, explaining exactly what data are to be collected and in what form; the leader giving reasons why the information is wanted and trying to make the team enthusiastic about the project;

(b) ensuring that each member of the team is not solely responsible for one area of the investigation. For example, if the project involves interviewing both girls and boys, one person should not do the boys and one the girls but both interviewers should question some boys and some girls. Otherwise, we cannot tell whether differences in the data collected arise from differences between the interviewers rather than differences between the children.

Exercise 3.1

Try to think of two investigations, connected with home, school or the local neighbourhood, that you are confident that you could complete by yourself. Think of two other investigations, that would need a small team of investigators. If you are going to be the leader of the team, how would you delegate the work? Give reasons.

Direct measurement and direct observation

Many investigations involve measurement or counting. Scientific experiments and biological surveys are often of this type. It is important to ensure that any apparatus or equipment is in good working order and that it has been checked for accuracy before use. If an experiment involves weighing, for example, then the balance should be correctly set by test weighing an object of known weight. Alternatively, if you are not sure that the zero of the scale is correctly set, it might be a good idea to weigh by difference, i.e. to weigh a container empty and then weigh it plus contents. The weight of the contents is given by the difference between the two recorded weights.

Preferably, measurements should be repeated under as near identical conditions as possible. This enables better estimates to be made. In a series of measurements, perhaps at different temperatures, try not to repeat the measurements in the same order. This is not always practicable as it might take far too long to keep waiting for an object to heat up and to cool down.

Some types of investigation involve observation of the behaviour of people or animals. It may be important that they do not know they are being observed since their behaviour might change. One large organisation monitored the telephone calls of its employees by recording the numbers dialled and the length of the calls. It did this for one month without telling the employees. It then informed employees that the calls were being monitored. In the next month, both the number and the length of the calls were reduced dramatically.

Exercise 3.2

1 A shop assistant weighs out coleslaw at the delicatessen counter of a local supermarket. She puts an empty container on the balance and sets the scale to zero. She then places a container holding coleslaw on the balance and removes the empty container. She adjusts the amount of coleslaw until the scale reads the quantity requested by the

customer. What is assumed by using this procedure? Do you think it is a reasonable assumption?

2 A researcher has to carry out the measurement at each of six different temperatures and wants to do them in random order. Suggest how a six-sided die could be used to decide on the order of the measurements.

3 Give two examples where your behaviour might change if you knew you were being observed.

Interviews

If an investigation involves a survey of personal opinions or habits, then it may be necessary to interview people to collect the data. This method can be expensive if paid interviewers are used or if a wide geographical area has to be covered. It is time-consuming because it is difficult to obtain useful information if people are rushed into giving answers.

Interviews are commonly used in market research and opinion research. Many professional interviewers carry identity cards to introduce themselves to members of the public. This encourages people to answer the questions freely.

An interviewer should be pleasant and should put the respondent at ease by explaining why the information is needed. The questions should be asked in a clear voice and in a logical order. If an answer seems as though it may not be correct, for example, a person may lie about his age, then the interviewer can make a visual check and note down a query on the answer sheet. If a person does not appear to understand the question, then the interviewer may give some further explanation but it is important that the interviewer should not influence the answers in any way. The interviewer should be impartial and should not show any reaction to the answers given. If a team of interviewers is used, they should each be instructed to ask the questions in the same way and to be careful to record the answers in the desired format.

People are usually willing to answer only a few simple questions when stopped in the street but, if it is possible to arrange for an interview at home, then longer interviews asking more detailed questions can be conducted. This is useful if the respondents need to refer to records, for example, to find out how much they spent on electricity in the past year. Personal interviewing usually has a good response rate, i.e. only a small proportion of people fail to reply.

Use of the telephone interview is growing in the UK and is widely used in the USA where a larger percentage of households have a telephone. It can be difficult to get people to answer questions over the telephone because they resent the invasion of their privacy, they have no way of checking the credentials of the person asking the question and they may not wish to disclose personal information, for example, voting intentions, if they live in a sensitive neighbourhood. The telephone method has achieved success, however, in getting a quick audience response to television programmes. Although it is easier for an interviewer to ring people up rather than to visit them at their homes, it is harder to ensure that questions are being answered honestly as there are no visual checks.

Exercise 3.3

'Please say what television programmes you watched yesterday evening and state what time you went to bed.'

You are asked to do this by (a) a researcher working for a television company, (b) your best friend, (c) a teacher at school, (d) a policeman. Would you give the same answers in every case? Discuss why you might not always give truthful answers.

Questionnaires

An alternative method of obtaining data from people is to use a questionnaire, i.e. a printed or typed list of questions on which the answers are to be put. This can be sent by post for a large scale survey or given out by hand for a local survey. The respondent fills in the form without any help from the investigator so, as a rule, only straightforward questions should be asked.

A postal questionnaire has many advantages;

(a) questionnaires can be distributed over a large area;

(b) uniformity, i.e. every person is asked the same questions in the same format at the same time;

(c) no interviewer costs, although there are the costs of printing and distributing the questionnaire;

(d) people can refer to records and not rely on memory.

The disadvantages are:

(a) low response rates as people may throw the questionnaire away and not bother to reply;

(b) responses may be received only from people who want to express strong views either for or against the subject of the enquiry;

(c) there is no one to explain any questions that are not understood.

To overcome these problems, clear instructions should be given and it is important to stress the reasons for the questionnaire, so as to encourage people to respond. If possible, a reply-paid envelope should be provided. Many official data are collected by post, for instance, income tax returns and electoral registration forms, but these have legal backing to ensure that they are returned.

Design of questions and questionnaires

In any survey, whether by interview or by questionnaire, great care has to be taken to ensure that the questions are phrased in a suitable way. The layout of a questionnaire is also important. The following guidelines are suggested:

(a) the questionnaire should be as short as possible but you must be able to get all the information you need from the questions asked;

(b) questions should be clear and concise; questions requiring simple answers, such as Yes, No or a number, are best;

(c) ensure that the questionnaire is clearly laid out and that there is enough space for people to write in their answers;

(d) questions should not use technical terms nor words that may not be understood;

(e) avoid leading questions, i.e. questions that may steer a respondent towards a particular answer. For instance, 'Do you agree that Brand X frozen peas are better than Brand Y frozen peas?' is a question that leads towards the answer 'Yes'. People tend to try to agree with a question rather than disagree.

(f) avoid questions that may be offensive or too personal, on grounds of race, religion, personal habits or health;

(g) avoid questions relying on memory or requiring calculation;

(h) try to include questions that provide checks, for example, ask for age last birthday as well as date of birth, since many people write down the current year instead of the year of their birth;

(i) it is often helpful to use a multiple-choice format where the respondent has to mark the appropriate box. This may encourage a suitable response, for example, a worker may not want to give his exact age but will state that he is between 45 and 59 years old as follows:
Please indicate age last birthday

under 18	18–24	25–34	35–44	45–59	60 and over
☐	☐	☐	☐	☐	☐

This type of question helps in processing the data because everyone is placed in just one of six categories. Categories must not overlap and everyone should be able to decide which category is appropriate. In some situations it is useful to have a category 'Other, please specify' to make sure every possible option has been covered.

(j) avoid questions that are biased, such as ones that express a point of view. The question 'Why do you think Brand X frozen peas are better than Brand Y frozen peas?' starts from the assumption that Brand X *is* better than Brand Y.

(k) try to test the questionnaire in a **pilot survey**, i.e. a small preliminary survey, and then modify any questions, instructions or design problems before the main survey.

Exercise 3.4

1 In a survey of household expenditure, the following questions were asked. Criticise them, where appropriate, and say how each might be better phrased.

(a) How old are you?
(b) How much do you spend each week on food?
(c) Which brand of tomato ketchup do you buy?
(d) What household detergent do you use?
(e) Do you prefer Heinz Baked Beans to a supermarket's own brand?
(f) Does anyone in your household make a habit of smoking?
(g) Do you have an illness requiring a special diet?
(h) Do you agree that prices have risen because of the policies of the present government?
(i) Indicate how often you serve cheese to your family:
Two or three times a week;
Once a week;
Once a month;
Never.
(j) What is your primary reason for shopping at Ocset's supermarket?

Convenience	Cheapness	Variety of goods
☐	☐	☐

2 You are trying to conduct a survey on computer games by interviewing people in your school. You want to know what computer games each person has played in the past three months, what computer they used for each game and how much they enjoyed playing each game.

Write down a list of the questions you would ask and decide how you will record the answers. Carry out a few interviews and see whether you need to alter any of the questions and the way in which you record the answers.

3 You want to find out whether the most popular television programmes as shown in the press each week, for BBC1, BBC2, ITV and Channel 4, are the same as the television programmes most popular with pupils in your school. Design a suitable questionnaire and test it out on a few people. Are there any problems? Make improvements to your questionnaire if possible.

Secondary data

It is expensive to collect data, whatever method is used, and it may be that the data you need have already been collected by someone else. If you are able to use their data, it will save much time and effort.

Data that have been collected by someone else for some other purpose are referred to as **secondary** data. You must take care that the definitions and units are as you require and that the data have been collected reliably. Data gathered by the Central Statistical Office and government departments are particularly useful. Some of the main official publications are described in Chapter 19. They are usually available in good reference libraries.

Books and newspapers can be suitable sources but books may be out-of-date and newspapers may be selective in their coverage, especially if they are trying to put forward a particular point of view. Company reports and accounts published annually are reliable sources as they have been scrutinised by auditors. Public companies will send copies of their reports on request.

For historical information, records may be more reliable than memory. For example, if you want to investigate whether the numbers of absences of GCSE pupils in the past five years are related to their final grades in GCSE mathematics, the pupils concerned will have forgotten how many times they have been absent. It will be much better to refer back to the attendance registers where the absences were recorded at the time.

Computer storage of data is increasing but it may be expensive to gain access. British Telecom's PRESTEL system, for example, is now available in many schools, colleges and libraries. This provides up-to-date details of many commercial and government data.

Exercise 3.5

Try to obtain the following data from suitable sources

(a) the total number of pupils registered to attend your school this term;

(b) the number of births and deaths in your local area in one week last month;

(c) the total rainfall in England and Wales last year;

(d) the amount spent on education by your local education authority in the last financial year;

(e) the share price on the London Stock Exchange last Friday of a large public company;

(f) official figures for the number of people unemployed last month in your area;

(g) the trading profit of a large public company last year.

Class exercise 3.6

1 Your class is considering setting up a weather station at your school. What measurements would you make? What apparatus and equipment is needed? How can you find out about the cost? Where will it be sited? How often are you going to make measurements? Is one person going to be in charge of all measurements? If you decide to use a team to record the results, what instructions would you give them? Where is the nearest weather station to your school? Are the data from that station available to you? Do you think it might be better to use data from that station?

2 The Head of your school is concerned about the litter in the grounds and asks your class to report on the problem. The Head wants to know

- what types of litter are dropped;
- when litter is dropped;
- who drops litter;
- why litter is dropped;
- what to do to prevent litter being dropped.

Discuss how you might obtain this information and the difficulties you foresee.

4 Approximation and errors

Rounding

Sometimes we need to record numbers or quantities exactly. If you have a savings account, the money you pay in and the money you draw out are recorded in pounds and pence. When the Chancellor of the Exchequer presents the Budget for the UK, he does not give his money figures in pounds and pence. He is concerned with such large sums of money that it is irrelevant to consider the pence and he usually gives his figures in millions, or even billions, of pounds.

(In the UK, a billion used to be one million million, 1 000 000 000 000, but, nowadays the American billion which is one thousand million, 1 000 000 000, is more usual.)

The Chancellor uses **rounded** figures that are approximately correct but they are detailed enough for his purposes.

Rules for rounding

1 Round off at the end of a calculation. Do not round off in the middle of a calculation.
2 If the first digit in the group of decimal digits to be dropped is greater than or equal to 5, the last digit kept is increased by 1.
3 If the first digit in the group of decimal digits to be dropped is less than 5, the last digit kept remains unchanged.

Example

253 216.196 25	is
253 216	to the nearest whole number
253 216.2	to 1 decimal place or to the nearest tenth
253 216.20	to 2 decimal places
253 216.196	to 3 decimal places
253 216.196 3	to 4 decimal places
253 220	to the nearest ten
253 200	to the nearest hundred
253 000	to the nearest thousand

250 000 to the nearest ten thousand
300 000 to the nearest hundred thousand
Instead of 'to 1 decimal place', we can write 'to 1 dec. pl.'

Exercise 4.1

1 Round the following numbers:
(a) 2123 to the nearest thousand;
(b) 2 342.76 to the nearest whole number;
(c) 352.762 to 2 decimal places;
(d) 23 456 375 to the nearest million;
(e) 62 394 to the nearest hundred;
(f) 54.982 to 1 decimal place.

2 Round the following quantities:
(a) £27.32 to the nearest pound;
(b) £28 543.68 to the nearest thousand pounds;
(c) 33.94 cm to the nearest centimetre;
(d) 31.49 cm to the nearest millimetre;
(e) 125.78 kg to the nearest kg;
(f) £92 916 200 to the nearest million pounds.

Absolute error

The difference between an approximate value and the true value is called the absolute error.

$$\text{absolute error} = \text{approximate value} - \text{true value}$$

If the true value is greater than the approximate value, the error is negative. If the true value is less than the approximate value, the error is positive.

In statistics, an error is not the same thing as a mistake. A mistake is some incorrect procedure or calculation resulting in a wrong value. By careful checking, mistakes can be eliminated completely. An error, on the other hand, usually cannot be avoided or is acceptable because it simplifies the situation.

In an opinion poll, the results from a sample may be used to predict the proportions in the whole population that intend to vote for each political party. The results from the sample will not be exactly the same as would be obtained if the whole population were surveyed. The differences or errors cannot be avoided, however, unless a census rather than a sampling procedure is used.

When we make measurements, we have to decide what apparatus or equipment to use. An ordinary ruler will enable us to measure the dimensions of a piece of paper correct to the nearest millimetre. The largest difference or error between the true dimension and our measurement can be at most half a millimetre. At a medical examination, a doctor measures a person's height to the nearest centimetre, so the maximum possible error of measurement will be half a centimetre.

Exercise 4.2

1 Work out the absolute errors in your answers to Questions 1 and 2 of Exercise 4.1.

2 State the maximum possible error when
(a) a distance is measured to the nearest kilometre;
(b) a time is measured to the nearest minute;
(c) a weight is measured to the nearest gram.

3 Packets of biscuits were weighed correct to the nearest gram. Records show that there were 30 packets of biscuits with weights in the 196–200 g category. Write down the minimum and maximum possible weights of a packet in this category.

4 The scheduled departure times of flights from an airport during one half-hour period in the afternoon are:

14.00 14.07 14.12 14.17 14.25 14.30

Last Friday all the actual departure times, recorded to the nearest minute, were exactly the same as the scheduled times. Write down the minimum and the maximum intervals between actual departure times which could have occurred between 14.00 and 14.30 on that day.

Calculations with rounded numbers

When we use a number that has been rounded, we know it is approximate and, when we make calculations with such numbers, our final answers will be approximate. We need to be able to estimate the maximum possible error in our calculations. The procedure is to work out the maximum value of the answer and the minimum value of the answer.

Example

The Head of Zedbury School estimates his intake of new pupils next year will be 150 correct to the nearest 10. The Head of Wyebury School estimates her new intake as 180 correct to the nearest 20.

1 (Addition) Estimate the total number of new pupils next year in the two schools together.

Zedbury School

$$\text{maximum number of pupils} = 150 + 5 = 155$$
$$\text{minimum number of pupils} = 150 - 5 = 145$$

Wyebury School

$$\text{maximum number of pupils} = 180 + 10 = 190$$
$$\text{minimum number of pupils} = 180 - 10 = 170$$

Both schools

$$\text{maximum number of pupils} = 155 + 190 = 345$$
$$\text{minimum number of pupils} = 145 + 170 = 315$$

We give the answer as the value halfway between these extremes:

$$\frac{315 + 345}{2} = 330$$

The true value could be as much as 15 higher or 15 lower so the maximum possible error is 15. The answer can be written concisely as 330 ± 15.

To summarise:

$$(150 \pm 5) + (180 \pm 10) = 330 \pm 15$$

Note that the error in the sum (15) is equal to the sum of the errors (5 + 10).

2 (Subtraction) Estimate the difference between the numbers of new pupils in the two schools.

The maximum difference will occur if Wyebury School has its maximum possible intake and Zedbury School has its minimum possible intake.

$$\text{maximum difference} = 190 - 145 = 45$$

Similarly,

$$\text{minimum difference} = 170 - 155 = 15$$

$$\text{estimate of difference} = \frac{45 + 15}{2} = \frac{60}{2} = 30$$

$$\text{maximum possible error} = 15$$

To summarise:

$$(180 \pm 10) - (150 \pm 5) = 30 \pm 15$$

Note that the error in the difference (15) also equals the sum of the errors (5 + 10).

3 (Multiplication) The Head of Zedbury School has to order English textbooks for all the new intake. The textbooks are not yet published but the publisher estimates that they will cost £4.50 each, correct to the nearest 50 p. Estimate the total cost of the books.

$$\text{maximum cost per book} = £4.50 + £0.25 = £4.75$$

$$\text{minimum cost per book} = £4.50 - £0.25 = £4.25$$

$$\text{maximum total cost of books} = 155 \times £4.75 = £736.25$$

$$\text{minimum total cost of books} = 145 \times £4.25 = £616.25$$

$$\text{estimate of total cost} = \frac{£736.25 + £616.25}{2} = £676.25$$

$$\text{maximum possible error} = £60$$

To summarise:

$$(150 \pm 5) \times (£4.50 \pm £0.25) = £676.25 \pm £60$$

4 (Division) The Head of Wyebury School has been told that the PTA intends to use some of its funds to provide metal lockers for the new intake of pupils. The treasurer of the PTA estimates that there will be £2500 available, correct to the nearest £500. Estimate how much the Head will have per pupil to spend on lockers.

$$\text{maximum PTA funds} = £2500 + £250 = £2750$$

$$\text{minimum PTA funds} = £2500 - £250 = £2250$$

$$\text{maximum amount available per pupil} = \frac{\text{maximum PTA funds}}{\text{minimum number of pupils}}$$

$$= \frac{£2750}{170}$$

$$= £16.18 \text{ to nearest p}$$

$$\text{minimum amount available per pupil} = \frac{\text{minimum PTA funds}}{\text{maximum number of pupils}}$$

$$= \frac{£2250}{190}$$

$$= £11.84 \text{ to nearest p}$$

$$\text{estimate of funds per pupil} = \frac{£16.18 + £11.84}{2}$$

$$= £14.01$$

$$\text{maximum possible error} = £2.17$$

To summarise:

$$\frac{£(2500 \pm 250)}{(180 \pm 10)} = £14.01 \pm £2.17$$

Exercise 4.3

1 To follow an architect's plans, a rectangular garden for a house must be 35 m by 20 m, both measured to the nearest metre. Calculate (a) the maximum perimeter of the garden, (b) the minimum area enclosed correct to the nearest square metre, each of which would be consistent with the plans.

2 A motorist set out for home, a distance of 45 km, at 17.01. He arrived at 17.52. What is the maximum possible value of his average speed (distance travelled per hour)? The times are correct to the nearest minute and the distance is correct to the nearest kilometre.

3 In 1983 the total number of staff in the prison service was 27 000, correct to the nearest thousand. The prison population, was 51 000 correct to the nearest thousand. In 1961, the corresponding numbers were 18 000 and 33 000, respectively. Estimate the number of prisoners per member of staff in 1961 and in 1983. State the maximum possible errors in your estimates. Comment on your estimates.

Compensating and cumulative errors

Rounding down

It is common practice in some situations to round down. For instance, when you ask a person's age, they usually tell you just the completed number of years and they do not mention the months. Rounding down is also called truncation.

Rule for rounding down

The digits to be kept are left unchanged.

Example

16.23 = 16 rounded down to a whole number

16.95 = 16 rounded down to a whole number

Rounding up

Occasionally it is wise to round up, particularly when budgeting for estimated future expenditure so as to be certain of having sufficient funds. For example, if you are going on holiday abroad, you will probably take more foreign currency and travellers cheques than you think you will actually need, so as not to run out of money if unforeseen circumstances arise.

Rule for rounding up

The last digit to be kept is increased by 1.

Example

16.23 = 17 rounded up to a whole number

16.95 = 17 rounded up to a whole number

When we round to the nearest whole number the possible error is between −0.5 and 0.5, i.e. our approximate value could be at most 0.5 too low or 0.5 too high. When we truncate or round down to a whole number, the error is between −1 and 0, i.e. our approximate value will always be too low. When we round up to a whole number, the error is between 0 and 1, i.e. our approximate value will always be too high. Rounding to the nearest whole number tends to keep the error smaller in size.

When we add a series of rounded numbers, these facts become especially important, because, as we noted earlier, the error in the sum is the sum of the errors. If we round to the nearest number, positive and negative errors tend to cancel out in the sum and we say that the errors are **compensating** or **unbiased.** If we truncate or round up, the errors are all of the same sign, so, the more numbers we add, the larger the error in the sum. We say that these errors are **cumulative** or **biased**.

Exercise 4.4

My bill from a supermarket last Saturday was as follows:

Butter	0.54
Meat	2.46
Tea	0.69
Sardines	0.27
Coconut	0.29
Cereal	0.62
Milk	0.23
Sauce	0.36
	£5.46

(a) Round each price correct to the nearest 10 p and find the total of the rounded prices.

(b) Round down each price to the nearest 10 p below and find the total of the rounded prices.

(c) Round up each price to the nearest 10 p above and find the total of the rounded prices.

What is the absolute error in the total you have found in each of (a), (b), (c)? Comment on the values.

Significant figures

When we measure a length correct to the nearest millimetre, it is recorded as a whole number of millimetres, e.g. 63 mm. If we measure correct to the nearest tenth of a millimetre, we might find the length is 63.2 mm. If the length came to exactly 63 mm when we measured to the nearest tenth of a millimetre, we record it as 63.0 mm to show clearly the precision with which our measurements have been made. The accurate digits in a number are called the significant figures in the number. Zeros at the start of a number less than one are not counted as significant figures as they merely position the decimal point. In the example above, 63 mm is correct to 2 significant figures (2 sig. figs.) whereas 63.2 mm and 63.0 mm are correct to 3 significant figures.

Numbers arising from counting are exact so all their digits are accurate.

When you do calculations with numbers that are correct to a given number of significant figures, you must be careful to quote the final answer to the appropriate number of significant figures. Your calculator may show many digits but these are not all accurate. You can assess the appropriate number of significant figures using the same procedure we used for calculating with rounded numbers.

Example

Work out 1.31×2.52, giving the answer to the appropriate number of significant figures. Using a calculator, we get

$$1.31 \times 2.52 = 3.3012$$

1.31 and 2.52 are both given correct to 3 significant figures, so the maximum possible error in each is ± 0.005.

$$\text{maximum value of product} = 1.315 \times 2.525 = 3.320\,375$$

$$\text{minimum value of product} = 1.305 \times 2.515 = 3.282\,075$$

Since the product can be anywhere between these two extremes, we should write the answer as:

$$1.31 \times 2.52 = 3.3 \text{ correct to 2 sig. figs.}$$

The remaining digits given by the calculator are not accurate.

Exercise 4.5

1 Work out the following calculations, giving your answers to the appropriate number of significant figures.

(a) 2.3×4.2; (b) $\frac{6.0}{2.1}$; (c) 12.3 m + 17.12 m + 15 m; (d) 2.73 kg − 2.15 kg

2 A rectangle has sides measured to be of length 2.8 cm and 5.2 cm. Calculate, giving each answer to 1 decimal place, (a) the maximum possible perimeter of the rectangle and (b) the minimum possible area of the rectangle.

Relative error

An absolute error has the same units as the quantity being estimated or approximated. It is often convenient to express the absolute error as a proportion or as a percentage of the quantity being estimated. This is called the relative error and enables us to compare the precision of different measurements, regardless of their units.

$$\text{relative error} = \frac{\text{absolute error}}{\text{true value of quantity}}$$

$$\text{percentage error} = \frac{\text{absolute error}}{\text{true value of quantity}} \times 100\%$$

The true value of the quantity will not always be known so, if this is the case, we put:

$$\text{relative error} = \frac{\text{absolute error}}{\text{approximate value of quantity}}$$

$$\text{percentage error} = \frac{\text{absolute error}}{\text{approximate value of quantity}} \times 100\%$$

Example

	True value	Estimated value	Absolute error	Relative error	Percentage error
length A	118 mm	120 mm	2 mm	2/118 = 0.017	1.7
length B	8 mm	10 mm	2 mm	2/8 = 0.25	25

Although the absolute error has the same size for both A and B, the relative error in the estimated length of A is very much smaller than that for length B.

If you need to calculate with quantities containing relative errors, first work out the size of the absolute errors and then use the same procedure as for calculation with rounded numbers. Quote the final answer giving the maximum possible error in percentage form.

Example

A toy manufacturer makes wooden building cubes which are intended to be of height 4 cm. The machine that makes the cubes can make an error of up to 4% in cutting any dimension. Estimate the volume of one of the cubes and give the maximum percentage error in the estimate.

$$\begin{aligned}
\text{absolute error in height of cube} &= 4\% \text{ of } 4 \text{ cm} \\
&= \frac{4}{100} \times 4 \text{ cm} = 0.16 \text{ cm} \\
\text{maximum height of cube} &= 4.16 \text{ cm} \\
\text{minimum height of cube} &= 3.84 \text{ cm} \\
\text{maximum volume of cube} &= 4.16 \text{ cm} \times 4.16 \text{ cm} \times 4.16 \text{ cm} \\
&= 71.991\,296 \text{ cm}^3 \\
\text{minimum volume of cube} &= 56.623\,104 \text{ cm}^3 \\
\text{estimate of volume of cube} &= \frac{71.991\,296 + 56.623\,104}{2} \text{ cm}^3 \\
&= 64.3 \text{ cm}^3 \text{ to 1 dec.pl.}
\end{aligned}$$

$$\text{absolute error} = 64.3 - 56.6 \text{ cm}^3$$
$$= 7.7 \text{ cm}^3$$
$$\text{percentage error} = \frac{7.7}{64.3} \times 100\%$$
$$= 12\% \text{ to nearest whole number.}$$

Exercise 4.6

1 A plank of actual length 1 m is measured as 0.95 m. What is (a) the absolute error, (b) the relative error, (c) the percentage error?
2 A rectangular carpet was estimated as 8.5 m by 3.5 m but its actual size is 9.0 m by 4.0 m. Calculate the absolute error and the percentage error in (a) the perimeter of the carpet, (b) the area of the carpet.
3 A car manufacturing company is introducing a new model. The cost accountant estimates that materials for each car will cost £2400, correct to the nearest £100, and that labour and other costs will be £1500 per car, with a possible error of 3%. Estimate the total cost of producing 2000 cars. What is the percentage error in your estimate?

Practical exercise 4.7

Work in pairs. Each pair needs a stop-watch.

One pupil has to try to estimate an interval of 10 seconds. Without looking at the stop-watch, that pupil starts the watch and then stops it after an interval that he or she thinks is 10 seconds. The other pupil records the actual interval as shown by the stop-watch but does not let the first pupil know the result. Repeat the procedure until the first pupil has made 10 estimates. Change over and repeat the experiment with the second pupil estimating the time interval.

Each pupil should work out the absolute error in each of his or her estimates. How many times was the estimate too high? How many times was the estimate too low? Work out the relative error in each estimate. Did the size of the errors get smaller as you made more estimates?

Repeat the experiment and calculations but this time you should try to estimate an interval of 20 seconds. Are the absolute errors greater? Are the relative errors greater? Repeat the experiment and calculations but after each estimate the pupil should be told whether the estimate was too high or too low. Do the errors decrease in size? Comment on the results.

5 Assembly of data

Data recording

After you have decided on a suitable method of collecting the data you require, the next stage in an investigation is the actual collection, observation or measurement and to gather together all your findings.

If you have used a questionnaire, whether filled in by the respondent or by you in an interview, the data will come back to you on the questionnaire in standard form and all you need to do is to check that all the questions have been answered and to keep a record of those not returned so that you can follow up any non-response later.

If you are making observations or taking measurements yourself, you must be methodical in your recording to keep track of all the data and so that you will have all the necessary details when you come to analyse them. It is very important to have headings, dates and units clearly marked. If you need to make only a small number of observations, you may be able to keep a record of them all on one piece of paper, see Table 5.1, but if you are making many observations you may need to have a filing card for each item observed, see Table 5.2.

Table 5.1 Traffic survey at roundabout near school

Date: 15 October

Time	Number of cars in queue (westbound)
09.05	6
09.10	4
09.15	4
09.20	6
09.25	3
09.30	2
12.30	3
12.35	2
12.40	1
12.45	2
12.50	0
12.55	2
13.00	1
15.45	8
15.50	9
15.55	7
16.00	7
16.05	6
16.10	2
16.15	2

Table 5.2 Survey of vital statistics of fourth-year pupils

Date:		Length of left foot	cm
Name:		Span of right hand	cm
Class:		Girth of right wrist	mm
Sex:		Waist	cm
Age: y m		Girth of left ankle	mm
Height	cm	Length of nose	mm
Weight	kg		

Exercise 5.1

1 Design a suitable form for recording which television programmes were watched by each of your classmates last week.

2 How would you record details of the make, registration letter and colour of every car in the staff car park?

3 Show how you would keep a complete record of the movement in share prices for British Telecom, National Westminster Bank and GEC for a period of two months.

4 Design a form to record, for a month, the time taken for you to travel between home and school or college, together with the method of transport used.

Data base

Once all the data have been recorded, the next stage is to store them conveniently, ready for preliminary checks and then for detailed analysis. One way of doing this is to form a data base.

I have a box containing 50 partly-used pencils, some of which are shown in Fig. 5.1. Data has been collected from these pencils in several different ways. I have stuck a label on each pencil so that each has an identity number (ID Number) between 00 and 49. (I used two digits to number each pencil because for later work it was important that each should be labelled in the same way.) I have put all the data I obtained from the pencils in Table 5.3. This is my data base. You will see that

(a) the observations are stored in the same way for each pencil;

(b) we can extract the data for a particular pencil once we know its ID number;

(c) it is easy to add further pencils to the list and to correct or update any entries.

If you are storing data about a large number of items under many different headings, it will be a good idea to use a computer data base such as Quest (Advisory Unit for Computer Based Education). Usually these are able to do some of the analysis for you as well. For smaller amounts of data, a box to keep your filing cards or a large piece of paper such as Table 5.3 will be sufficient. The data base contains **raw data**. This is the term given to observations before we have done any analysis or summarisation.

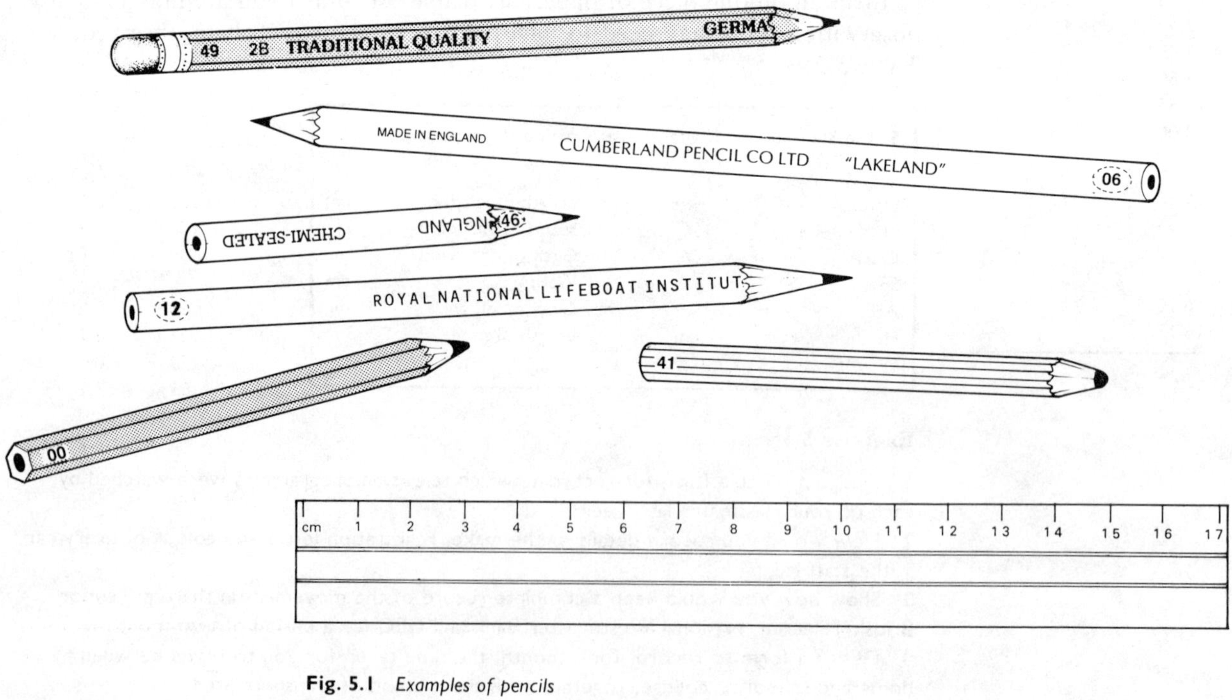

Fig. 5.1 *Examples of pencils*

Table 5.3 Pencil data base

ID number	Eraser	Graphite	Main colour of casing	Number of colours on casing	Number of complete letters on casing	Length (mm)	Maximum diameter (mm)
00	no	no	green	1	0	84	6.6
01	no	yes	green	2	22	132	7.0
02	no	no	green	2	43	147	8.0
03	yes	yes	yellow	2	2	60	7.4
04	no	no	brown	2	12	62	7.3
05	no	yes	yellow	1	0	77	7.0
06	no	no	orange	2	42	163	8.0
07	no	yes	blue	2	35	148	6.9
08	no	no	purple	2	59	172	7.9
09	no	no	blue	2	24	72	8.2
10	no	yes	white	1	0	84	7.7
11	no	yes	blue	2	50	164	7.0
12	no	yes	bare wood	0*	30	131	6.9
13	no	yes	red	2	51	175	7.6
14	no	yes	yellow	2	8	67	7.0
15	no	yes	red	2	13	79	7.0
16	no	yes	green	1	0	131	7.7
17	no	no	red	2	43	147	8.0
18	no	no	blue	2	20	84	8.0
19	no	no	yellow	2	16	64	7.8
20	no	no	orange	2	20	81	8.0
21	no	no	yellow	2	40	124	7.2
22	no	no	yellow	2	33	80	8.1
23	no	no	yellow	2	16	111	7.8
24	no	yes	red	2	22	88	7.7
25	no	yes	yellow	4	7	57	7.2
26	no	yes	green	2	0	108	7.0
27	no	no	red	2	14	147	6.9
28	no	yes	bare wood	0*	0	100	6.9
29	no	yes	grey	1	0	72	7.5
30	no	no	red	2	13	43	7.5
31	no	no	blue	2	35	127	8.0
32	no	yes	gold	2	100	133	7.2
33	no	yes	yellow	1	0	73	7.0
34	no	yes	blue	1	0	106	6.9
35	no	no	blue	2	16	159	7.8
36	yes	yes	yellow	1	12	109	7.8
37	no	yes	green	2	20	116	7.5
38	no	no	purple	2	44	168	8.0
39	no	yes	white	4	49	138	6.9
40	no	no	green	2	46	171	8.0
41	no	yes	blue	2	0	85	7.2
42	no	no	purple	2	33	84	8.0
43	no	yes	yellow	2	17	94	7.1
44	no	yes	red	1	0	47	7.9
45	no	yes	blue	4	45	157	7.5
46	no	yes	yellow	2	17	69	7.1
47	no	no	white	2	31	167	7.6
48	no	no	brown	2	16	74	7.9
49	yes	yes	red	2	25	133	7.5

*denotes bare wood, i.e. no painted casing

Notes: Length measured to the nearest mm

Diameter measured to the nearest 0.1 mm

Preliminary checks

Table 5.4 Coded data (a) and (b)

ID number	Eraser	Graphite
00	0	0
01	0	1
02	0	0
03	1	1
04	0	0
05	0	1
06	0	0
07	0	1
08	0	0
09	0	0
10	0	1
11	0	1
12	0	1
13	0	1
14	0	1
15	0	1
16	0	1
17	0	0
18	0	0
19	0	0
20	0	0
21	0	0
22	0	0
23	0	0
24	0	1
25	0	1
26	0	1
27	0	0
28	0	1
29	0	1
30	0	0
31	0	0
32	0	1
33	0	1
34	0	1
35	0	0
36	1	1
37	0	1
38	0	0
39	0	1
40	0	0
41	0	1
42	0	0
43	0	1
44	0	1
45	0	1
46	0	1
47	0	0
48	0	0
49	1	1

Qualitative data

The qualitative variables used to describe the pencils in Table 5.3 are:
(a) eraser/no eraser,
(b) graphite/non-graphite (coloured),
(c) main colour of the outside casing.

For variables (a) and (b) there are just two possible categories labelled 'yes' and 'no' in Table 5.3. It is a good idea to code these categories, either to single letters Y and N or to the numbers 1 and 0. One advantage of coding is less writing; it also makes it easier to notice interesting relationships within the data. Table 5.4 shows the data for variables (a) and (b) coded in this way. If you study the table, you will see that a 1 in the eraser column is always associated with a 1 in the graphite column (although not the other way round). In this way we can confirm that erasers are present only on graphite pencils, i.e. the combination (eraser, non-graphite) or (1, 0) is forbidden.

With a qualitative variable that can take more than two categories, such as (c), the simple 0, 1 coding is not possible. In some investigations we may know all the categories before we collect the data. For example, if you wanted to compare the numbers in the fifth-year at your school taking each different GCSE subject, you can find out from the school timetable what subjects are studied. With the pencil colours, however, we do not know what colours might be present before we start the investigation. Thus, although we could code the data on GCSE subjects before or as we collected it, we can code the colour data only after collection.

There is a second difficulty with coding the colours, since there is the possibility that you and I might disagree on the coding because colour is a subjective rather than an objective assessment. You might code a turquoise coloured pencil as 'blue', whereas I might put it as 'green'. If you can foresee possible difficulties such as this, it might be better to keep a separate category and code for 'turquoise' and then we have full details for further analysis.

If we know all the categories of classification we can extend our number-coding, for example,

green = 00	yellow = 01	brown = 02	orange = 03
blue = 04	purple = 05	white = 06	bare wood = 07
red = 08	grey = 09	gold = 10	

Table 5.5 shows the data for variable (c) coded in this way. It is easy to make mistakes when there are many categories so great care must be taken to check the coding.

Exercise 5.2

1 Think of other qualitative variables that could be used to distinguish between pencils. How would you code the data for these variables?
2 Search through your own pencils and decide whether the colour codes used in Table 5.5 would be adequate for your pencils. Extend the coding, as necessary, so you could include data from your pencils.

Table 5.5 Coded data (c)

ID number	Main colour of casing
00	00
01	00
02	00
03	01
04	02
05	01
06	03
07	04
08	05
09	04
10	06
11	04
12	07
13	08
14	01
15	08
16	00
17	08
18	04
19	01
20	03
21	01
22	01
23	01
24	08
25	01
26	00
27	08
28	07
29	09
30	08
31	04
32	10
33	01
34	04
35	04
36	01
37	00
38	05
39	06
40	00
41	04
42	05
43	01
44	08
45	04
46	01
47	06
48	02
49	08

Discrete numerical data

The discrete variables used to describe the pencils are:
(a) number of colours on the casing,
(b) number of complete letters on the casing.

In both cases the observations will be non-negative integers, i.e. 0, 1, 2 ... We can see at once from Table 5.3 that there is a much smaller range of values taken by (a) than by (b).

The pencils made of bare wood with no painted casing have been noted as a special case and were considered to have zero colour on the casing.

Exercise 5.3

Can you think of other discrete variables that could be used to describe the pencils? Have you any idea of the ranges of values these variables might take?

Continuous numerical data

The continuous variables used to describe the pencils are:
(a) length,
(b) maximum diameter.

I had to decide what units of measurement to use, what apparatus or equipment was appropriate and available and the precision that was possible. I decided to measure the lengths in millimetres using an ordinary ruler so I could record them correct to the nearest millimetre. The diameters were also measured in millimetres but I used a micrometer for this so I was able to record them correct to the nearest tenth of a millimetre, i.e. to the nearest 0.1 mm.

From Table 5.3 we can see at a glance that there is less spread in the diameters than in the lengths, as one would expect.

In this initial data analysis, it is useful to check for any **outliers** or **outlying observations**. These are observations that seem to be out-of-line or not typical of the rest of the data. For instance, a pencil whose length has been recorded as 321 mm in Table 5.3 would immediately be noticeable since there are no values of 200 mm or more. It is always worth checking outliers to see whether they are correct observations and not just mistakes in recording. Further checks might show that the unusual pencil length should have been 123 mm and not 321 mm or it could be that the pencil was a 'fun' pencil won at a fairground and was indeed a giant. In this case, outlying observations may have been noted for other variables as well, as it might be fatter and more highly decorated than the others. You would then have to decide whether to treat this pencil as a special case on its own or to include it in the analysis with all the others.

Exercise 5.4

Think of other continuous variables you could use to describe the pencils. What units would you use? What apparatus or equipment would you need to make each measurement? Do you have this equipment available? What precision do you think you can achieve? Would the manufacturer of the pencil be able to measure some variables that you would find difficult? Do any of your proposed measurements involve destroying the pencil? What spread of values would you expect for each variable?

Practical exercise 5.5

1 Each member of the class should bring an apple to the lesson. Discuss how you would label the apples so you knew who owned which. In what ways could you collect data from the apples? Do any of these involve a subjective assessment, i.e. does your opinion on the appropriate category differ from your neighbour's? Do any of them involve destructive measurement, i.e. will the apples be intact afterwards?

Are there any difficulties you foresee in collecting the data?

Choose one qualitative variable, one discrete numerical variable and one continuous variable from the ones suggested and prepare a data base recording your observations for the complete set of apples. What practical difficulties did you find? If you were to collect data from more apples, what ranges of values would you expect for your numerical variables? Give an example of how an outlying observation might arise.

2 The teacher should bring a bunch of grapes to the class. Discuss how you would identify each grape so that you can collect data from each one. Would you be able to use the same variables for a data base as you chose in Question 1? What variables would no longer be of interest? Prepare a data base as in Question 1. What do you notice about the expected ranges of the numerical variables?

3 Repeat Question 1 with a collection of leaves brought in by different members of the class.

4 Make a collection of leaves all from the same tree or plant. Would you be able to use the same variables for a data base as you chose in Question 3? What variables would no longer be of interest? Prepare a data base as in Question 3. What do you notice about the expected ranges of the numerical variables?

6 One variable analysis – qualitative data

Tabulation

The next stage in a statistical investigation is to put raw data in a form where we can see the observations clearly and concisely so that it is easier to make comparisons and interpretations. Tables and diagrammatic presentations, i.e. charts or graphs, can be used, followed by calculation of statistics, where appropriate. Different methods of analysis are suitable for the various types of data and we shall consider each in turn.

Tables are appropriate for summarising information about any data set, whether qualitative or quantitative.

The process of putting data in the form of a table is called tabulation.

To plan a table:

(a) decide what categories of classification are to be represented in each row and column;

(b) put numbers to be added in the same column, where possible;

(c) place numbers to be compared as close together as possible;

(d) use a ruler to draw any lines separating categories or totals; spacing can be used instead of lines to separate categories;

(e) label the categories, giving units of measurement;

(f) insert totals where appropriate;

(g) give the table a brief title;

(h) indicate the source of the data or when and where it was collected, if appropriate.

Look closely at the tables in this book and check that they follow these rules.

Exercise 6.1

1 In April, Mr and Mrs Jaybury had total earnings of £950, after tax, national insurance and pension contributions had been paid. Their expenditure on food and drink was £200. Housing costs amounted to £140. Their motoring expenditure was £60, with fares and other travel costs amounting to £40. They spent £80 on fuel and light, £70 on clothes and £70 on household goods. Spending on personal goods and services was £50. They invested £100 and the money remaining went into savings for their summer holiday.

(a) How much money went into holiday savings?

(b) Draw up a table to display this information.

2 In the twelve months to February 1987, the Department of Employment was notified of 350 work stoppages, involving 357 600 workers, arising from grievances about wage rates and 27 stoppages, involving 19 900 workers, concerning overtime pay and fringe benefits. Questions of redundancy gave rise to 93 stoppages involving 86 900 workers and 32 stoppages for trade union matters involved 45 700 workers.

Put this information in a table, showing the total number of stoppages and the total numbers of workers involved.

3

Unemployment in selected countries

	UK	France	Germany	Japan	US
Numbers unemployed (thousands)					
1983	3105	2068	2258	1561	10 717
1984	3160	2310	2265	1608	8 539
1985	3271	2424	2305	1563	8 312
1986	3289	2517	2223	1668	8 237

Source: *Employment Gazette*

(a) Which country had the highest number unemployed in 1985?
(b) Which country had the lowest number unemployed in 1986?
(c) Which country had the greatest increase in the number unemployed between 1985 and 1986?
(d) Which country had the greatest decrease in the number unemployed between 1984 and 1985?
(e) Which countries showed an increase in the numbers unemployed in every year from 1983 to 1986?
(f) Which country showed a decrease in the numbers unemployed in every year from 1983 to 1986?
(g) Suggest reasons why the figures for different countries might not be strictly comparable.

Two categories of classification

Tabulation

Table 6.1 Pencils classified by eraser

	Number of pencils (Frequency)
With eraser	3
Without eraser	47
Total	50

From either Table 5.3 or 5.4, we find that three pencils have an eraser and 47 pencils have no eraser. This information is displayed in Table 6.1. The number of observations in a particular category is referred to as the **frequency**. It is useful to include the total frequency in the table to make sure that we have not left out any pencils.

We can say that three pencils have the **attribute** of having an eraser. There are more pencils without an eraser. We state that the **modal** category, i.e. the category with the higher frequency, is no eraser.

A proportion of 3 out of 50, i.e. $3/50 = 0.06$, has an eraser. A proportion of 47 out of 50, i.e. $47/50 = 0.94$, has no eraser. We say that the **relative frequency** of an eraser is 0.06 and the relative frequency of no eraser is 0.94. We can quote the figures as percentages if we multiply each by 100. Six % have an eraser and 94% have no eraser.

Alternatively we can say that the ratio of the number of pencils with an eraser to those without an eraser is 3 to 47 or 3 : 47.

Diagrammatic presentation

Simple bar chart

This is one of the simplest and clearest forms of presentation. The vertical scale represents the frequency in each category. It must start at zero and needs to be at least as long as the highest frequency. To show the eraser data from Table 6.1, the vertical scale must cover the range 0 to 47 and it is convenient to draw the scale from 0 to 50, marking if off in tens (see Fig. 6.1). It is easier to draw the chart on graph paper or squared paper but you will often see bar charts presented in the press and on TV screens with a plain background.

For each category, we draw a bar with length proportional to the frequency it represents. The width of the bar is not important although it must be the same for each category and it is clearer if there is a gap between the bars. The bars can be shaded or coloured if desired.

It is important to

- label all axes and categories
- give the chart a title
- indicate the source of data, if appropriate.

In Fig. 6.1, the bars have been drawn vertically. Horizontal bar charts can also be drawn.

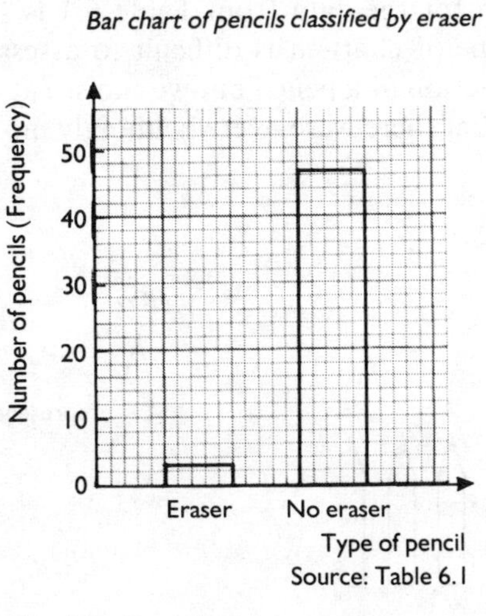

Fig. 6.1 *Simple bar chart*

Component, sectional or composite bar chart

In this chart we draw a bar to represent the total frequency and then divide the bar into **components** or **sections** whose lengths are proportional to the frequencies of the categories they represent. The data from Table 6.1 is shown in Fig. 6.2 as a horizontal component bar chart. The chart can also be drawn in percentage form with the bar representing 100% as in Fig. 6.3.

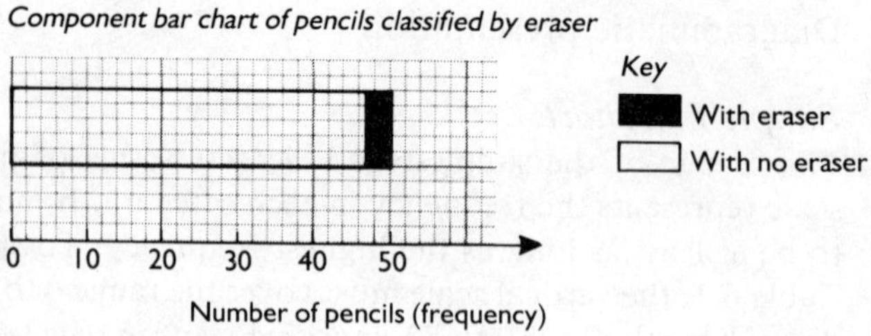

Fig. 6.2 *Component bar chart*

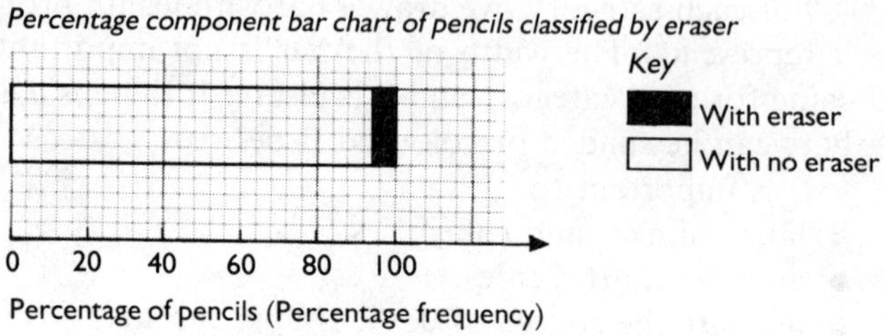

Fig. 6.3 *Percentage component bar chart*

Pictogram, picturegram, ideograph or isotype diagram

In a pictogram we use an appropriate logo to represent a given number of items. A pictogram for the data from Table 6.1 is shown in Fig. 6.4. When interpreting this type of chart, it is difficult to assess exactly what number is represented by a fraction of a pencil but we can see at a glance that the data are about pencils and that there were overwhelmingly more pencils with no eraser.

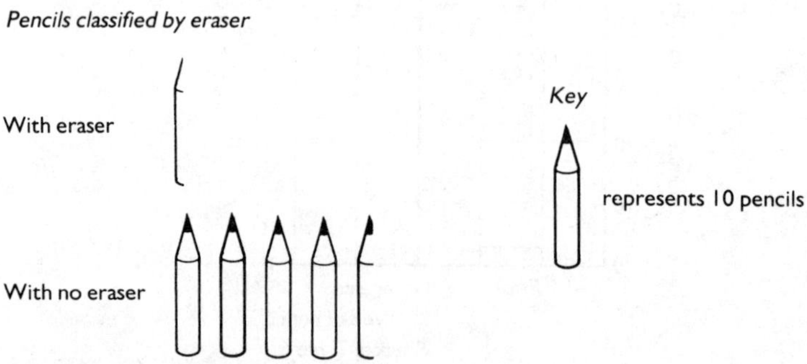

Fig. 6.4 *Pictogram*

Pie chart or circular diagram

This is a circle divided into sectors or 'pieces of a pie' whose areas are proportional to the frequencies of the categories they represent. To do this we must make the angles of the sector proportional to the frequencies. There are 360° in the complete pie, so, using the data from Table 6.1, 47/50 of the pie must represent pencils with no eraser and the remaining 3/50 of the pie those with erasers.

$$\text{The angle for the no eraser category} = \frac{47}{50} \times 360^\circ = 338^\circ \text{ to the nearest degree}$$

$$\text{The angle for the eraser category} = \frac{3}{50} \times 360^\circ = \ \ 22^\circ \text{ to the nearest degree}$$

$$\text{Check: Total } \overline{360^\circ}$$

Using a pair of compasses to draw the circle and a protractor to measure the angles, the chart is constructed as in Fig. 6.5(a). It is not usual to label the angles on the final diagram. The sectors can be labelled, Fig. 6.5(b), or shaded and a key given, Fig. 6.5(c). If desired, the frequency or the percentage frequency can be put on the diagram.

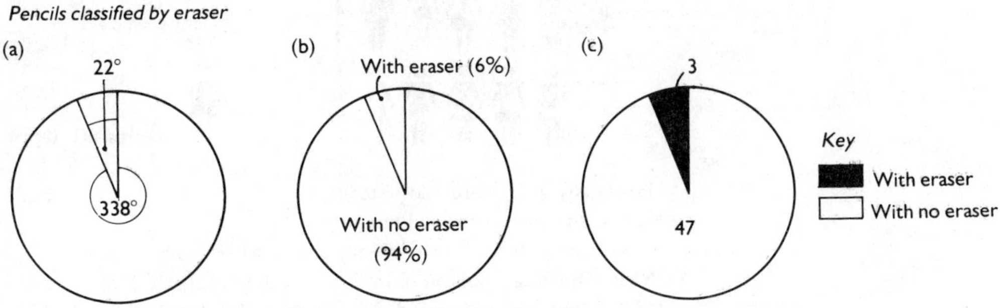

Fig. 6.5 *Pie chart (a) angles (b) percentages (c) frequencies*

Exercise 6.2

1 Refer to the column headed Graphite in Table 5.3. Find
(a) the frequency of graphite pencils,
(b) the proportion of graphite pencils,
(c) the percentage of graphite pencils,
and then find (a), (b) and (c) for non-graphite pencils.

2 Using the component bar chart shown below find
(a) the number of boys in the fourth year,
(b) the number of girls in the fourth year,
(c) the proportion of boys in the fourth year,
(d) the percentage of girls in the fourth year.

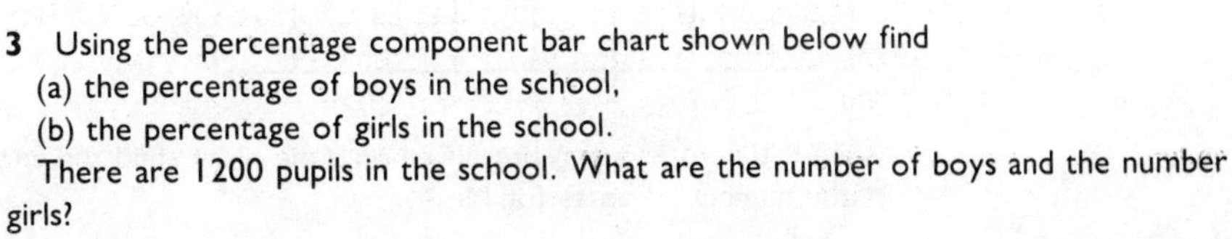

3 Using the percentage component bar chart shown below find
(a) the percentage of boys in the school,
(b) the percentage of girls in the school.
There are 1200 pupils in the school. What are the number of boys and the number of girls?

Percentages of boys and girls at Bebury School

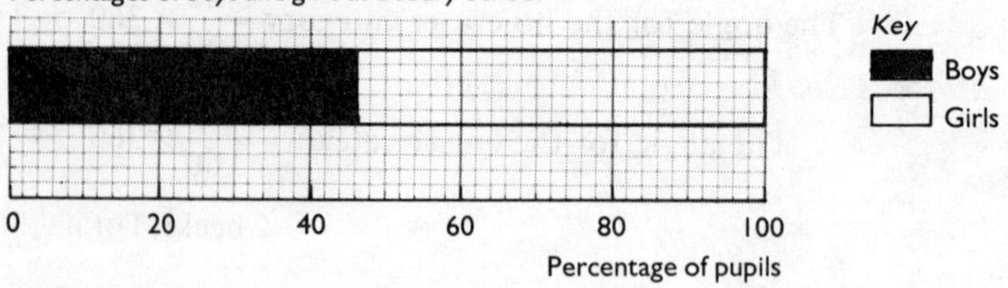

4 Sally did a survey of the girls in her year at school. She asked them whether they preferred hockey or netball. The results, including her own preference, are displayed in the pictogram.

Pictogram

(a) How many girls preferred netball?
(b) How many girls preferred hockey?
(c) How many girls are there in Sally's year at school?
(d) What difficulties did you have in answering (a), (b) and (c)?
(e) What other diagram would you use to show these data and why?

5 The numbers of men and women employed in a department store are shown in the pie chart below.

Pie chart of employees in a department store

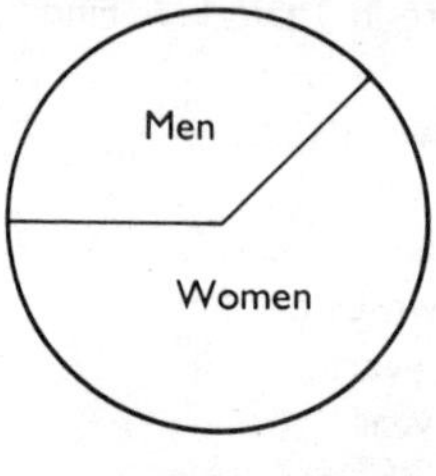

(a) Measure the angle of the sector representing men.
(b) What proportion of the employees are men?
(c) There are 720 employees altogether. How many of them are men? How many are women?

6 In an election for leadership of a trade union, the votes cast for the two candidates, Mr A and Miss B, are in the ratio 7 : 9.

(a) The votes are to be represented by the bar shown. Make a copy of the bar on graph paper, divide the bar in the ratio 7 : 9, shade and label each portion.

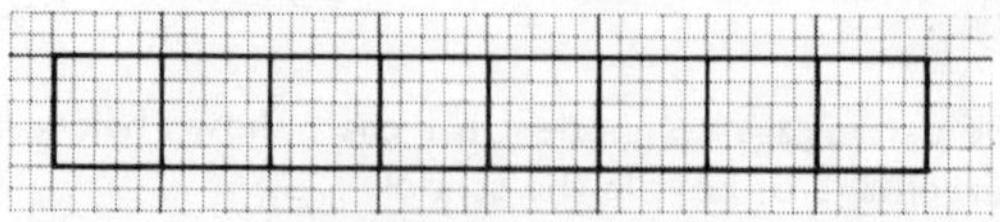

(b) If the votes are represented on a pie chart, find the angle of the sector representing the number of votes for Mr A.

Diagrammatic presentation of several sets of related data

We may want to compare our data set with other similar data sets and it is convenient to be able to do this on one diagram rather than having several separate charts. I have two further sets of pencils. The data is summarised in Table 6.2.

Table 6.2 Three pencil sets classified by eraser

Set	1		2		3	
	Frequency	%	Frequency	%	Frequency	%
With eraser	3	6	8	8	10	16
Without eraser	47	94	92	92	50	83
Totals	50	100	100	100	60	100

Dual bar chart

We draw two bars (hence the name **dual**) side-by-side for each pencil set with a gap between the bars for the different sets as shown in Fig. 6.6.

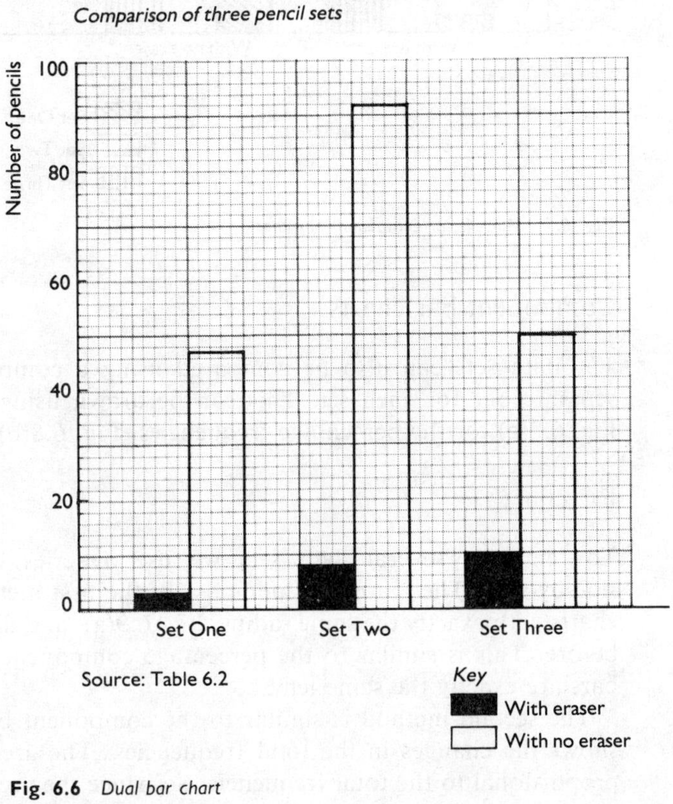

Fig. 6.6 *Dual bar chart*

Multiple bar chart

Alternatively, we can group together the data about pencils with erasers to form a **multiple** or **compound** bar chart as shown in Fig. 6.7.

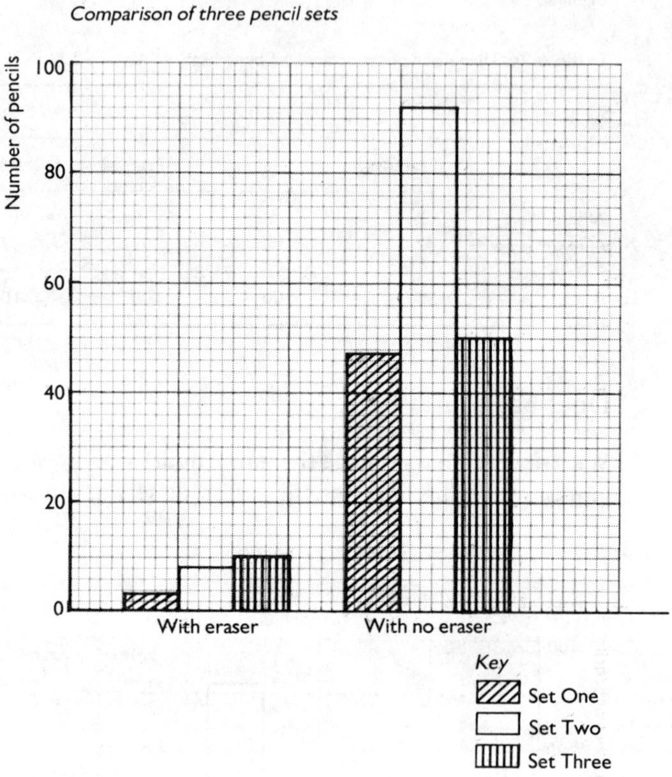

Fig. 6.7 *Multiple (or compound) bar chart*

Component bar charts

The data sets can also be compared using a component bar chart with a separate bar for each set. This can be drawn using the actual frequencies, Fig. 6.8(a), or the percentage frequencies, Fig. 6.8(b).

Pie chart

To represent several data sets we use a series of pie charts arranged side-by-side. There are two methods. In the first method we draw all the pie charts with exactly the same radius, Fig. 6.9(a), and divide each into sectors as before. This is similar to the percentage component bar chart where all the bars are exactly the same length.

The second method is similar to the component bar chart because it also shows the changes in the total frequencies. The areas of the pie charts are proportional to the total frequencies so, since the area of a circle equals πr^2,

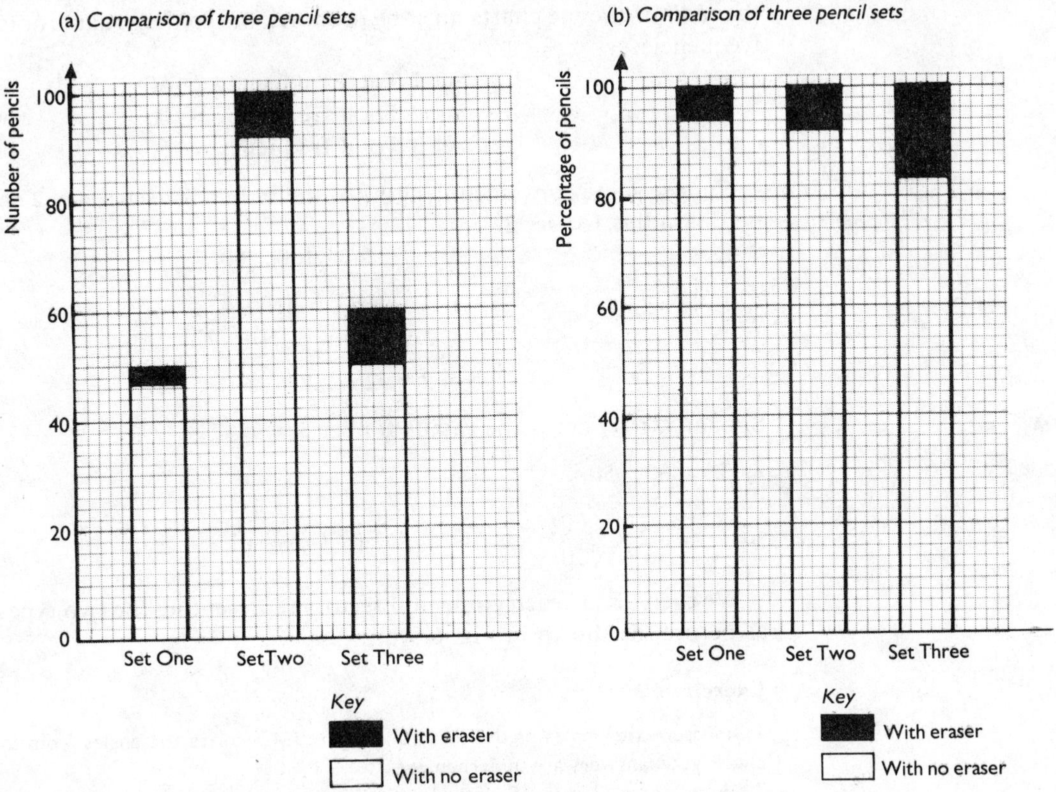

Fig. 6.8 *(a) Component bar chart (b) percentage component bar chart*

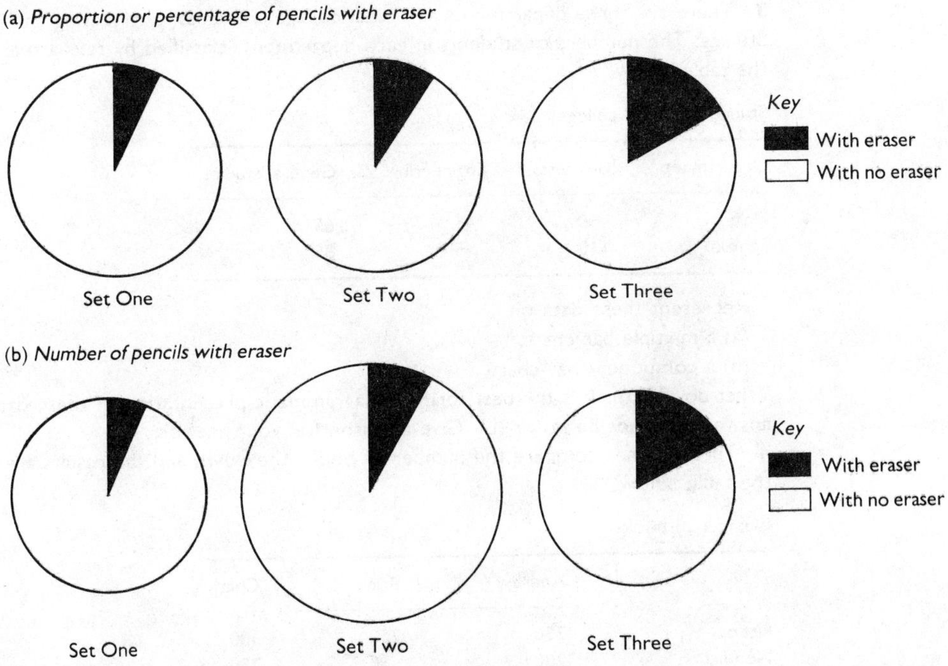

Fig. 6.9 *Pie charts of related data (a) equal area (b) area proportional to frequency*

the radii of the pie charts must be proportional to the square roots of the total frequencies.

Set 1 Total frequency = 50
Set 2 Total frequency = 100
Set 3 Total frequency = 60

Choose some convenient length for the radius for set 1, say 2 cm. Let r_2 cm be the radius for set 2.

$$r_2 : 2 = \sqrt{100} : \sqrt{50}$$

i.e.
$$\frac{r_2}{2} = \frac{\sqrt{100}}{\sqrt{50}} = \sqrt{\frac{100}{50}} = \sqrt{2}$$

$$r_2 = 2 \times \sqrt{2} = 2.8 \text{ to 1 dec. pl.}$$

Similarly, if r_3 cm is the radius for set 3,

$r_3 : 2 = \sqrt{60} : \sqrt{50}$

so $\quad r_3 = 2 \times \sqrt{\frac{60}{50}} = 2 \times \sqrt{1.2} = 2.2$ to 1 dec. pl.

We then divide each circle into sectors representing the two types of pencils, as before, as shown in Fig. 6.9(b).

Exercise 6.3

1 Measure the angles of the sectors in Fig. 6.9. Calculate the angles from the data and check your answers are in agreement.
2 A pie chart of radius 5 cm is drawn to illustrate a total population of 60 000 in a town in 1960. What radius of pie chart is needed to represent the town's population of 75 000 in 1985?
3 There are three departments at a local college: Business, Engineering and General Studies. The numbers of students in each department, classified by sex, are as shown in the table below.

Students at local college

Department	Business	Engineering	General studies
Male	90	145	65
Female	110	5	85

Represent these data on
(a) a multiple bar chart,
(b) a component bar chart.

What do you think is the best form of diagrammatic presentation of these data? Your answer need not be (a) or (b). Give a reason for your answer.
4 Three friends compare the number of books they own and the results are shown in the table below.

Number of books

	Andrew	Brian	Charles
Fiction	350	200	300
Non-fiction	200	50	250

(a) Draw a dual bar chart to illustrate these data.

(b) What feature of the data would have been shown more clearly on a component bar chart?

5 Sketch the type of bar chart you would draw which will best show the relationship between the number of imported cars and the number of home-produced cars sold per year in the UK over a period of three successive years. Give reasons for your choice.

More than two categories of classification

Frequency table

From Tables 5.3 and 5.5 we can draw up a frequency table, Table 6.3, showing the pencils classified by the main colour of the casing. We go through the data pencil by pencil and put a tally mark in the appropriate category. When we come to the fifth pencil in a category, we put its tally mark across the previous four, 𝍸, to form a group of five. This makes it easier to add up the frequencies in each category at the end.

You might think it is just as easy to go through the data, colour by colour, and to count up the number in each category in this way. For very small amounts of data, this may be true but here we have 11 different colour categories so this method would involve going through the data 11 times instead of the single time using the tally method. You should always check that the total frequency does come to the expected number. It is easy to make mistakes so it is a good idea to repeat the whole process to check your frequencies.

From Table 6.3 we see at once that yellow is the single most popular colour of casing. We say that the mode is yellow or that the modal category is yellow.

We can also work out the proportions and percentages of pencils in each category, Table 6.4.

We can use all the methods mentioned before to represent our results diagrammatically but the charts will be more complex as we have more categories.

Table 6.3 Pencils classified by predominant colour of casing

Colour	Code	Tally	Frequency
Green	00	𝍸 II	7
Yellow	01	𝍸 𝍸 II	12
Brown	02	II	2
Orange	03	II	2
Blue	04	𝍸 IIII	9
Purple	05	III	3
White	06	III	3
Bare wood	07	II	2
Red	08	𝍸 III	8
Grey	09	I	1
Gold	10	I	1
Total			50

Source: Table 5.3

Table 6.4 Proportions and percentages of pencils classified by predominant colour of casing

Colour	Frequency	Proportion	Percentage
Green	7	$\frac{7}{50} = 0.14$	14
Yellow	12	0.24	24
Brown	2	0.04	4
Orange	2	0.04	4
Blue	9	0.18	18
Purple	3	0.06	6
White	3	0.06	6
Bare wood	2	0.04	4
Red	8	0.16	16
Grey	1	0.02	2
Gold	1	0.02	2
Totals	50	1.00	100

Simple bar chart

A simple bar chart is shown in Fig. 6.10(a), with the bars in the same order as in Table 6.4. To enable us to make comparisons more easily we can redraw the chart with the bars in order of frequency. We can do this with a qualitative variable because there is no natural order to the categories themselves.

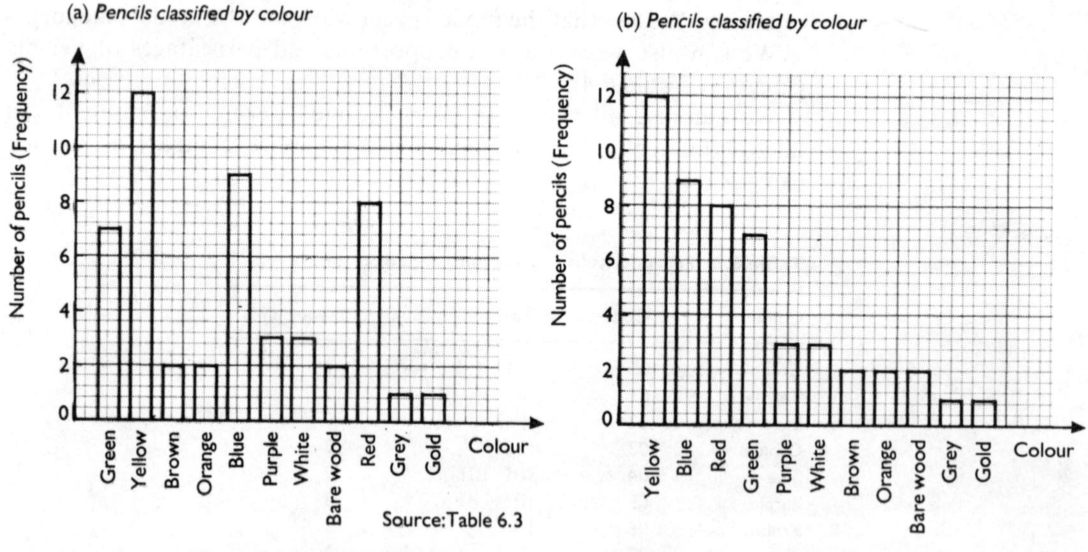

Fig. 6.10 *Simple bar charts (a) in same order as Table 6.3 (b) in frequency order*

Component bar chart

A component bar chart and a percentage component bar chart for the data are shown in Figs. 6.11(a) and (b). These diagrams are usually clearer if the

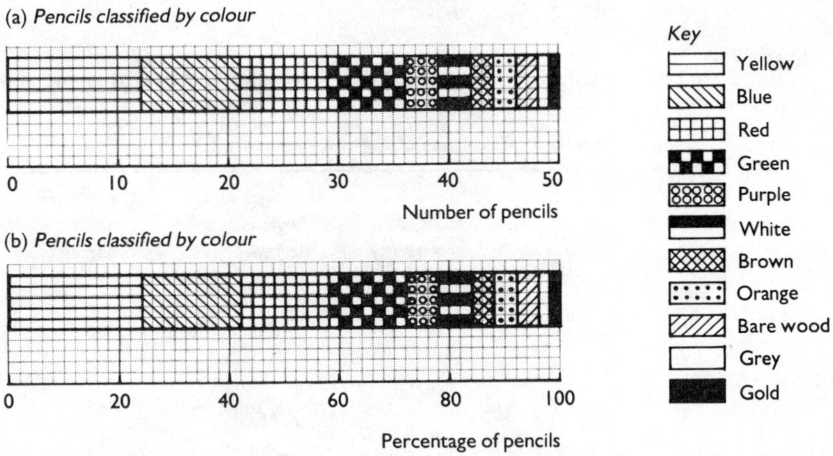

Fig. 6.11 *(a) Component bar chart (b) percentage component bar chart*

components are arranged in order of size. It is a good idea to add up the frequencies category by category so you know where on the scale to draw the end of a component. These frequencies are called **cumulative frequencies** and are given in Table 6.5(a) with the categories arranged in order of frequency. We have 12 yellow pencils, $(12 + 9) = 21$ yellow or blue pencils, $(21 + 8) = 29$ yellow, blue or red pencils and so on until we have 50 pencils in all. The whole bar is drawn from 0 to 50 and then we mark off the ends of the components at 12, 21, 29 and so on. The corresponding calculations for drawing the percentage component bar chart are shown in Table 6.5(b). We can label each component or use colour/shading and a key to identify the different sections.

Table 6.5 Calculations for component bar charts (a) cumulative frequencies; (b) cumulative percentage frequencies

(a)			(b)	
Colour	Frequency	Cumulative frequency	Percentage frequency	Cumulative percentage frequency
Yellow	12	12	24	24
Blue	9	21	18	42
Red	8	29	16	58
Green	7	36	14	72
Purple	3	39	6	78
White	3	42	6	84
Brown	2	44	4	88
Orange	2	46	4	92
Bare wood	2	48	4	96
Grey	1	49	2	98
Gold	1	50	2	100
Totals	50		100	

Pie chart

Table 6.6 gives the angles for the sectors of a pie chart.

Table 6.6 Calculation of angles for pie chart

Colour	Frequency	Angle in degrees	Angle to nearest degree
Yellow	12	$\frac{12}{50} \times 360 = 86.4$	86
Blue	9	$\frac{9}{50} \times 360 = 64.8$	65
Red	8	57.6	58
Green	7	50.4	50
Purple	3	21.6	22
White	3	21.6	22
Brown	2	14.4	14
Orange	2	14.4	14
Bare wood	2	14.4	14
Grey	1	7.2	7
Gold	1	7.2	7
Totals	50	360.0	359

It is usual to round the angles off to the nearest degree and the total of the column of rounded numbers may not come to exactly 360°.

If possible label each sector by name. If some of the sectors are too small for this, you may need to put the label outside the diagram, see Fig. 6.12. Alternatively, colour in the sectors appropriately or use different shading for each category and include a key.

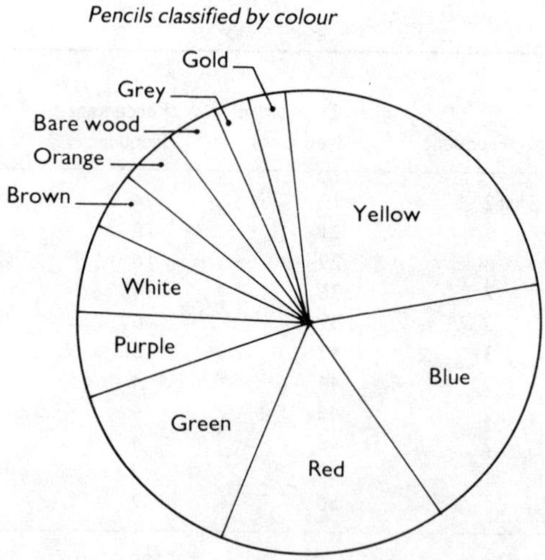

Fig. 6.12 *Pie chart*

Exercise 6.4

1 Use the pie chart below to answer the following questions.

Pie chart showing how 120 pupils travel to school

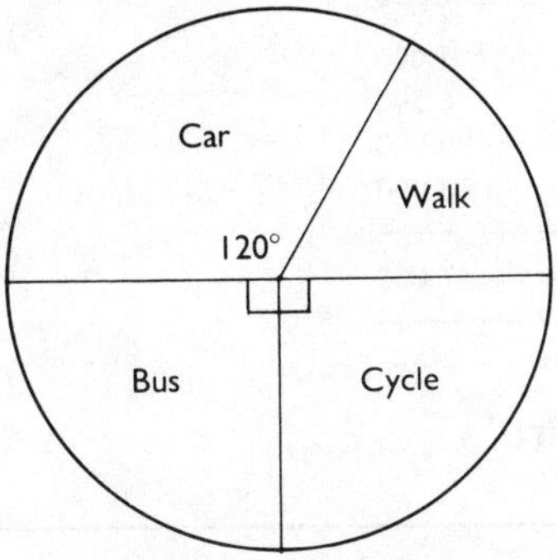

(a) What proportion of pupils cycle to school?
(b) How many pupils cycle to school?
(c) How many pupils travel to school by bus?
(d) What fraction of pupils travel to school by car?
(e) What fraction of pupils walk to school?
(f) How many pupils either walk to school or travel by car?

Accident type	Number of deaths
Poisoning	500
Fall	3000
Fire	750
Suffocation	500
Other†	500

†Accidents caused by explosive, hot substances, corrosive liquid, electric shock etc.
Source: *Social Trends 1985*

2 The table shows the approximate numbers of deaths in Great Britain in 1986 from accidents in the home. Represent the data (a) on a simple bar chart, (b) on a pie chart. Which do you think is the more effective form of presentation for these data?

UK population (millions)

Country	1972	1982
England	46.3	46.8
Scotland	5.2	5.2
Wales	2.7	2.8
Northern Ireland	2.5	1.6

Source: *Social Trends 1985*

3 (a) Represent the data shown in the table on a component bar chart, i.e. one bar for 1972 and one bar for 1982.
(b) Calculate the percentage of people in each region and represent the data on a percentage component bar chart.
(c) Comment on what your charts show.

4 The pie chart shows the number of cups of various drinks dispensed by a vending machine during one week. There were 600 cups of tea dispensed.

Drinks dispensed by vending machine

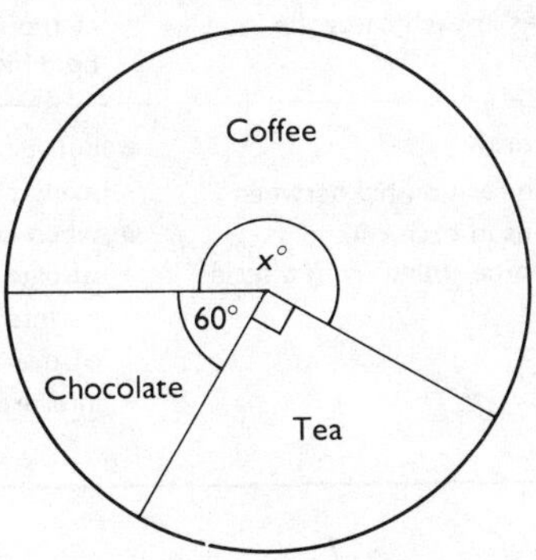

(a) How many cups of chocolate were dispensed?
(b) What is the value of x?
(c) How many cups of coffee were dispensed?

5 The number of persons employed by a large public company during a particular year is shown in the table below. Represent these data on (a) a bar chart, (b) a pie chart. Comment on what your charts show.

Employees classified by sector

Sector	Number
General merchanting	10 000
Insurance	2 500
Marine and specialist services	4 000
Motor	6 500
Tea	20 000
Other	4 000
Total	47 000

Comparisons between pie charts and bar charts

	Advantages	*Disadvantages*
Pie chart	• eye-catching • easy to compare the proportion in each category with the whole	• calculation needed • protractor and pair of compasses needed • difficult to compare more than one set of data • difficult to compare and draw very small sectors • frequencies/percentages cannot be read directly from a scale
Simple bar chart	• simple to draw • easy to understand • frequencies can be read from a scale	• does not show any information about the total frequency
Component bar chart	• fairly easy to draw • frequencies can be found from a scale • shows total frequency as well as the frequencies in each category • emphasises the relationships between the frequencies in each category	• difficult to interpret when there are many categories • when comparing more than one set of data, the categories start at different heights (apart from the one at the foot of the column) so it can be difficult to interpret
Percentage component bar chart	• fairly easy to draw • emphasises the relationship between the proportions in each category • percentage can be found from a scale	• difficult to interpret when there are many categories • when comparing more than one set of data, the categories start at different heights (apart from the one at the foot of the column) so it can be difficult to interpret

Other applications of bar charts and pie charts

Bar charts and pie charts can be used to represent the frequencies with which values of quantitative data occur. Simple bar charts are particularly good for showing discrete data, see Fig. 7.2.

The charts are also used to represent quantities other than frequencies, for

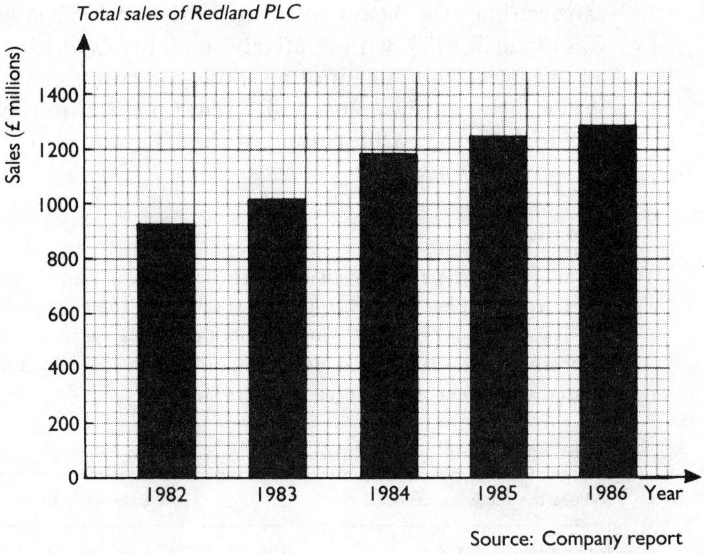

Fig. 6.13 *Bar chart of sales*

example, the value of a company's sales, see Fig. 6.13. The units of measurement must be clearly shown. From the figure, we can see clearly that there was an increase in sales every year but, in the most recent years, the increase was less than in the earlier years.

A simple bar chart or a multiple bar chart can show both positive and negative values, as might occur, for example, when showing the profit/loss of a company. A loss is shown as a negative profit, see Fig. 6.14. From the chart we

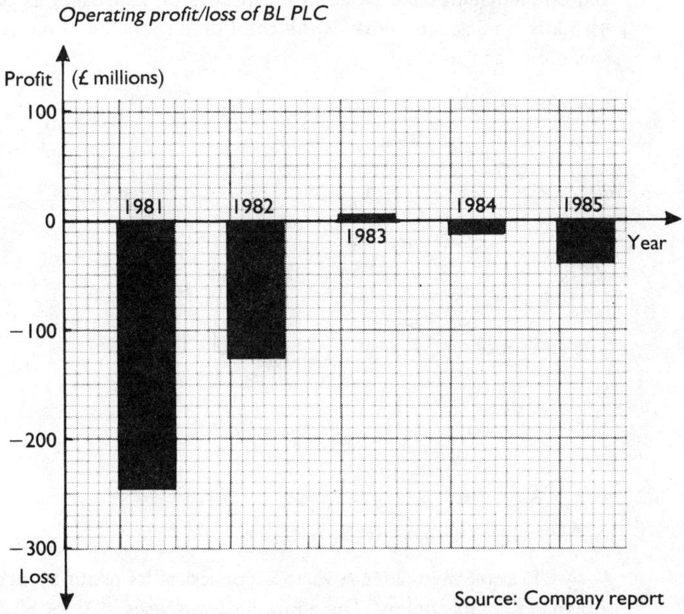

Fig. 6.14 *Bar chart showing positive and negative amounts*

can see that after heavy losses in 1981 and 1982, a very small operating profit was made in 1983, with relatively small losses in 1984 and 1985. Mixed positive and negative values cannot be shown on component bar charts and pie charts. When each bar represents a different time, it is preferable to draw vertical bars and to have the earliest time on the left.

Exercise 6.5

1 Sketch the type of bar chart which, for a particular company dealing in rice, nuts and dried fruit, will best illustrate the total sales and their constituent parts over several years.
2 The cash flow of a UK company in a particular year was as given in the table below. Represent these data (a) on two component bar charts of the same length; (b) on two pie charts. Comment on what your charts show.

Cash flow (£million)

Where the funds came from		How they were used	
Income before UK tax	750	Capital investment	720
Depreciation	300	UK tax	40
Other	50	Additional working capital	60
		Dividends	80
		Repayment of borrowing	200
Total	1100		1100

3 The pie chart below shows the amount of time spent by a pupil on homework in various subjects in a particular week. The pupil spends the same amount of time on English and on Humanities and twice as much time on Languages as on Mathematics. He spent $4\frac{1}{2}$ hours on Science. What is the total time spent on homework? How much time did he spend on each subject?

Time spent on homework

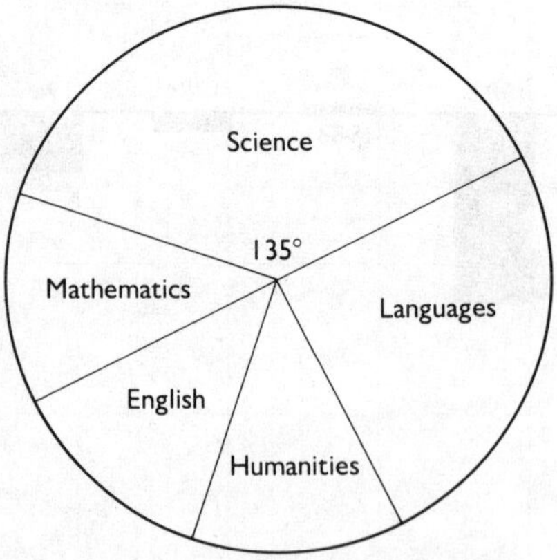

4 A UK company trades in various countries. Its profit before tax, for a particular year, is shown in the table below. The entry in parentheses, ( ), for SE Asia denotes a loss. Represent the data on a bar chart. Comment on what the chart shows.

Profit of UK company (£000)

Geographical market	Profit
Africa	2 600
Europe (excl UK)	6 300
SE Asia	(10 300)
India	9 700
UK	20 100
N and S America	2 300
Australasia	1 000
Far East	24 300
Middle East	3 400

5 A family kept a record of all its expenditure on transport last year. Represent these data on a pie chart.

Expenditure on transport	£
Purchase of motor vehicles, spares and accessories	505
Maintenance and running of motor vehicles	720
Railway fares	64
Bus and coach fares	67
Other travel and transport	104

What expenditure do you think is covered in the 'other travel and transport category'? Comment on the data.

6 At a sixth form college, all students who used the canteen at lunchtime were asked to assess as Good, Reasonable or Poor

(a) the quantity of food provided

(b) the value for money of the food provided.

600 students responded and it was found that one third of the students thought that the quantity of food was good while 250 thought it was reasonable. Half the students thought the meals were good value for money, while one tenth of them thought they were poor value for money.

(a) Consider the quantity of food provided. How many students thought it was

(i) Good (ii) Reasonable (iii) Poor?

(b) Consider the value for money of the food provided. How many students thought it was

(i) Good (ii) Reasonable (iii) Poor?

(c) Represent the results on a dual bar chart.

(d) What do you conclude from this survey?

7 In December a retailer sold 72 calculators, 54 cassette recorders and 90 video recorders. Display these data on a pie chart with a radius of 4 cm. In February he sold 18 calculators, 14 cassette recorders and 22 video recorders. Calculate the radius of the pie chart to show the February sales. Draw the pie chart for the February sales.

Practical exercise 6.6

1 Refer to the data you collected in Practical exercise 5.5. Choose a qualitative variable with just two categories and find the frequency, the proportion and the percentage in each category. Make diagrammatic presentations of the data using (a) a simple bar chart, (b) a component bar chart, (c) a percentage component bar chart, (d) a pictogram and (e) a pie chart.

2 Refer to the data you collected in Practical exercise 5.5. Choose a qualitative variable with more than two categories. Construct a frequency table similar to Table 6.2. Can you find the modal category? Represent your data using (a) a bar chart, (b) a component bar chart, (c) a percentage component bar chart and (d) a pie chart. Comment on what your diagrams reveal. Note any difficulties you had.

3 (a) Toss a coin 30 times and record the outcome using a table like the one shown below, i.e. after the toss put a tally mark in either the head or the tail category and also put a tally mark in the tosses column regardless of the outcome. Continue tossing the coin and recording the results until you have recorded 30 tosses. It will be easy to see when you have reached 30 from the tosses column. Draw a percentage component bar chart and a pie chart to represent your results.

Outcome	Tally of outcome	Frequency	Tally of tosses
Head			
Tail			
Total		30	

(b) Continue the experiment for another 30 tosses and draw a percentage component bar chart and a pie chart, with the same radius as before, to represent the results of all 60 tosses.

(c) Repeat (b) until you have 90 tosses and then continue to 120 tosses.

(d) How do the charts change as the number of tosses increases? Is this what you expected to happen? Explain.

4 Take a well-shuffled pack of 52 ordinary playing cards. Remove one card and record in a table whether its suit is hearts, clubs, diamonds or spades. Return the card to the pack. Shuffle and take another card. Record its suit similarly. Continue until you have taken 36 cards in all. Draw a bar chart and a pie chart to represent your results. Continue the experiment and draw another bar chart and a pie chart of the same radius (a) after 72 cards, (b) after 108 cards, (c) after 144 cards. Describe the changes you have noticed in your charts. What do you think the pie chart might look like after 1080 cards? Why?

7 One variable analysis – quantitative data, ungrouped or discrete (1)

Exploratory data analysis

Range

With quantitative data we have a numerical variable and the first step in the analysis is to look for the smallest observation and the largest observation. Referring to the pencil data base in Table 5.3, the variable 'number of colours on casing' has smallest value 0 and largest value 4. Similarly the variable 'maximum diameter' has minimum value 6.6 mm and maximum value 8.2 mm.

The difference between the largest and smallest observations is termed the **range** of the data.

$$\text{range of number of colours on casing} = 4 - 0 = 4$$

$$\text{range of maximum diameters} = 8.2 - 6.6 \text{ mm} = 1.6 \text{ mm}$$

Representation on a line

One method of getting a 'feel' for the data is to represent all the values on a line so that we have some idea of the clustering at the different values. We draw a scaled line to cover the range of the data. We go through the data, pencil by pencil, and use either a cross or a dot to represent each value at its appropriate position on the line.

From Fig. 7.1(a), we see at once that two colours occur by far the most often and that none of the pencils had three colours. From Fig. 7.1(b), we notice that all diameters between 6.9 and 8.2 mm are represented with diameters 7.0 mm and 8.0 mm occurring most frequently. There is just one pencil at the very small value of 6.6 mm.

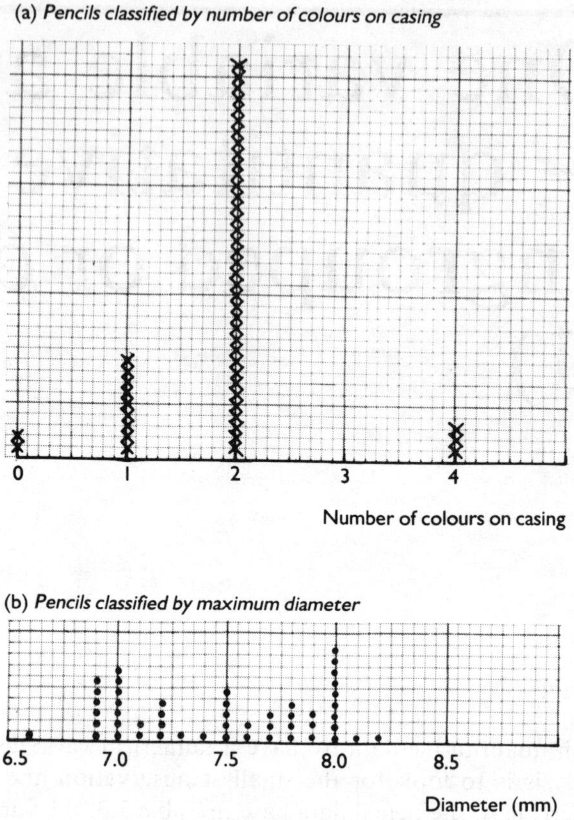

Fig. 7.1 *Representation of data on a line*

Stem-and-leaf diagram

Another method of exploratory data analysis is to use a stem-and-leaf diagram.

For the data on maximum diameters, we have noted already that the observations are in the interval 6.6 to 8.2 mm. First we write down the whole number part of these measurements, 6, 7, 8 in a column on the left of the diagram as shown in Table 7.1. Next we draw a vertical line to separate the units (mm) from the tenths of a unit (0.1 mm) which are put to the right of the line. We go through the data systematically working from the data base, Table 5.3, and we write down the tenths of a unit on the appropriate row. For pencil number 00 with diameter 6.6 mm we write 6 to the right of the line on row 6;

Table 7.1 Initial layout of a stem-and-leaf diagram

Maximum diameter of pencils	I unit = I mm
(units)	(tenths)
6	
7	
8	

Table 7.2 Incomplete stem-and-leaf diagram
(Data up to pencil number 08)

Maximum diameter of pencils	1 unit = 1 mm
(units)	(tenths)
6	69
7	04309
8	00

for pencil 01, diameter 7.0 mm we put 0 on row 7; for pencil 02, diameter 8.0 mm, we put 0 on row 8; for pencil 03, diameter 7.4 mm, we put 4 on row 7 next to the 0 already there and so on. Table 7.2 shows the diagram after 9 pencils and Table 7.3 shows all the data.

Table 7.3 Stem-and-leaf diagram, unordered leaves

Maximum diameter of pencils	1 unit = 1 mm
(units)	(tenths)
6	6999999
7	04309706007828720552088521951695
8	00200010000

Each row of the diagram is a stem and each piece of information on a stem is a leaf. It is better to redraw the diagram with the leaves in order of size so that the final form is as shown in Table 7.4. It is important to have the leaves evenly spaced and as close together as possible.

Table 7.4 Stem-and-leaf diagram, final form

Maximum diameter of pencils	1 unit = 1 mm
(units)	(tenths)
6	6999999
7	00000001122223455555667778888999
8	00000000012

The number of colours on the casing can be displayed similarly, as shown in Table 7.5. It is helpful to record the number of leaves on each stem, i.e. the frequency, and this can be put in parentheses at the right of the diagram, as shown.

Table 7.5 Further example of a stem-and-leaf diagram

Number of colours on casing of pencils	1 unit = 1	
(units)	(units)	
0	00	(2)
1	111111111	(9)
2	222222222222222222222222222222222222	(36)
3		(0)
4	444	(3)

The outline of a stem-and-leaf diagram gives a simple graphical display of the data and at the same time we have full details of all the observations in order of size.

Exercise 7.1

1 In a chemistry lesson, ten pupils have to find the mass of a small piece of rock. The teacher asks them to work in two groups of five and everyone has to find the mass correct to the nearest gram.

The results in grams are

Group 1 102, 98, 97, 101, 98

Group 2 100, 100, 100, 100, 100

(a) Represent the results of each group on a line, using a separate line for each group. Comment on the results. What do you think is the mass of the rock? Why might you be wrong?

(b) If the teacher knows that the true mass is 100 g, what should she say to each group of pupils?

(c) If the teacher knows the true mass is 98 g, what should she say to each group of pupils?

2 Refer to Table 5.3 and represent the variable 'number of complete letters on the casing' of the 50 pencils on a line.

A stem-and-leaf diagram for the data up to pencil number 09 is shown in Table 7.6. Copy out and complete the diagram. Redraw the diagram with the leaves in order on each stem. Comment on what your diagrams show.

Table 7.6 Incomplete stem-and-leaf diagram
(Data up to pencil number 09)

Number of complete letters on casing 1 unit = 1

(tens)	(units)
0	020
1	2
2	24
3	5
4	32
5	9
6	
7	
8	
9	
10	

3 Using stems 4, 5, 6, ... 17 in units of 10 mm, construct a stem-and-leaf diagram for the lengths of the 50 pencils, Table 5.3. Indicate the frequency of leaves on each stem.

Discrete data

Frequency table

For a discrete variable, the data can be presented compactly in a frequency table, Table 7.7, which shows the number of times each different value of the variable was recorded. The frequencies can be found from the stem-and-leaf diagram, Table 7.5. Alternatively, we can work directly from the data base, Table 5.3, and construct a tally chart as shown in Table 7.8.

Table 7.7 Frequency table: number of colours on casing

Number of colours (x)	Frequency (f)
0	2
1	9
2	36
3	0
4	3
Total	50

Table 7.8 Tally chart: number of colours on casing of pencils

Number of colours	Tally	Frequency
0	II	2
1	~~IIII~~ IIII	9
2	~~IIII~~ ~~IIII~~ ~~IIII~~ ~~IIII~~ ~~IIII~~ ~~IIII~~ ~~IIII~~ I	36
3		0
4	III	3
Total		50

(a) *Pencils classified by number of colours on casing*

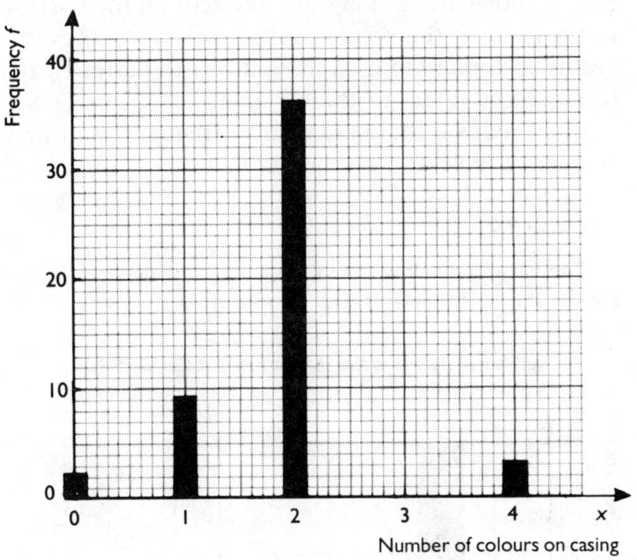

(b) *Pencils classified by number of colours on casing*

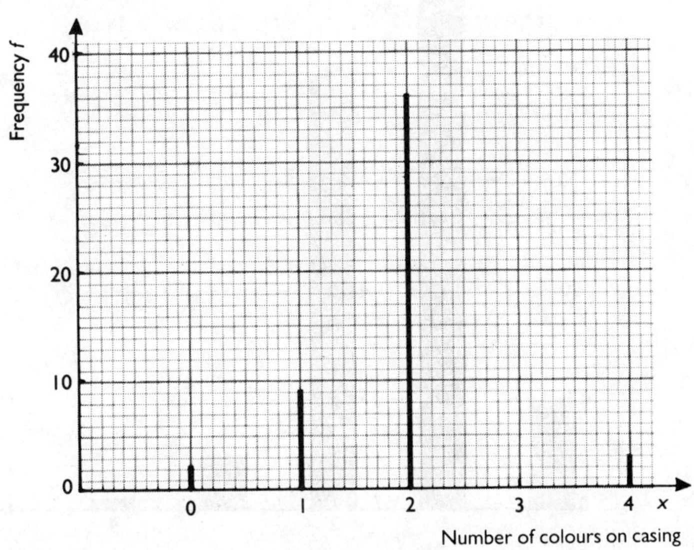

Fig. 7.2 *(a) Frequency bar chart (b) line diagram*

Frequency bar chart

The most usual way to represent discrete data graphically is on a frequency bar chart, Fig. 7.2(a). The same rules of presentation apply as given for simple bar charts in Chapter 6, with two exceptions. Firstly, frequency bar charts are always drawn with vertical bars. Secondly, with a quantitative variable, we also have a numerical scale on the horizontal axis. This means that we have to draw the bars at the correct position on this scale and we cannot rearrange the order of the bars to suit ourselves.

Sometimes, each bar is drawn as a line, emphasising that with a discrete variable only these specific values are possible. The bar chart is then called a **line diagram**, Fig. 7.2(b). To make sure that the line representing 0 colours is clearly shown in this diagram, the zero on the horizontal scale has been moved to the right of the vertical axis.

It is customary to use the symbol f to represent frequency and the symbol x to represent values of the variable.

If desired, we could use relative frequencies or percentage frequencies in the frequency table and on the bar chart.

Exercise 7.2

1 The bar chart below shows the number of siblings, i.e. brothers and sisters, of each pupil in the fourth year at Cebury school.

Number of siblings of fourth-year pupils at Cebury School

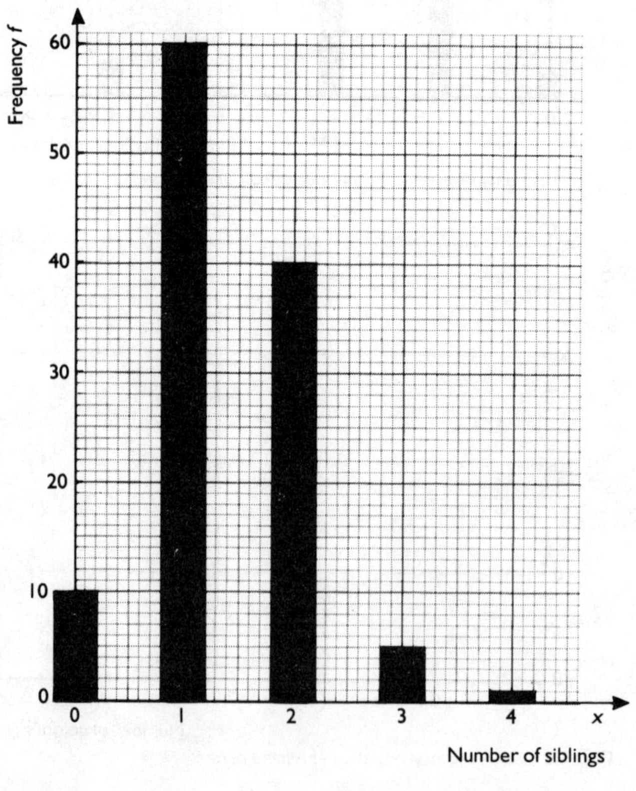

(a) How many pupils have two siblings?
(b) How many pupils have two or more siblings?
(c) How many pupils are in the fourth year at Cebury school?
(d) What is the range of the data?

2 David counted the number of people in each car entering a supermarket car park between 10.00 and 11.00 on a Saturday morning. His tally sheet is given in the table.
Draw a frequency bar chart to show the data David collected.

Number of people in car (x)	Tally
1	𝍸 𝍸 𝍸 𝍸 𝍸 I
2	𝍸 𝍸 𝍸 𝍸 𝍸 𝍸 𝍸 𝍸 𝍸 II
3	𝍸 𝍸 𝍸 𝍸 𝍸 𝍸 𝍸 II
4	𝍸 𝍸 𝍸 𝍸 𝍸 I
5	𝍸

3 In a survey of 60 families in Deebury, each was asked 'How many pets do you have?' The replies were:

0 1 0 3 0 1 3 5 0 2
5 4 5 1 1 6 1 2 7 5
5 2 2 1 2 4 2 3 2 5
1 1 2 1 1 7 1 1 2 1
2 1 0 7 1 6 3 4 4 1
2 2 5 2 1 6 2 1 3 4

Construct a frequency table for the data and draw a line diagram to show the results graphically.

Introduction to measures of location

Mode

We have noticed already in Fig. 7.1(a) and Fig. 7.2(a) that two colours was the number of colours that occurred most often on the pencils. We say that the **mode** is two colours or that the **modal number** of colours is two.

The mode is one value or statistic that we have extracted from the data but there are other methods of finding a value that is representative or typical of the data. The representative values are called **measures of location, measures of central tendency** or **averages.**

Median

If we arrange our data in order of size, we can pick out the middle value in the array. This middle value is called the **median**. If we have an odd number of observations, there will be just one middle value. If there is an even number of observations, there will be two values in the middle, so the median is halfway between these two middle values.

For example

(1) Seven observations

Raw data 3, 2, 1, 1, 5, 4, 4

Array 1, 1, 2, 3, 4, 4, 5

↑ median

median = 3

(2) Six observations

Raw data (cm) 7.2, 5.4, 2.6, 1.9, 10.3, 4.6

Array (cm) 1.9, 2.6, 4.6, 5.4, 7.2, 10.3

Median is halfway between 4.6 cm and 5.4 cm.

$$\text{median} = \frac{4.6 + 5.4}{2}$$

$$= 5.0 \text{ cm}$$

When there are seven observations, the median is the 4th value from the start of the array. When there are six observations, it is halfway between the 3rd and 4th values in the array so we can say it is the $3\frac{1}{2}$ th item. In general, when we have n observations, the median is the $(n + 1)/2$ th value from the start of the array.

Arithmetic mean

The arithmetic mean, usually referred to as **the mean**, is found by adding up all the observations and dividing by the number of observations. It is what most people think of as the average but its correct name is the mean and you must try not to use the word average except as a collective term for all measures of location or central tendency.

For example

(1) Seven observations

Raw data 3, 2, 1, 1, 5, 4, 4

$\text{sum} = 3 + 2 + 1 + 1 + 5 + 4 + 4 = 20$

$\text{arithmetic mean} = 20/7 = 2\frac{6}{7} = 2.86$ to 2 dec. pl.

(2) Six observations

Raw data (cm) 7.2, 5.4, 2.6, 1.9, 10.3, 4.6

$\text{sum} = 7.2 + 5.4 + 2.6 + 1.9 + 10.3 + 4.6 = 32.0$ cm

$\text{arithmetic mean} = 32.0/6 = 5.33$ cm to 2 dec. pl.

We can write down a formula to show this procedure. We have n observations each giving a value, x, of the variable. We need to add up these x values and divide by n. The Greek letter Σ, capital sigma, is used as a summation sign so Σx is a shorthand way of telling us to add up all the x values. We have

$$\text{arithmetic mean} = \frac{\Sigma x}{n}$$

The symbol $\bar{x}$, xbar, is often used to stand for the arithmetic mean so

$$\bar{x} = \frac{\Sigma x}{n}$$

Exercise 7.3

1 The numbers of words on 9 consecutive lines of a book are

14, 12, 16, 12, 13, 13, 11, 13 and 13

(a) What is the modal number of words?
(b) What is the median number of words?
(c) What is the mean number of words?

2 The numbers of pupils absent in the 25 classes of school last Wednesday were

2, 3, 2, 0, 1 2, 4, 6, 3, 2 2, 0, 5, 7, 2 3, 2, 1, 4, 4 3, 2, 2, 6, 11

(a) What was the total number of absentees that day?
(b) Find the mean number of absentees per class.
(c) Find the mode of the number of absentees.

3 The ages, in years, of 14 people attending a family party were

12, 14, 42, 42, 7, 9, 35, 36, 6, 9, 37, 38, 67 and 68

Find the modal age. Find the median age. Find the mean age.
The 67- and 68-year old grandparents decide to leave the party early. What now are the values of the mode, the median and the mean? Comment on your results.

4 The heights in centimetres, measured correct to the nearest centimetre, of seven students are 142, 176, 154, 162, 168, 173, and 158. Find the mode, median and mean of these heights. Comment on your results.

If you had to investigate the heights of another group of seven students, how many measurements do you think you would need to make in order to determine (a) their median height, (b) their modal height, (c) their mean height?

5 A workshop employs 15 men. The total weekly wage bill is £2890.15. What is the mean weekly wage? Can you deduce what are the modal wage and the median wage?

6 Anna carried out a survey of shoe sizes in her class at school. She drew a line diagram to show her results.

Shoe sizes of my classmates

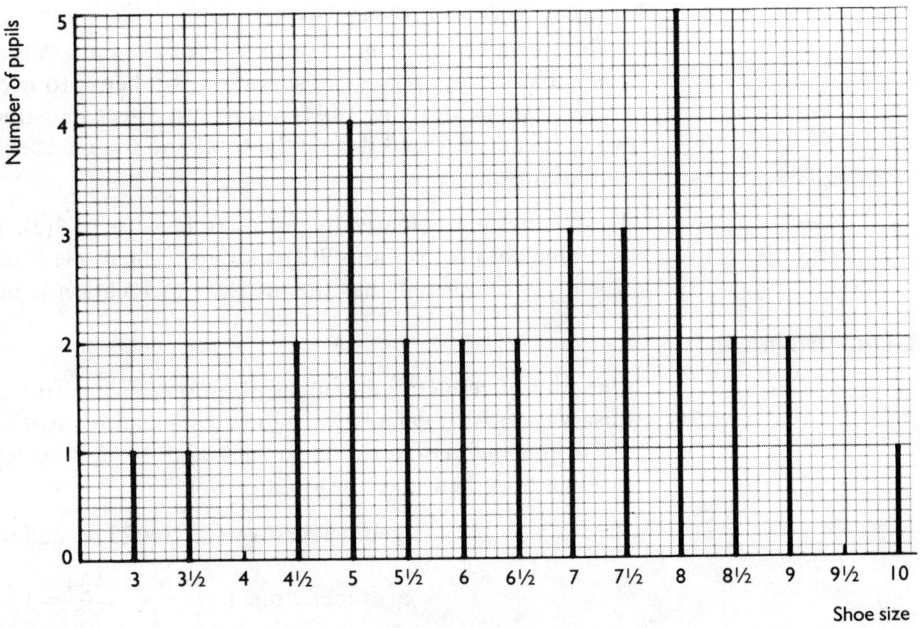

(a) What is the modal shoe size?
(b) How many pupils are in Anna's class?
(c) What is the median shoe size?
(d) Do you think it would be useful to work out the mean shoe size? Give reasons for your answer.
(e) Do you think Anna goes to a single-sex school or to a co-educational school? Why?
(f) Write a short letter to the shoe stockist for Anna's school, giving him any information from the survey that you think it would be useful for him to know.

7 Use your answer to Exercise 7.1 Question 2 to find the median and the mode for the number of complete letters on the pencils, Table 5.3.

8 Find the median pencil length using the stem-and-leaf diagram you drew in Exercise 7.1 Question 3.

Comparison of mode, median and mean

1 Mode
(a) It does not always exist.
(b) It may not be unique.
(c) It is easy to find.
(d) It is always one of the data values.
(e) The values of the other observations are not used.
(f) It may be an extreme value, i.e. either the largest or the smallest value.

2 Median
(a) It is easy to find.
(b) It will always be one of the data values or halfway between two data values.
(c) The values of the rest of the data are not used.
(d) Its value is not affected by an outlying observation.
(e) Half the data values are less than or equal to the median and half the data values are greater than or equal to the median.

3 Mean
(a) A calculation is needed to find it.
(b) Its value is not necessarily one of the data values.
(c) The value of every observation is taken into account in its calculation.
(d) A single outlying observation can affect its value greatly.
(e) It can be found if only the total and the number of the observations are known.

The mean is mathematically preferred because of 3(c). The median is preferred for some data for reasons 2(d) and 3(d). The mode is preferred for reason 1(d) when it is important that the measure of location is one of the data values.

Geometric mean

One way of reducing the effect of an outlier but still using the value of every observation is to calculate a geometric mean instead of an arithmetic mean.

To find the geometric mean of 9 and 25, for example, we work out their product and then take the square root.

$$\text{geometric mean} = \sqrt{9 \times 25} = \sqrt{225} = 15$$

$$\text{arithmetic mean} = \frac{9 + 25}{2} = \frac{34}{2} = 17$$

We can see that the geometric mean is less than the arithmetic mean in this example. In fact, the geometric mean is never greater than the arithmetic mean. It cannot be used, however, when one of the values is negative or zero.

To find the geometric mean of n values, we find their product and then take the nth root. For example, for the values 9, 25, and 120

$$\begin{aligned} \text{geometric mean} &= \sqrt[3]{9 \times 25 \times 120} \\ &= \sqrt[3]{27\,000} \\ &= (27\,000)^{1/3} \\ &= 30 \text{ (using a calculator or by inspection)} \end{aligned}$$

$$\text{Check: } 30 \times 30 \times 30 = 27\,000$$

The geometric mean is particularly useful when we wish to find an average in a situation of constant growth or constant decay, for example, in population growth studies, reproduction of bacteria, radioactive emissions and measurement of share price changes.

Exercise 7.4

1 Calculate (a) the arithmetic mean (b) the geometric mean of the numbers

1, 3, 5, 7, 9

2 40 bacteria were counted on a petri dish at 10.00 and 6250 were counted at 10.30. Use the geometric mean to estimate the number of bacteria on the dish at 10.15. Why do you think this will be a better estimate than the arithmetic mean?

3 The proportion of income spent on food by three families was 0.1, 0.4 and 0.2. What is the geometric mean proportion of income spent on food by these families?

Cumulative frequency

To find the median for a small number of observations, we have used an array. For larger numbers of observations, we found the median from a stem-and-leaf diagram, see Exercise 7.3 Questions 7 and 8. If the data set is in the form of a frequency table, we can find the median directly from the table by counting up the observations from the lowest value until we reach the median.

For the pencil data there are 50 observations, so the median is the $(50 + 1)/2$ th observation, i.e. the $25\frac{1}{2}$th observation, which is halfway between the 25th and 26th observations when they are arranged in order of size. Using Table 7.7, there are two pencils with 0 colours, $(2 + 9) = 11$ pencils with 0 or 1 colours and $(11 + 36) = 47$ with 0, 1 or 2 colurs. This tells us that the 25th and 26th values must both be 2 colours since 25 and 26 are between 11 and 47. Hence the median is 2 colours. (You can confirm this by counting the leaves in Table 7.5.)

The frequencies added up in this way are called **cumulative frequencies** and we can show all their values as in Table 7.9. They tell us how many observations were less than the stated value of the variable. We can represent the cumulative frequencies graphically on a **step diagram**, see Fig. 7.3, which is also referred to as a **cumulative frequency step polygon.** There were no values less than 0, so the cumulative frequency is zero until $x = 0$. Then we have two pencils with $x = 0$, so the graph 'steps up' to 2. It continues at 2 until the value

Table 7.9 Cumulative frequency table

Number of colours	Frequency	Cumulative frequency
		$0 < 0$
0	2	$2 < 1$
1	9	$11 < 2$
2	36	$47 < 3$
3	0	$47 < 4$
4	3	$50 < 5$
Total	50	

Number of colours on casing of pencils

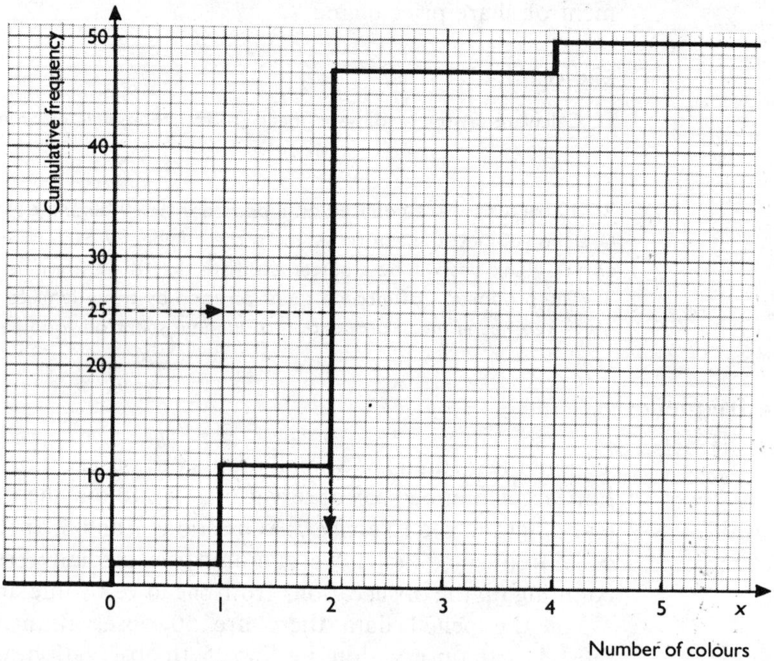

Fig. 7.3 *Cumulative frequency step diagram*

$x = 1$ is reached. Then we add on the nine pencils with $x = 1$ so the graph steps up to 11 and so on. Once we have added on the three pencils with $x = 4$, we have accounted for all the 50 pencils and the graph has reached its highest level at which it continues for any value of x greater than 4.

We can use the step diagram to find the median. The median is the value such that half the observations are less than or equal to it. The convention used is to work out half the total frequency, $50/2 = 25$, and to find the value of x corresponding to this cumulative frequency. The construction is shown by a dashed line in Fig. 7.3 and we find as before that the median is 2 colours. It could happen with some data that the cumulative frequency corresponding to the median is in line with one of the horizontal portions of the step diagram and we will not obtain a unique value of x. The convention in this case is to take the value of x halfway along the horizontal portion.

Exercise 7.5

1 Use the data of Exercise 7.3 Question 2. Make a cumulative frequency table and use it to find the median. Draw a cumulative frequency step diagram and use it to confirm that your calculated value of the median is correct.

2 The table shows the weekly number of TV sets sold by a shop for a period of 40 weeks.

Number of sets sold (x)	4	5	6	7	8	9	10
Number of weeks (f)	2	8	10	5	5	6	4

Work out the cumulative frequencies, draw a cumulative frequency step diagram and estimate the median.

Arithmetic mean for a frequency table

When the data are in a frequency table, we can find the arithmetic mean, $\bar{x}$, more quickly by modifying the original formula $\bar{x} = \Sigma x/n$.

Using the data from Table 7.7, which is given again in Table 7.10, we first need to find the total number of colours on all 50 pencils. There are 0 colours on the first 2 pencils in the table, 9 colours on the next 9 pencils as there is just 1 colour on each, 72 colours on the 36 pencils with 2 colours. There were 0 pencils with 3 colours and 3 pencils with 4 colours adding another 12 colours to the total. Altogether there are $0 + 9 + 72 + 0 + 12 = 93$ colours. Hence we have

$$\text{arithmetic mean} = \frac{93}{50} = 1.86 \text{ colours}$$

What we have done is to work out the product $f \times x = fx$ for each of the different values of x, as shown in the final column of Table 7.10, and then we added them up, i.e. we found Σfx. (You can write this with parentheses, $\Sigma(fx)$, to emphasise that you must work out each product first and then do the addition, but it is more usual to omit the parentheses.) We divide the sum by the total number of observations, n. n is equal to the sum of the frequencies so $n = \Sigma f$.

The modified formula for the mean becomes:

$$\bar{x} = \frac{\Sigma fx}{n} \quad \text{or} \quad \bar{x} = \frac{\Sigma fx}{\Sigma f}$$

Table 7.10 Frequency table: calculation of $\bar{x}$

Number of colours x	Frequency f	fx
0	2	0
1	9	9
2	36	72
3	0	0
4	3	12
Totals	50	93

Exercise 7.6

1 Use the frequency table in Exercise 7.5 Question 2 to find the mean number of TV sets sold per week.

2 Calculate the arithmetic mean of the set of numbers

0, 1, 1, 1, 1, 2, 2, 2, 2, 2, 2, 3, 3, 3, 4, 4.

3 The table shows the number of goals scored by local football teams in club matches one weekend last season. What is the mean number of goals scored per team?

Number of goals	0	1	2	3	4	5	6
Number of teams	27	26	29	15	2	0	1

4 I counted the number of cars passing my house in 60 consecutive one-minute intervals. The results are as shown.

Number of cars in one-minute interval	4	5	6	7	8
Number of intervals	10	14	16	8	12

(a) Draw a bar chart to represent the data.
(b) What is the modal number of cars per minute that pass my house?
(c) How many cars passed my house in this hour?
(d) What is the mean number of cars per minute that pass my house?
(e) Find the median number of cars per minute that pass my house.

Practical exercise 7.7

1 Refer to the data you collected in Practical exercise 5.5 and look at data for a discrete variable.
(a) Represent your data on a line.
(b) Construct a stem-and-leaf diagram.
(c) Make a frequency table.
(d) Draw a frequency bar chart.
(e) Find the mode, median and mean.
(f) Comment on what you have found.

2 Take a six-sided die and throw it 96 times. Keep a record of the score each time and of the number of throws using a table like the one shown.
(a) Represent your data on a frequency line diagram.
(b) Find the mode, median and mean score.
(c) Are the results as you expected? Explain.

Score on die	Tally	Tally of throws
1		
2		
3		
4		
5		
6		

8 One variable analysis – quantitative data, ungrouped or discrete (2)

Measures of dispersion

When comparing data sets, it is important to be able to measure the **spread** or **variation** in the observations as well as finding measures of location. For example, two data sets might have the same mean but in one set the observations are all close to the mean and in the second set some of the observations are close to the mean, while others are far away from the mean. There are several different measures of dispersion or measures of variation that we can use.

Range

At the start of any analysis, we use the simplest measure of spread, the range:

$$\text{range} = \text{largest observation} - \text{smallest observation}$$

It is easy to find but it is very crude as it uses the values of only two observations and its value is distorted by any outliers.

Referring to the pencil data base, Table 5.3, for the variable 'number of complete letters on casing'

$$\text{range} = 100 - 0 = 100$$

If pencil number 32 is not included, however, we have:

$$\text{range} = 59 - 0 = 59$$

Just the one pencil has made a very large difference to the value of the range and to get a better measure of the spread we need to use more of the information from the data set.

Quartiles

As the rame suggests, quartiles are related to quarters. We first arrange the data in order of size. The quartiles are defined as the values which divide this array into four parts, each containing equal numbers of observations. One quarter of the observations is less than or equal to the lower or first quartile, Q_1, two quarters, or one half, are less than or equal to the second quartile, Q_2, and three quarters are less than or equal to the upper or third quartile, Q_3. Thus the second quartile is the same as the median.

To find the quartiles in practice, we can use the following procedure which approximates to the theoretical definition above.

To find Q_1

Work out one quarter of the total frequency, $(n/4)$. If $n/4$ is exactly a whole number, k, Q_1 is halfway between the kth and the $(k+1)$th observations in the array. If $n/4$ is not exactly a whole number but lies between the whole numbers k and $k+1$, Q_1 is the value of the $(k+1)$th observation.

To find Q_3

Work out three quarters of the total frequency, $3n/4$ and then use the same procedure as for Q_1.

For example

(1) 10 observations

Raw data 1, 6, 1, 6, 5, 7, 0, 4, 8, 1

Array 0, 1, 1, 1, 4, 5, 6, 6, 7, 8

$$\text{median} = \text{value of } (10+1)/2 \text{ th observation}$$
$$= \text{value of } 5\tfrac{1}{2}\text{th observation}$$

$$\text{median} = \frac{4+5}{2} = 4.5$$

$$n/4 = 10/4 = 2.5$$
$$Q_1 = \text{value of 3rd observation}$$
$$Q_1 = 1$$
$$3n/4 = 3 \times 10/4 = 7.5$$
$$Q_3 = \text{value of 8th observation}$$
$$Q_3 = 6$$

(2) 11 observations

Raw data 3, 5, 4, 1, 1, 7, 8, 9, 8, 7, 0

Array 0, 1, 1, 3, 4, 5, 7, 7, 8, 8, 9

$$\text{median} = \text{value of } (11+1)/2 \text{ th observation}$$
$$= \text{value of 6th observation}$$
$$\text{median} = 5$$

$$n/4 = 11/4 = 2.75$$

$$Q_1 = \text{value of 3rd observation}$$

$$Q_1 = 1$$

$$3n/4 = 3 \times 11/4 = 8.25$$

$$Q_3 = \text{value of 9th observation}$$

$$Q_3 = 8$$

(3) 12 observations

Raw data 3, 5, 2, 3, 0, 6, 6, 8, 5, 2, 5, 0

Array 0, 0, 2, 2, 3, 3, 5, 5, 5, 6, 6, 8

$$\text{median} = \text{value of } (12 + 1)/2 \text{ th observation}$$

$$= \text{value of } 6\tfrac{1}{2}\text{th observation}$$

$$\text{median} = \frac{3 + 5}{2} = 4$$

$$n/4 = 12/4 = 3$$

Q_1 is halfway between the 3rd and 4th observations

$$Q_1 = \frac{2 + 2}{2} = 2$$

$$3n/4 = 3 \times 12/4 = 9$$

Q_3 is halfway between the 9th and 10th observations

$$Q_3 = \frac{5 + 6}{2} = 5.5$$

Interquartile range

The difference between the lower and upper quartile is called the **interquartile range** and it measures the spread of the middle 50% of the data.

$$\text{interquartile range} = \text{upper quartile} - \text{lower quartile}$$

$$= Q_3 - Q_1$$

The **semi-interquartile range,** sometimes called the **quartile deviation,** is also used as a measure of dispersion.

$$\text{semi-interquartile range} = \text{quartile deviation} = \frac{Q_3 - Q_1}{2}$$

For the examples (1), (2) and (3) above we have

	(1)	(2)	(3)
Upper quartile	6	8	5.5
Lower quartile	1	1	2
Interquartile range, $Q_3 - Q_1$	5	7	3.5
Semi-interquartile range, $(Q_3 - Q_1)/2$	2.5	3.5	1.75

These measures tell us that the spread of the middle values was greatest for example (2) and least for example (3).

If the data are in a stem-and-leaf diagram, we find the positions of Q_1 and Q_3 using the procedures given above and then count up the leaves until we reach the required values. For the data in Table 7.4, for example, we have 50 observations.

$$n/4 = 50/4 = 12.5$$

$$Q_1 = \text{value of 13th observation}$$

Counting up to the 13th leaf, we find $Q_1 = 7.0$ mm.

$$3n/4 = 3 \times 50/4 = 37.5$$

$$Q_3 = \text{value of 38th observation}$$

Counting up to the 38th leaf, we find $Q_3 = 7.9$ mm.

$$\text{interquartile range} = 7.9 - 7.0$$
$$= 0.9 \text{ mm}$$

$$\text{semi-interquartile range} = 0.45 \text{ mm}$$

For data in a frequency table, we first find the positions of Q_1 and Q_3 using the procedures given above and then we use the cumulative frequency table to find their values.

For the data in Table 7.9, for example, we again have 50 observations.

$$n/4 = 50/4 = 12.5$$

$$Q_1 = \text{value of 13th observation}$$

13 lies between the cumulative frequencies 11 and 47.

$$Q_1 = 2$$

$$3n/4 = 3 \times 50/4 = 37.5$$

$$Q_3 = \text{value of 38th observation}$$

38 lies between the cumulative frequencies 1 and 47.

$$Q_3 = 2$$

$$\text{interquartile range} = 2 - 2 = 0$$

Here we see that the spread of the middle 50% of the data is zero, with so many pencils having 2 colours on their casings.

Alternatively, we can use the cumulative frequency step diagram, Fig. 7.3. For Q_1, we work out one quarter of the total frequency ($50/4 = 12.5$) and find the value of x corresponding to this cumulative frequency. It can be seen that 12.5 on the vertical scale corresponds to the value $x = 2$ so $Q_1 = 2$. Similarly for Q_3, we work out three quarters of the total frequency ($3 \times 50/4 = 37.5$) and find the corresponding value of x. Again we find $Q_3 = 2$.

The values of the quartiles are unaffected by an outlying observation. To find the quartiles we do not use the value of every observation. The interquartile range or the quartile deviation is usually used as a measure of dispersion when the median is used as a measure of location.

Box-and-whisker plot

We can display the values of the smallest observation, the largest observation, the quartiles and the median of a data set on a box-and-whisker plot as shown in Fig. 8.1. The 'box' runs from the lower quartile to the upper quartile and is divided at the median value. One 'whisker' runs from the lower edge of the box to the lowest observation and another whisker goes from the highest edge of the box to the highest observation. Both whiskers end in large dots. A scaled line is included alongside the plot to show the values of the variable. The width of the box is not important but it is usually chosen to be about 1 cm. The box plots shown in Fig. 8.1 refer to the data sets (1), (2) and (3) on pp 68–9. From the plots we notice:

(a) each set has a smallest value of zero;
(b) the range of data set (2) is greater than that of data sets (1) and (3);
(c) the range of set (3) is the same as the range of set (1);
(d) set (3) has the smallest interquartile range and set (2) has the largest;
(e) in data set (3) the median is exactly midway between the extreme observations;
(f) in data set (3) the spread of each quarter of the data is very similar;
(g) in data set (2) the middle 50% of the data is much more spread out than either the lowest 25% or the highest 25%;
(h) in data set (1) the greatest spread is between Q_1 and the median with the lowest 25% having the smallest spread.

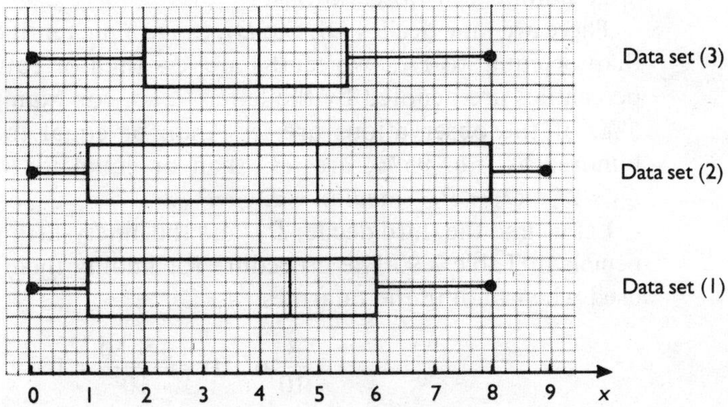

Fig. 8.1 *Box-and-whisker plots*

Exercise 8.1

1 Refer to Table 5.3 and find the range of the pencil lengths.
2 Find the median and the upper and lower quartiles of the following data sets.

(a) 3, 5, 2, 3, 0, 6, 6, 8, 5, 2, 5, 0, 3, 9, 5;
(b) 2, 9, 9, 3, 5, 8, 2, 1, 7, 1, 0, 5, 6, 8, 5, 8.

Draw box-and-whisker plots and compare the data sets.

3 The scores when a six-sided die was tossed 48 times were as follows:

2	3	3	3	5	6	2	5	1	3	5	5
5	4	4	6	1	2	4	4	6	6	4	1
2	1	2	5	2	3	5	1	6	4	4	4
2	1	5	2	6	5	6	2	4	6	3	2

(a) Construct a frequency table to show the data.
(b) Find the cumulative frequencies.
(c) Find the median and the quartiles from the cumulative frequency table.
(d) Draw a cumulative frequency step diagram and use it to find the median and the quartiles.
(e) What is the interquartile range?
(f) Find the semi-interquartile range.
(g) What is the difference in value between the median and the lower quartile? What is the difference in value between the upper quartile and the median? Comment on your answers.

4 Use your answer to Exercise 7.1 Question 2 to find the interquartile range of the number of complete letters on the pencils, Table 5.3.

5 Use your answer to Exercise 7.1 Question 3 to find the quartile deviation of the pencil lengths, Table 5.3.

Deciles and percentiles

When we require measures that divide up the data more finely, we can use deciles, which divide the array into ten parts, or percentiles, which divide the array into one hundred parts. They are particularly useful when dealing with large numbers of observations.

There are nine deciles $D_1, D_2, D_3, \dots D_9$. One tenth of the observations is less than or equal to D_1, two tenths are less than or equal to D_2 and so on. The percentiles are denoted by the letter P, so, for example, five hundredths, i.e. 5%, of the observations are less than or equal to P_5, whereas ninety-five hundredths, i.e. 95%, are less than or equal to P_{95}. You will notice that $Q_1 = P_{25}$, $Q_3 = P_{75}$, median $= D_5 = P_{50}$.

Let us find the third decile, D_3, and the ninety-fifth percentile, P_{95}, for the 50 pencils in Table 7.9. The procedure for finding them is exactly similar to that used when finding the quartiles.

$$\frac{3}{10} \text{ of } 50 = \frac{3 \times 50}{10} = 15$$

This is exactly a whole number so D_3 is halfway between the 15th and the 16th observations. From Table 7.9, both 15 and 16 lie between 11 and 47 so $D_3 = 2$.

$$\frac{95}{100} \text{ of } 50 = \frac{95 \times 50}{100} = 47.5$$

P_{95} is the value of the 48th observation. From Table 7.9, 48 lies between 47 and 50 so $P_{95} = 4$. We could also have counted the leaves in Table 7.5 to obtain the same results. Alternatively, using the cumulative frequency step diagram, Fig. 7.3, we can see that a cumulative frequency of 15 corresponds to $x = 2$, so $D_3 = 2$, and cumulative frequency of 47.5 corresponds to $x = 4$, giving $P_{95} = 4$ as above.

Exercise 8.2

1 Using your cumulative frequency table and step diagram for Exercise 8.1 Question 3, find D_2, D_8 and P_{15}.

2 A record was kept of motor vehicles passing in one direction along a main road. The number of cars in each group of 10 vehicles was noted for a total of 200 successive groups.

Number of cars in a group of 10 vehicles	0	1	2	3	4	5	6	7	8	9	10
Number of groups	0	0	15	19	31	50	31	27	16	11	0

(a) What is the range of the data?
(b) Find the fifth and ninety-fifth percentiles. What is the difference in their values?
(c) Find the first and ninth deciles. What is the difference in their values?
(d) Find the interquartile range.
(e) Comment on your results.

3 Use your answer to Exercise 7.2 Question 2 to find all the deciles for the number of complete letters on the pencils, Table 5.3. Comment on your results.

Mean (absolute) deviation (from the mean)

This measure of dispersion is based on the difference between each observation, x, and the mean, $\bar{x}$, of a data set. This difference is called the **deviation.** We work out $x - \bar{x}$ for each observation and then find the mean of all n deviations. For observations less than $\bar{x}$, $x - \bar{x}$ is negative, but we ignore the minus signs. In symbols we write $|x - \bar{x}|$ to show that we are taking the positive value of the difference. ($|x|$ is called the **modulus** or **absolute value** of x.)

$$\text{mean deviation} = \frac{\Sigma|x - \bar{x}|}{n}$$

For example
7 observations
Raw data (x) 4, 2, 1, 1, 5, 4, 4

$$\text{mean } \bar{x} = \frac{\Sigma x}{n} = \frac{21}{7} = 3$$

Table 8.1 Calculation of mean deviation for ungrouped data

x	$x-\bar{x}$	$\|x-\bar{x}\|$
4	1	1
2	−1	1
1	−2	2
1	−2	2
5	2	2
4	1	1
4	1	1
Total		10

From Table 8.1 mean deviation $= \frac{10}{7} = 1.43$ to 2 dec. pl.

When the data are in a frequency table, the formula becomes:

$$\text{mean deviation} = \frac{\Sigma f|x - \bar{x}|}{n} \text{ or } \frac{\Sigma f|x - \bar{x}|}{\Sigma f}$$

It is usually easiest to set out the calculation in a table. The calculation for the data from Table 7.7 is shown in Table 8.2.

$$\bar{x} = \frac{\Sigma fx}{n} = \frac{93}{50} = 1.86$$

$$\text{mean deviation} = \frac{\Sigma f|x - \bar{x}|}{n} = \frac{22.92}{50} = 0.46 \text{ to 2 dec. pl.}$$

Table 8.2 Calculation of mean deviation for a frequency table

Number of colours x	Frequency f	fx	$(x-\bar{x})$	$\lvert x-\bar{x}\rvert$	$f\lvert x-\bar{x}\rvert$
0	2	0	−1.86	1.86	3.72
1	9	9	−0.86	0.86	7.74
2	36	72	0.14	0.14	5.04
3	0	0	1.14	1.14	0
4	3	12	2.14	2.14	6.42
Totals	50	93			22.92

To work out the mean deviation we use the value of every observation. If the mean deviation is small, the observations are, on average, close to the mean and there is little spread in the data. If the mean deviation is large, the observations are, on average, far from the mean and there is large variation in the data. Although we use the value of every observation in its calculation, the mean deviation is not much used in advanced statistical work because the modulus function $\lvert x \rvert$ is difficult to work with mathematically.

The deviations from the median can be used instead of deviations from the mean but in an examination assume the mean is to be used unless you are specifically told otherwise.

Standard deviation and variance

The standard deviation is the most important and widely used measure of dispersion. It uses the values of every observation and is easy to manipulate mathematically in advanced statistical work.

We work out the deviation $x-\bar{x}$ for each observation, as before, but we now square all these deviations. You will remember that $(-1)\times(-1)=+1$ so all the squared deviations will be positive. If we find the mean of the squared deviations, we have a measure of variation, called the **variance**.

$$\text{variance} = \frac{\Sigma(x-\bar{x})^2}{n}$$

Unfortunately, this measure has square units. For example, if our data are in units of pence, the variance has units 'square pence'. It is convenient to have a measure in the same units as the data so we take the square root of the variance. The result is the **standard deviation.**

$$\text{standard deviation} = \sqrt{\text{variance}} = \sqrt{\frac{\Sigma(x-\bar{x})^2}{n}}$$

Note: variance = (standard deviation)^2

For example:

7 observations

Raw data (x) 4, 2, 1, 1, 5, 4, 4

$$\text{mean } \bar{x} = \frac{\Sigma x}{n} = \frac{21}{7} = 3$$

Table 8.3 Calculation of standard deviation for ungrouped data

x	$x-\bar{x}$	$(x-\bar{x})^2$
4	1	1
2	−1	1
1	−2	4
1	−2	4
5	2	4
4	1	1
4	1	1
Total		16

From Table 8.3

$$\text{variance} = \frac{16}{7} = 2.29 \text{ to 2 dec. pl.}$$

$$\text{standard deviation} = \sqrt{\text{variance}}$$
$$= 1.51 \text{ to 2 dec. pl.}$$

When the data are in a frequency table, the formula becomes:

$$\text{standard deviation} = \sqrt{\text{variance}}$$
$$= \sqrt{\frac{\Sigma f(x-\bar{x})^2}{n}} \text{ or } \sqrt{\frac{\Sigma f(x-\bar{x})^2}{\Sigma f}}$$

Make sure that you square only $(x-\bar{x})$. The frequency, f, is not squared. The calculation for the data in Table 7.7 is shown in Table 8.4 with the working rounded to 2 decimal places.

$$\bar{x} = \frac{\Sigma fx}{n} = \frac{93}{50} = 1.86$$

$$\text{variance} = \frac{\Sigma f(x-\bar{x})^2}{n} = \frac{28.04}{50} = 0.56 \text{ to 2 dec. pl.}$$

$$\text{standard deviation} = \sqrt{\text{variance}} = 0.75 \text{ to 2 dec. pl.}$$

Table 8.4 Calculation of standard deviation for a frequency table

Number of colours x	Frequency f	fx	$(x-\bar{x})$	$(x-\bar{x})^2$	$f(x-\bar{x})^2$
0	2	0	−1.86	3.46	6.92
1	9	9	−0.86	0.74	6.66
2	36	72	0.14	0.02	0.72
3	0	0	1.14	1.30	0
4	3	12	2.14	4.58	13.74
Totals	50	93			28.04

The values of both the mean deviation and the standard deviation are affected by outliers. The standard deviation is affected more than the mean deviation because of the squaring process. For this reason it may be preferable to use the interquartile range as a measure of spread with some sets of data.

Exercise 8.3

1 Kevin regularly buys packets of fruit gums. He has noticed that the number of green ones, which he does not like, varies from packet to packet. He recorded the number in the last 8 packets he bought.

Number of green gums 3, 4, 2, 4, 3, 6, 4, 6

(a) What is the mean number of green gums per packet?
(b) Find the mean deviation of the number of green gums per packet.
(c) Calculate the variance of the number of green gums per packet.
(d) What is the value of the standard deviation?

2 Jayne buys fruit gums but she does not like the red ones. In her last 10 packets she found:

Number of red gums 2, 4, 2, 3, 4, 2, 2, 3, 3, 4

Find the mean number of red gums per packet. Also calculate the mean deviation, the variance and the standard deviation.

Compare the results with your answers to Question 1.

3 You are asked to compare the weekly outputs of two factories A and B. Do this by calculating the mean and the mean deviation for each factory using the data given.

Weekly output (number of batches)

Week	Factory ABC	Factory UVW
1	88	126
2	91	82
3	88	100
4	97	26
5	91	92
6	80	47
7	90	98
8	96	71
9	90	146
10	84	107

4 The matron at a school kept a record of the number of accidents she had to deal with each day during one school year.

Number of accidents per day	0	1	2	3	4
Number of days	108	45	36	21	10

(a) Find the mean number of accidents per day.
(b) Find the mean deviation of the number of accidents per day.
(c) Calculate the variance and the standard deviation.

Some of the accidents were due to pupils using PE equipment without supervision. The next school year, the use of this equipment without supervision was banned. The matron's record of accidents was as follows:

Number of accidents per day	0	1	2	3	4	5
Number of days	120	48	29	15	7	1

Find the mean, the mean deviation, the variance and the standard deviation for these data and comment on the differences you find.

5 (a) Refer to Table 8.1. What is the sum of the deviations $\Sigma(x - \bar{x})$?
(b) Refer to Table 8.2. What is the sum of the deviations, $\Sigma f(x - \bar{x})$?

6 (a) Find the arithmetic mean and the standard deviation of the numbers

4 8 3 1 7 5

(b) Add 10 to each of the numbers to get

14 18 13 11 17 15

What is the arithmetic mean and the standard deviation of these numbers?
(c) Write down the arithmetic mean and the standard deviation of the numbers

104 108 103 101 107 105

(d) Use a similar method to find the arithmetic mean and the standard deviation of the numbers

1003 1006 1002 1004 1007

7 (a) Find the arithmetic mean and the standard deviation of the numbers

2 5 6 9 4

(b) Multiply each of the numbers by 4 to get

8 20 24 36 16

What is the arithmetic mean and the standard deviation of these numbers?

(c) What is the arithmetic mean and the standard deviation of the numbers

20 50 60 90 40

(d) Use a similar method to find the arithmetic mean and the standard deviation of the numbers

75 25 125 150

Methods of simplifying and checking calculations

Use of calculator

For project work you may find it useful to have a statistical calculator, i.e. one which has a standard deviation (SD) mode. In this mode, you enter each item of data using the appropriate key, often marked x_D or DATA. To find the mean, press the key marked $\bar{x}$ and to find the standard deviation, use the key marked σ or σ_n. Some calculators work out the variance, marked v, and you then take the square root to find the standard deviation.

Some makes of calculator, e.g. CASIO, allow you to enter data from a frequency table and this is a considerable saving of time. To enter the data from Table 7.7, for example, you press the following keys in SD mode:

$$0 \times 2\ x_D\ 1 \times 9\ x_D\ 2 \times 36\ x_D\ 4 \times 3\ x_D$$

Then press $\bar{x}$ to find the mean and σ_n for the standard deviation.

For examination purposes, you usually have to show full details of your working but, even so, remember to use the memory on your calculator to accumulate sums so that you do not need to re-enter previous results. For example, in Table 8.4, we first work out Σfx, as follows:

$0 \times 2 =$ **Min** (The first entry to the memory overwriting any previous entry)
$1 \times 9 =$ **M+** (Adds on to whatever is in the memory.)
$2 \times 36 =$ **M+**
$4 \times 3 =$ **M+**
MR (Recalls the memory, i.e. gives Σfx.)

You can write down the intermediate products 0, 9, 72 and 12 as they appear. So far the time saved is not great as the numbers were small but the next stage in finding the standard deviation is almost always quicker using the memory. The procedure is:

$$0 - 1.86 = x^2 \times \ \ 2 = \mathbf{M}\text{in}$$
$$1 - 1.86 = x^2 \times \ \ 9 = \mathbf{M}+$$
$$2 - 1.86 = x^2 \times 36 = \mathbf{M}+$$
$$4 - 1.86 = x^2 \times \ \ 3 = \mathbf{M}+$$
$$\mathbf{MR} \text{ (gives } \Sigma f(x - \bar{x})^2)$$

Use of working zero and scaling

It is better to work with as small numbers as possible because we are less likely to make mistakes.

From the results of Exercise 8.3, Question 6, you will have found that if we add (or subtract) a constant amount to (or from) each item in a data set, the standard deviation is unchanged and the mean is altered by the amount added (or subtracted).
For example:

Raw data 1203 1215 1204 1207

As these values are all just above 1200, substract 1200 from each value.

Transformed data 3 15 4 7

$$\text{new mean} = \frac{29}{4} = 7.25$$

$$\text{new standard deviation} = \sqrt{\frac{88.75}{4}} = 4.71 \text{ to 2 dec. pl.}$$

$$\text{mean of original data} = 7.25 + 1200 = 1207.25$$
$$\text{standard deviation of original data} = 4.71$$

We say we are working from a zero of 1200 or that we are working with an assumed mean of 1200.

From the results of Exercise 8.3, Question 7 you will have found that if you multiply (or divide) each item of a data set by a constant amount, the mean and the standard deviation are also multiplied (or divided) by that amount.
For example:

Raw data 0.001 0.020 0.015 0.009

To convert these to small whole numbers, multiply by 1000.

Transformed data 1 20 15 9

$$\text{new mean} = \frac{45}{4} = 11.25$$

$$\text{new standard deviation} = \sqrt{\frac{200.75}{4}} = 7.08 \text{ to 2 dec. pl.}$$

$$\text{mean of original data} = 11.25/1000 = 0.011\,25$$
$$\text{standard deviation of original data} = 7.08/1000 = 0.0708$$

This procedure is called scaling the data.

We can, of course, combine the use of a working zero and scaling as follows:

	Raw data	1.025	1.040	1.015	1.045
(1)	Subtract 1	0.025	0.040	0.015	0.045
(2)	Multiply by 1000	25	40	15	45
(3)	Divide by 5	5	8	3	9

	Mean	Standard deviation
Stage (3)	$\dfrac{25}{4} = 6.25$	$\sqrt{\dfrac{22.75}{4}} = 2.38$ to 2 dec. pl.
Stage (2)	$6.25 \times 5 = 31.25$	$2.38 \times 5 = 11.90$
Stage (1)	$31.25/1000 = 0.031\,25$	$11.90/1000 = 0.0119$
Raw data	$0.031\,25 + 1 = 1.031\,25$	0.0119

Alternative formulae for standard deviation

When you worked out the standard deviation in Exercise 8.3, Questions 1, 2 and 4, you probably thought that the calculation was 'not bad' when $\bar{x}$ came out to be a whole number because then the deviations were also whole numbers. When $\bar{x}$ is not a whole number, the calculation, even with a calculator, is much more tedious.

The formulae for the standard deviation can be rewritten to make the arithmetic easier using the following equalitier.

$$\frac{\Sigma(x-\bar{x})^2}{n} = \frac{\Sigma x^2}{n} - \left(\frac{\Sigma x}{n}\right)^2 = \frac{\Sigma x^2}{n} - \bar{x}^2$$

$$\frac{\Sigma f(x-\bar{x})^2}{\Sigma f} = \frac{\Sigma fx^2}{\Sigma f} - \left(\frac{\Sigma fx}{\Sigma f}\right)^2 = \frac{s fx^2}{\Sigma f} - \bar{x}^2$$

Table 8.5 Calculation of standard deviation of ungrouped data using alternative formula

	x	x^2
	4	16
	2	4
	1	1
	1	1
	5	25
	4	16
	4	16
Totals	21	79

Tables 8.5 and 8.6 show the calculations of the sums for the data sets used in Tables 8.3 and 8.4. From Table 8.5

$$\text{standard deviation} = \sqrt{\frac{79}{7} - \left(\frac{21}{7}\right)^2}$$
$$= \sqrt{11.2875 - 9}$$
$$= \sqrt{2.2857} = 1.51 \text{ to 2 dec. pl.}$$

From Table 8.6,

$$\text{standard deviation} = \sqrt{\frac{201}{50} - \left(\frac{93}{50}\right)^2}$$
$$= \sqrt{4.02 - 1.86^2}$$
$$= \sqrt{4.02 - 3.4596}$$
$$= \sqrt{0.5604}$$
$$= 0.75 \text{ to 2 dec. pl.}$$

Table 8.6 Calculation of standard deviation of a frequency table using alternative formula

Number of colours (x)	Frequency f	fx	fx^2
0	2	0	0
1	9	9	9
2	36	72	144
3	0	0	0
4	3	12	48
Totals	50	93	201

Our results are identical to those we obtained before. The alternative formulae are usually quicker to use than the original formulae when $\bar{x}$ is not a whole number.

Checking

Always check that the values you have obtained for measures of location and dispersion are reasonable. It is very easy to get digits transposed or a decimal point in the wrong place.

Points worth remembering are:

1 the values of the mean and median must be between the lowest observation and the highest observation;

2 a mode must be one of the values in the data set;

3 the interquartile range, the mean deviation and the standard deviation are all less than the range of the data set;

4 the standard deviation is approximately one sixth of the range;

5 from Exercise 8.3 Question 5, the sum of the deviations from the mean equals zero. If it does not, you have made a mistake in your arithmetic.

Exercise 8.4

1 Find the mean and the standard deviation of the following lengths.

(cm) 0.386 0.391 0.396 0.380 0.397 0.390

2 The diameters of 8 pieces of tubing in millimetres are:

6.33 6.33 6.30 6.36 6.39 6.37 6.38 6.41

Jack recorded the mean diameter as 6.63 mm with a standard deviation of 0.34 mm. Why do you know at once that these results are incorrect? Find the correct values.

3 Rework Questions 1, 2 and 4 of Exercise 8.3 using the alternative formulae for the standard deviation.

4 Samantha travels to and from school each day by bus, a total of 10 journeys each week. Sometimes the bus does not come so she has to walk and is late for school or late returning home. She decided to keep a record for a whole school year of the number of times each week that the bus did not arrive so that she could report to the bus company at the end of the year.

Her records show:

Number of times bus did not arrive (x)	0	1	2	3	4	5
Number of weeks (f)	10	12	10	5	2	1

(a) How many times altogether did the bus not arrive?
(b) What is this as a percentage of all Samantha's journey's?
(c) What is the mean number of times per week that the bus did not come?
(d) Find the standard deviation.
(e) Find the median and the interquartile range.
(f) What is the mode?
(g) Write a suitable report for Samantha to send to the bus company, incorporating the results of your calculations, without using technical terms.

5 The largest out of over 100 observations in a data set is replaced by an even larger observation.
(a) Name a measure of location which would be (i) affected, (ii) unaffected
(b) Name a measure of dispersion which would be (i) affected, (ii) unaffected.

Practical exercise 8.5

1 Refer to the data you collected in Practical exercise 5.5 and partially analysed in Practical exercise 7.7 Question 1. Continue your analysis by working out the interquartile range, the mean deviation and the standard deviation. Draw a box-and-whisker plot for your results. Comment on what you have found.

2 (a) Toss 2 coins 80 times and record the number of heads occurring at each toss. Find the relative frequencies of 0, 1 and 2 heads and show your results on a line diagram. Find the mean number of heads per toss and the standard deviation.
(b) Toss 3 coins 80 times and record the number of heads occurring at each toss. Find the relative frequencies of 0, 1, 2 and 3 heads and show your results on a line diagram. Find the mean number of heads per toss and the standard deviation.
(c) Repeat the procedure with 4 coins.
(d) Comment on your results. Are there any relationships you notice? What answers did you expect to get?

3 Select a fiction book either from your own collection or from a library. Open the book randomly and count the number of words in the first sentence on the right hand page. Repeat the procedure until you have 40 observations. Make a descriptive summary of your data, using any tables, diagrams and measures of location and dispersion that you think are appropriate.

You can extend the exercise, if desired, by repeating the procedure with a book by a different author and comparing the results.

9 One variable analysis – quantitative data, grouped frequency distributions (1)

Construction of a grouped frequency distribution

Need for grouping

In the analysis so far, using stem-and-leaf diagrams and frequency tables for a discrete variable, we have worked with the actual values of the data as they were recorded. In some circumstances it is more appropriate to put the observations into **groups** or **classes** containing a range of values. This can simplify the analysis and makes overall patterns in the data easier to see. We lose information in this process but, provided we are careful with the choice of classes, the errors introduced into our analysis by grouping are small in general. Grouping should be considered only for large numbers of observations. Usually we would not group fewer than 20 observations.

Grouping is often used for discrete data taking a wide range of values. For example, in Table 5.3, the variable 'number of complete letters on casing' takes values from 0 to 100. It would be acceptable to put the data into groups 0–9, 10–19, 20–29 etc. For the variable 'numbers of colours on casing', however, grouping would not be appropriate as this variable takes only the four values 0, 1, 2 and 4.

Grouping is most commonly used when we have a continuous variable. Measurements of a continuous variable are accurate only to within the limits of the measuring equipment. For example, there are four pencils in Table 5.3 with length recorded as 84 mm but, as they are measured to the nearest millimetre, their actual lengths could be anywhere from 83.5 mm to 84.5 mm. Since all we know is that the length lies in this interval rather that at 84 mm precisely, it is logical to count up the number of observations occurring in an interval instead of counting the number that happen to be recorded at one particular value.

Choice of classes

As with all data analysis, we look first at the range of the data. The classes must cover this range but they must not overlap, so that each observation belongs to one, and only one, class. The number of classes to use is between 5 and 20. If you use too few classes, too much information is lost in the grouping process. If too many classes are used, there is insufficient simplification of the analysis. Five classes would be appropriate for between 20 and 30 observations whereas 20 classes would be needed for a thousand or more observations. Between 7 and 10 classes should be used for about 100 observations.

Try to choose classes that are convenient to work with. For example, it is easier to use classes 0–9, 10–19, 20–29 etc. than classes 1–10, 11–20, 21–30 etc. because all the units go into one class, all the tens in the next, all the twenties in the next and so on, so that we need only look at the first digit when allocating the data to the appropriate groups.

Referring to the variable 'length of pencils', in Table 5.3, we find the 50 pencils range in length from 43 mm to 175 mm. Appropriate classes, lengths to the nearest mm, would be

40–59   60–79   80–99   100–119   120–139   140–159   160–179

Class limits and boundaries

The term 'class limits' is used for the smallest and largest observations that can be recorded in a class. With the pencil lengths, they are 40 mm and 59 mm for the first class, 60 mm and 79 mm for the second class and so on.

The term 'class boundary' is used for the value that divides one class from its neighbour. As the pencil lengths are recorded to the nearest millimetre, any pencil with actual length between 59.5 and 60.0 mm, for example, will be in the 60–79 class whereas a pencil with length between 59.0 and 59.5 mm will be in the 40–59 class. The dividing value is thus 59.5 mm. Hence the boundaries are 39.5 mm and 59.5 mm for the first class and 59.5 mm and 79.5 mm for the second class and so on.

The **length,** or **width, of a class interval** is the difference between the class boundaries, so for the pencil lengths in every class:

$$\text{length of class interval} = 20 \text{ mm}$$

The analysis is usually simpler if equal length intervals are used, as here. This is not appropriate in every case. For the variable 'number of complete letters on casing', Table 5.3, the range is from 0 to 100. Classes 0–9, 10–19, 20–29 etc. seem appropriate at first sight but, inspecting the data more closely, we see that 100 is an outlier and we would have several empty classes if we continued with 60–69, 70–79 up to 100–109. We could use a longer class interval for high values of the variable, e.g. 60–109. Alternatively we could have an **open-ended** class, 60 and over, which has no specific upper limit.

When grouping discrete data, we treat the values as though they were continuous, so the value 10, for instance, is considered to cover the interval from 9.5 to 10.5 and the value 0 goes from −0.5 to +0.5. The class boundaries for the 'number of complete letters on the casing' are −0.5 and

9.5, 9.5 and 19.5, ..., 59.5 and 109.5 using the classes mentioned previously. If the open-ended class, 60 and over, is used, then we cannot specify its upper class boundary.

The midpoint of a class interval is the value halfway between the class boundaries and is sometimes called the **class mark.** The midpoints are 49.5 mm, 69.5 mm, 89.5 mm, etc for the pencil lengths and 4.5, 14.5, 24.5, 34.5, 44.5 and 84.5 for the number of letters. If the open-ended class is used, we cannot work out the midpoint.

Allocation of data to classes

If a stem-and-leaf diagram has been drawn, the number of observations in the chosen classes can be totted up directly. If you are working directly from the raw data, it is convenient to use a tally chart. Using the data on pencil lengths from Table 5.3, we work systematically pencil by pencil. Pencil number 00 has length 84 mm so we put a tally mark against the class 80–99, pencil 01 has length 132 mm so we put a tally mark against the class 120–139 and so on. Table 9.1 shows the tally chart as it appears up to and including pencil 15.

Table 9.2 shows the completed chart with the frequencies written in. A **grouped frequency distribution** consists of the first and last columns of this table. Often when you are using data collected by someone else, you will be presented with just a grouped frequency distribution and you will have no details of the raw data from which it was constructed.

Table 9.1 Incomplete tally chart for lengths of 50 pencils

Length (mm)	Tally
40– 59	
60– 79	~~IIII~~ I
80– 99	II
100–119	
120–139	II
140–159	II
160–179	IIII

Table 9.2 Grouped frequency distribution for lengths of 50 pencils

Length (mm)	Tally	Frequency
40– 59	III	3
60– 79	~~IIII~~ ~~IIII~~ I	11
80– 99	~~IIII~~ IIII	9
100–119	~~IIII~~ I	6
120–139	~~IIII~~ III	8
140–159	~~IIII~~ I	6
160–179	~~IIII~~ II	7
Total		50

Exercise 9.1

1 The times taken for a businessman to drive between home and work are recorded correct to the nearest minute.

Time (minutes)

30	35	33	40	42	57	58	50
42	37	48	55	52	53	63	39
49	57	40	60	41	56	64	55
60	51	62	50	32	47	38	51

What is the range of times?

Copy out and complete the grouped frequency distribution using the class intervals shown overleaf.

Times (minutes)	Tally	Frequency
30–34		
35–39		
40–44		
45–49		
50–54		
55–59		
60–64		
Total		

2 The weights of 60 pebbles taken from Kaybury beach were recorded to the nearest gram.

Weight (g)

244	182	350	291	207	264	255	494	172	211
394	65	540	473	278	82	226	294	102	349
513	294	260	277	244	284	298	226	273	252
282	104	454	527	174	283	266	261	401	443
76	71	182	269	132	229	264	244	227	229
495	432	235	159	181	171	350	268	120	137

(a) What was the weight of the smallest pebble?
(b) What was the weight of the largest pebble?
(c) Using classes 0–99, 100–199, 200–299, 300–399, 400–499, 500–599, all measurements in grams, construct a grouped frequency distribution from the data.
(d) How many pebbles weighed less than 199.5 g?
(e) What proportion of pebbles weighed less than 199.5 g?
(f) What percentage of the pebbles weighed more than 199.5 g?

3 Students' weights were recorded in the following frequency distribution.

Weights (kg)	Frequency
50 up to 55	3
55 up to 60	6
60 up to 65	11
65 up to 70	12
70 up to 75	4
75 up to 80	8

(a) How many weighed 70 kg or more?
(b) What proportion weighed less than 60 kg?
(c) What percentage weighed 75 kg or more?

4 A local college asks students to state 'age last birthday' on their registration forms. If the college produces a grouped frequency distribution of student's ages, what is the actual age represented by the midpoint of the class 20–24 years? What is the upper class boundary of this class?

5 Observations of a continuous variable have been put into 3 classes whose midpoints are 17.5, 30 and 45. The lower class boundary of the first class is 15.

(a) What is the upper class boundary of the first class?
(b) What is the lower class boundary of the second class?

(c) What is the upper class boundary of the second class?
(d) What is the length of the second class interval?
(e) Work out the length of the third class interval.

6 The times taken to do a given task were recorded as shown.

Time (minutes)	5–	10–	15–	20 or more
Frequency	4	14	20	15

State the class boundaries of the first class if
(a) the times are measured correct to the nearest minute;
(b) the times are measured correct to the nearest second.

7 In order to test one of their products, a company recorded how long a sample of 100 light bulbs lasted. The results are shown in the table. No light bulb lasted more than 4000 hours and the life times are correct to the nearest hour.

Lifetime of at least	Frequency
2000 h	100
2400 h	90
2800 h	63
3200 h	28
3600 h	5

Construct a grouped frequency distribution from the given information.

8 Refer to Table 5.3 and construct a grouped frequency distribution for the variable 'number of complete letters on the casing' using classes 0–9, 10–19, 20–29, 30–39, 40–49, 50–59 and 60–109.

Graphical representations of a grouped frequency distribution

Histogram

In a histogram, the frequency in each class is represented by drawing a rectangle whose base is the class interval and whose area is proportional to the class frequency.

Class intervals of equal length

If the class intervals are all of the same length, the rectangles must be drawn so that their heights are proportional to the class frequencies.

- mark the class boundaries on a horizontal scale
- rule a vertical scale going from 0 to at least the highest class frequency
- draw each rectangle with base the class interval and height the class frequency
- the vertical axis can be labelled 'Frequency' or, preferably, 'Frequency density per class interval length'

The histogram for the lengths of the 50 pencils is shown in Fig. 9.1.

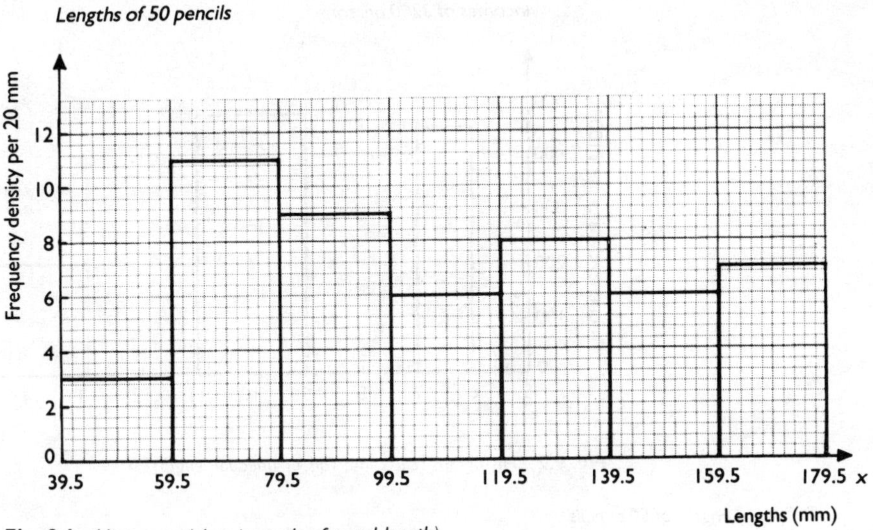

Fig. 9.1 *Histogram (class intervals of equal length)*

Class intervals of unequal length

- mark the class boundaries on a horizontal scale
- choose one of the class interval lengths as the standard
- work out the frequency density in each class relative to this standard length, which must be clearly stated on the vertical axis
- the vertical scale goes from 0 to at least the highest value of the frequency density
- draw each rectangle with base the class interval and height the frequency density per standard interval

In this way the areas are in correct proportion, whatever the lengths of the class intervals.

Table 9.3 shows a grouped frequency distribution of annual incomes which has unequal class intervals.
Choosing £1000 as the standard class interval length, the frequency densities per £1000 are shown in the final column of the table and the corresponding histogram is in Fig. 9.2. Assuming incomes are recorded correct to the nearest penny, the class boundaries are £4999.995, £5999.995, £6999.995 etc, but, for simplicity, these are written on the graph as £5000, £6000, £7000 etc.

Table 9.3 Grouped frequency distribution (class intervals of unequal length)

Income (£)	Number of persons	Class interval length (£)	Frequency density per £1000
5 000 and up to 6 000	200	1000	200
6 000 and up to 7 000	450	1000	450
7 000 and up to 9 000	800	2000	400
9 000 and up to 11 000	950	2000	475
11 000 and up to 15 000	800	4000	200
Total	3200		

Incomes of 3200 persons

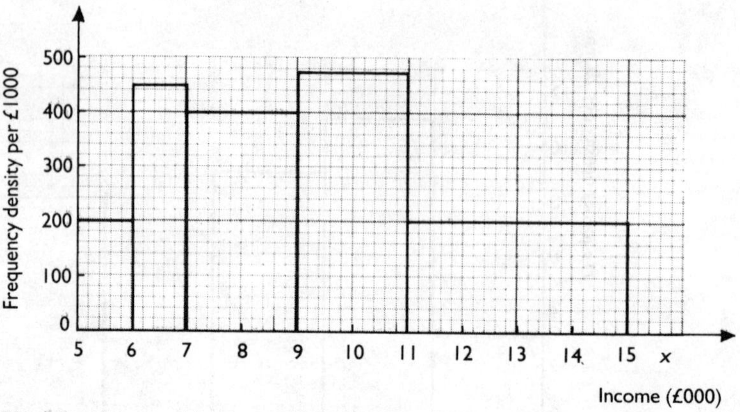

Fig. 9.2 *Histogram (class intervals of unequal length)*

Lengths of 50 pencils

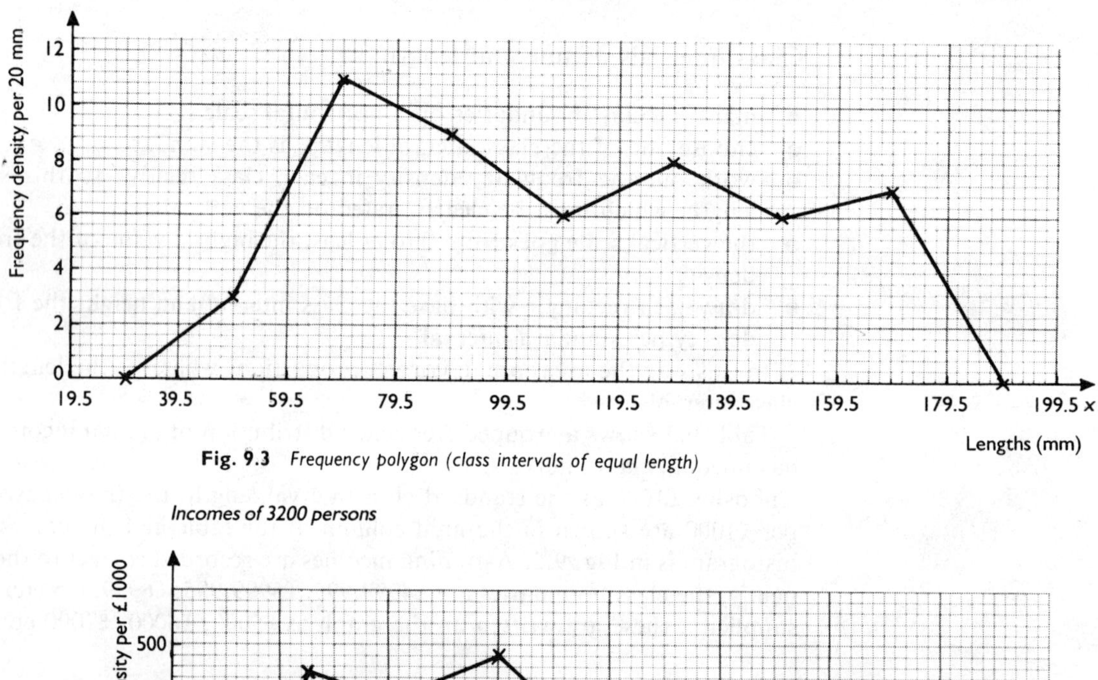

Fig. 9.3 *Frequency polygon (class intervals of equal length)*

Incomes of 3200 persons

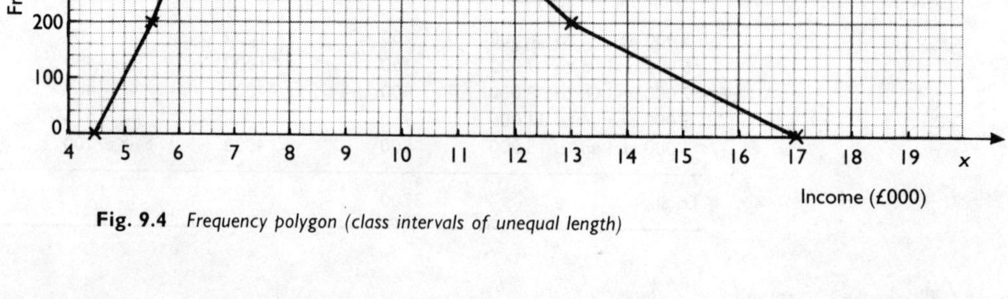

Fig. 9.4 *Frequency polygon (class intervals of unequal length)*

Frequency polygon

For each class, mark the point which would be at the middle of the top of each rectangle in the histogram, i.e. plot each class frequency density at the class midpoint. Join adjacent pairs of points with ruled lines. Add one class with zero frequency at each end of the distribution. These classes should be the same lengths as their neighbours. In this way the area enclosed by the frequency polygon will be the same as that enclosed by the histogram and will be proportional to the total frequency. Figures 9.3 and 9.4 show the frequency polygon for the pencil lengths and the income distributions.

Relative frequency and percentage frequency

Histograms and frequency polygons can be drawn using relative frequencies or percentage frequencies. This is particularly useful when comparing distributions of the same variable but with differing total numbers of observations. Table 9.4 shows the relative and percentage frequencies for the distribution of the pencil lengths.

Table 9.4 Relative and percentage frequency distributions

Length (mm)	Frequency	Relative frequency	Percentage frequency
40– 59	3	3/50 = 0.06	0.06 × 100 = 6
60– 79	11	11/50 = 0.22	0.22 × 100 = 22
80– 99	9	0.18	18
100–119	6	0.12	12
120–139	8	0.16	16
140–159	6	0.12	12
160–179	7	0.14	14
Totals	50	1.00	100

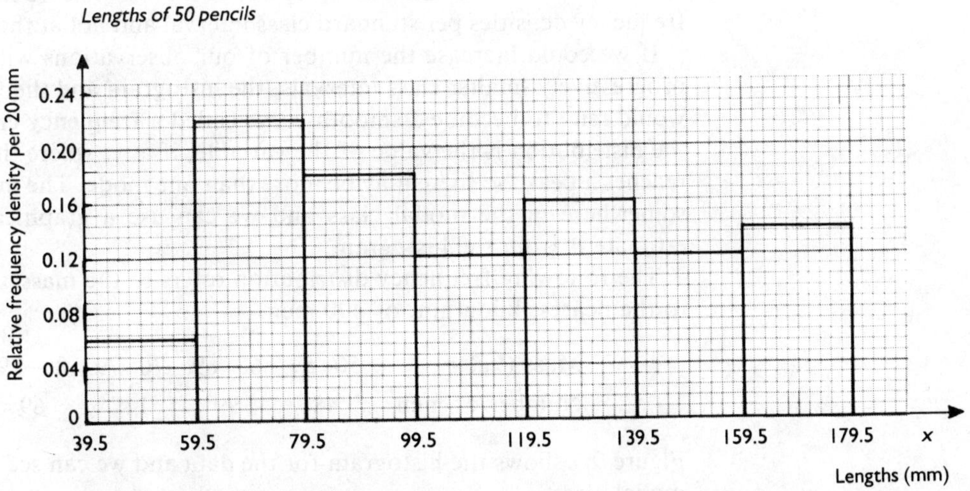

Fig. 9.5 *Relative frequency histogram*

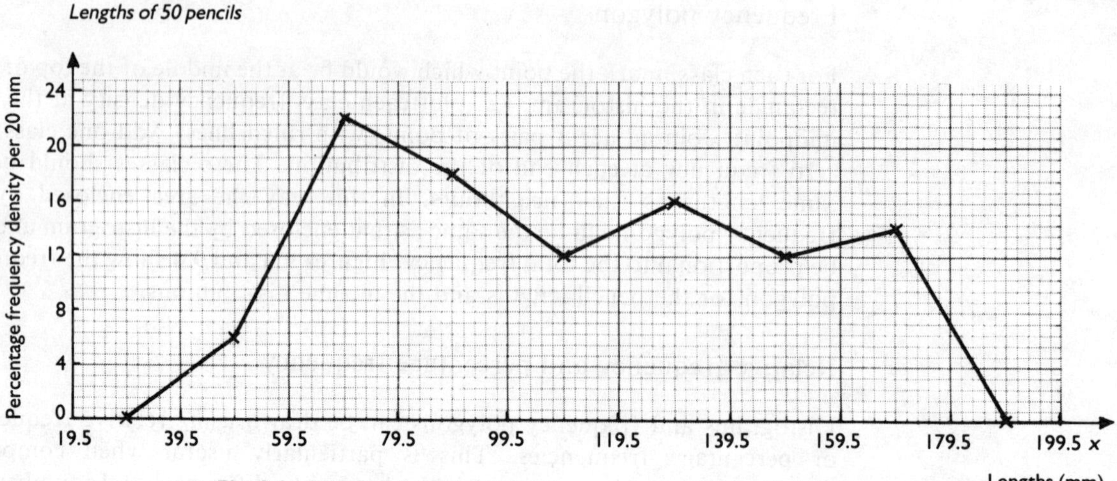

Fig. 9.6 *Percentage frequency polygon*

Figure 9.5 shows the relative frequency histogram and Fig. 9.6 shows the percentage frequency polygon. The relative shapes of the graphs are unaltered—it is just a change of scale on the vertical axis.

Modal class and mode

From the graphs or from the frequency distribution of pencil lengths, we can see at once that the class with the highest frequency density is the 60–79 class. This is called the **modal class**. For this distribution, there are two other peaks, although not as high, in classes 120–139 mm and 150–169 mm. These are also considered to be modal classes and we would call this a **trimodal** distribution because it has three modal classes. A distribution with one modal class is called **unimodal** and a distribution with two modal classes is called **bimodal**. The income distribution in Table 9.3 and Fig. 9.4 is bimodal. The modal classes are £6000 up to £7000 and £9000 up to £11 000. Note that we look for the highest frequency densities per standard class interval and not at the class frequencies.

If we could increase the number of our observations without limit, taking progressively smaller class intervals, the histogram and the frequency polygon would tend to become a smooth curve called a **frequency curve.** The mode of the distribution is the value of the variable, if any, where the frequency curve reaches a peak, so there may be more than one mode. The mode will always be somewhere in the modal class and we can use a graphical construction to estimate it from the histogram.

The following frequency distribution refers to the masses, recorded correct to the nearest kilogram, of 400 men.

Mass (kg)	50–59	60–69	70–79	80–89	90–99
Number of men	48	99	117	69	67

Figure 9.7 shows the histogram for the data and we can see that it has a single modal class.

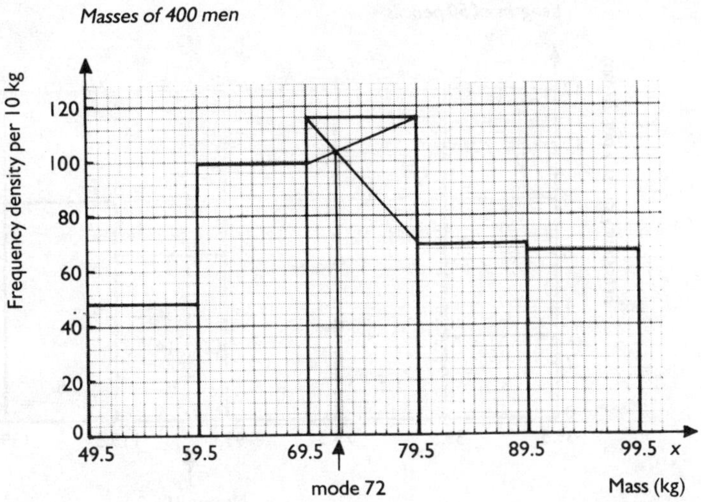

Fig. 9.7 *Estimation of mode from histogram*

To estimate the mode

Join the top left-hand corner of the rectangle for the modal class to the top left-hand corner of the rectangle for the class above the modal class.

Join the top right-hand corner of the rectangle for the modal class to the top right-hand corner of the rectangle for the class below the modal class.

The value of the variable where these lines cross is the estimate of the mode. From Fig. 9.7 we find:

$$\text{estimate of mode} = 72 \text{ mm}$$

Estimation of the median from the histogram

The median is the value of the variable such that half the observations are less than or equal to it. Since the area enclosed by the histogram represents the total number of observations, we can find the median by finding the value of the variable which divides the histogram into two equal halves.

Figure 9.8 shows the histogram of pencil lengths with the frequencies written on each rectangle. The total frequency is 50 so we need to divide the histogram into two halves, each containing 25 observations. Counting up the frequencies, $3 + 11 = 14$, $14 + 9 = 23$, we find the median is in the 99.5–119.5 class. We need to divide this class after 2 observations to reach a total of 25 observations. There are 6 observations in this class altogether so the median is 2/6 of the way along this class interval. We have:

$$\text{median} = 99.5 + \frac{2 \times 20}{6} = 99.5 + 6.7 = 106.2 \text{ mm to 2 dec. pl.}$$

From Exercise 7.3 Question 8, we found the median length from the stem-and-leaf diagram to be 107.0 mm so the results are in good agreement.

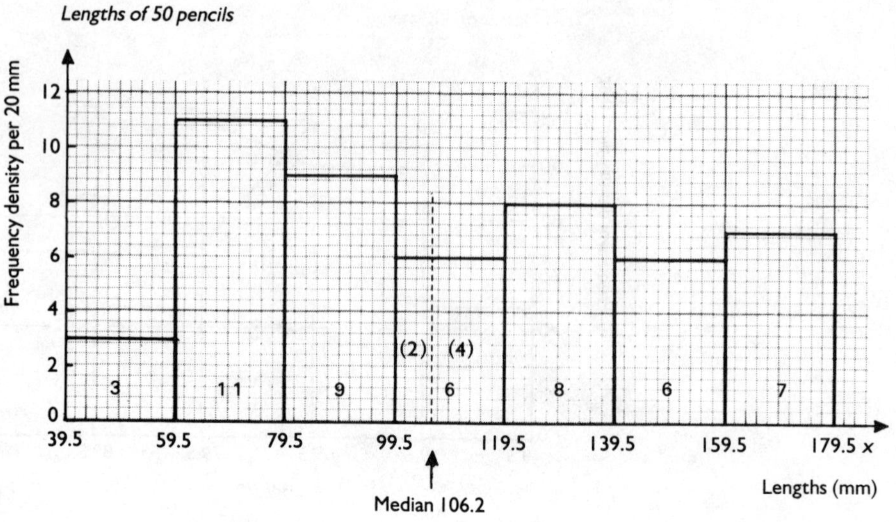

Fig. 9.8 *Estimation of median from histogram*

Important note

To draw any histogram or frequency polygon, we need to know the class boundaries of every class. If there is an open-ended class at the extreme of a distribution, we have to make an assumption about its boundary. Sometimes we can refer to the raw data and determine the appropriate value. On occasions we have background knowledge that will enable us to fix the boundary.

For example, with the variable 'age of car worker', we know the minimum working age in the UK is 16 years, so the open-ended class 'under 20' must have a lower class boundary equal to 16. If no other information is available, it is the convention to assume that an open-ended class has the same length of class interval as its neighbour.

Exercise 9.2

1 Draw a histogram for the following distribution of heights, measured correct to the nearest centimetre.

Height (cm)	155–159	160–164	165–169	170–174	175–179
Frequency	8	16	32	20	4

2 Draw a histogram for the following distribution of weights, recorded correct to the nearest gram.

Weight (g)	20–34	35–44	45–49	50–54	55–69
Frequency	120	100	150	100	150

3 The histogram shows the blood pressure, to the nearest millimetre, of a sample of men.

(a) Write down the class boundaries for each class.

(b) Find the number of men in each class.

(c) How many men are in the sample?

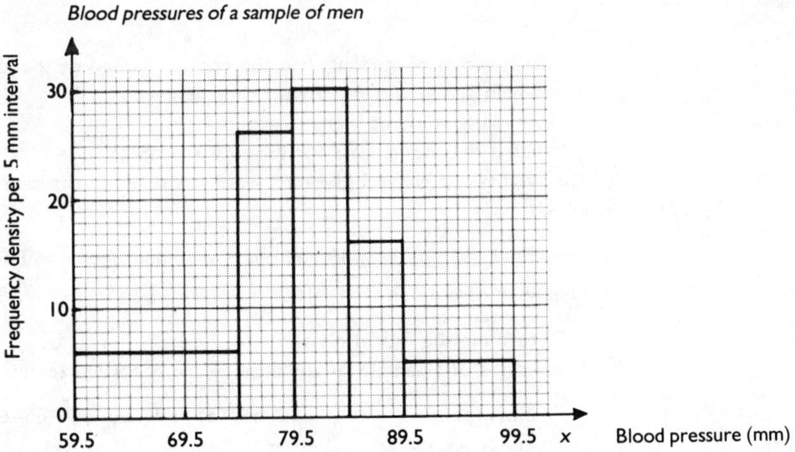

4 Draw a frequency polygon for the following distribution of masses, measured correct to the nearest kilogram.

Mass (kg)	40–49	50–59	60–69	70–79	80–89	90–99
Frequency	24	46	50	40	32	8

5 Draw a frequency polygon for the following distribution of ages of workers in a factory.

Age last birthday (years)	15–19	20–24	25–34	35–44	45–59
Number of workers	20	30	80	60	30

6 Two frequency polygons are shown in the graph. They show the times, in minutes, taken by two groups, A and B, of typewriting students to type a document.

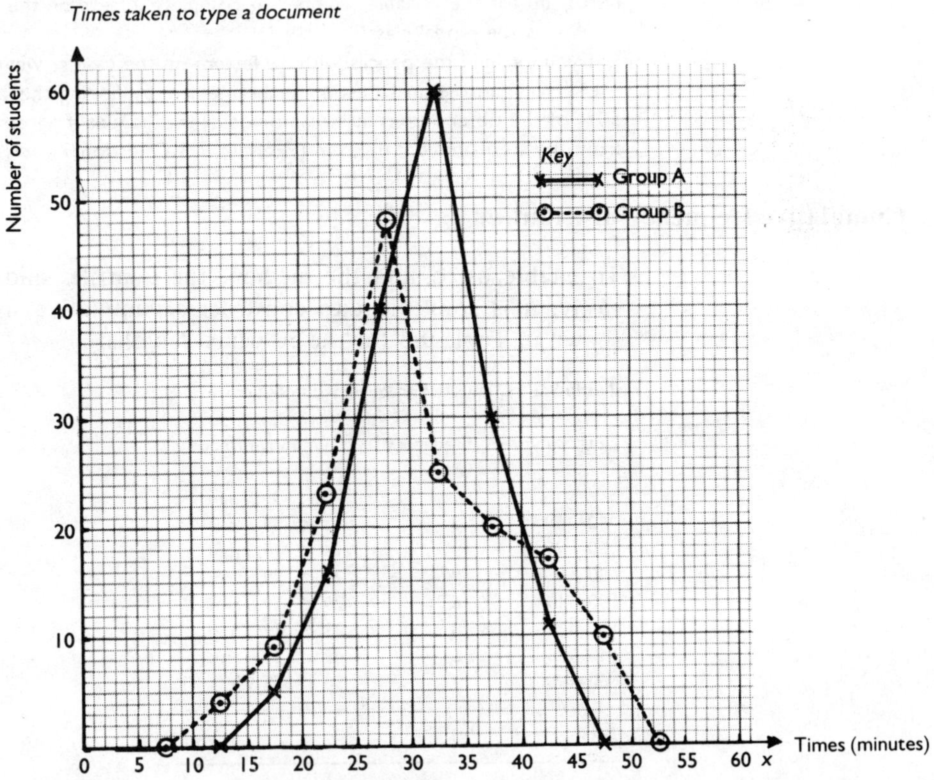

(a) Which group of students had the greater spread of speeds?
(b) In which group was the lowest time achieved?
(c) How many students were in group A?
(d) What is the modal class for group B students?

7 The heights of a group of women were measured to the nearest centimetre and recorded as follows.

Height (cm)	140 and over	150 and over	160 and over	170 and over
Number of women	100	84	56	24

Determine the modal class.

8 The masses of a sample of tomatoes were recorded to the nearest gram.

Mass (g)	50–54	55–59	60–64	65–69	70–74	75–79
Number of tomatoes	5	15	20	25	15	10

(a) Draw a histogram of the distribution.
(b) Use your histogram to estimate the mode of the data.

9 The maximum speeds of 100 merchant ships correct to the nearest knot (nautical mile per hour) are shown in the table.

Maximum speed (knots)	7–9	10–12	13–15	16–18	19–21	22–24
Number of ships	13	23	36	20	6	2

(a) Draw a histogram of the distribution.
(b) Use your histogram to estimate the median maximum speed.
(c) Draw a relative frequency polygon of the distribution.

10 Use your results from Exercise 9.1 Question 8 to draw a percentage frequency histogram for the variable 'number of complete letters on the casing'.

What is the modal class?

If you exclude the pencils with no letters on the casing, what is the modal class?

Use your histogram to estimate the median, by finding the value of the variable that has 50% of the observations less than or equal to it. Does it agree with the value you obtained from the stem-and-leaf diagram (Exercise 7.3 Question 7)?

Cumulative frequency distribution

To enable us to find the median, the quartiles and other percentiles more easily, it is convenient to construct a cumulative frequency distribution as shown in Table 9.5 for the 50 pencil lengths.

Table 9.5 Cumulative frequency distribution

Length (mm)	Frequency	Cumulative frequency
		0 < 39.5 mm
40– 59	3	3 < 59.5 mm
60– 79	11	14 < 79.5 mm
80– 99	9	23 < 99.5 mm
100–119	6	29 < 119.5 mm
120–139	8	37 < 139.5 mm
140–159	6	43 < 159.5 mm
160–179	7	50 < 179.5 mm
Total	50	

We go through the frequency distribution class by class and count up how many observations are less than the upper class boundary of each class. There are no observations below 39.5 mm so we include this value as well. There are 3 observations in the 40–59 mm class, so 3 observations are less than 59.5 mm. There are 11 observations in the 60–79 mm class, so 3 + 11 = 14 observations are less than 79.5 mm. We continue in this way until we have accounted for all 50 observations.

Ogive or cumulative frequency diagram

The graph of a cumulative frequency distribution is called an ogive. Each cumulative frequency is plotted at the upper boundary of its class (not at the class midpoint). The points can be joined with ruled lines to form a cumulative frequency polygon. This is appropriate if the data are the only values of interest and are a complete population. Alternatively, the points can be joined with a smooth curve. This is appropriate if the data are a sample from a larger population and we are trying to estimate summary values for this population.

The ogive for the 50 pencil lengths is shown in Fig. 9.9. The steeper the ogive, the greater the concentration of observations in that class, so we can see at a glance that the 59.5–79.5 mm class is the modal class. This ogive is close to a straight line above 99.5 mm as there is approximately the same number of observations in each of these higher classes. In general, an ogive has a characteristic elongated-S shape.

Open-ended classes can be ignored when drawing an ogive because, for

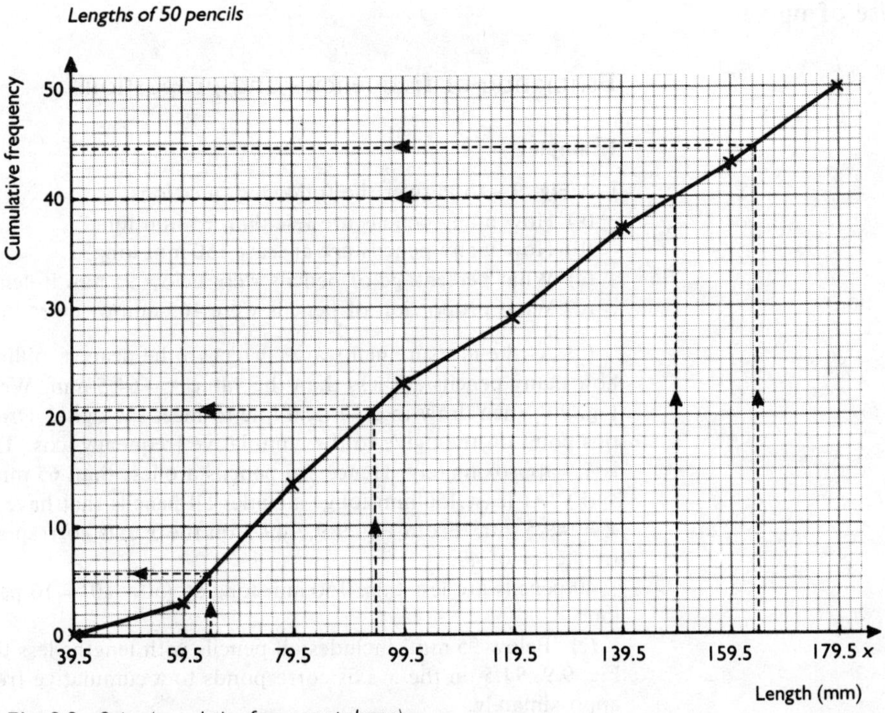

Fig. 9.9 *Ogive (cumulative frequency polygon)*

estimation purposes, we are usually not interested in the extremes of the ogive.

It is sometimes convenient to draw the ogive in percentage form. To work out the cumulative percentage frequency distribution either

(a) find the cumulative frequencies and convert them to percentages of the total frequency, or

(b) change the class frequencies to percentages of the total frequency and then find the cumulative percentage frequencies.

The cumulative percentage frequency distribution for the 50 pencil lengths is shown in Table 9.6.

Table 9.6 Cumulative percentage frequency distribution

Length (mm)	Frequency	Cumulative frequency	Cumulative percentage frequency
		0	$0 < 39.5$ mm
40– 59	3	3	$\frac{3}{50} \times 100 = 6 < 59.5$ mm
60– 79	11	14	$\frac{14}{50} \times 100 = 28 < 79.5$ mm
80– 99	9	23	$46 < 99.5$ mm
100–119	6	29	$58 < 119.5$ mm
120–139	8	37	$74 < 139.5$ mm
140–159	6	43	$86 < 159.5$ mm
160–179	7	50	$100 < 179.5$ mm
Total	50		

Use of ogive

Estimation of frequencies and proportions

Example

Use Fig. 9.9 to answer the following questions:

(a) How many pencils are less than 65 mm long?
(b) How many pencils are at least 150 mm long?
(c) What percentage of pencils were below 95 mm in length?
(d) What proportion of pencils were 165 mm or more in length?

(a) As the measurements are correct to the nearest millimetre, we need to find how many pencils are less than the value $x = 64.5$ mm. We find 64.5 on the x axis in Fig. 9.9, then draw in a vertical line to meet the ogive. Draw a horizontal line from this point on the ogive to the cumulative frequency axis. The cumulative frequency is 5.5 approximately. Hence 5.5 pencils are less than 65 mm long.

(b) 'At least 150 mm long' includes all pencils that have lengths greater than $x = 149.5$ mm. From Fig. 9.9, 149.5 on the x axis corresponds to a cumulative frequency of 40.

40 pencils are less than 150 mm long so $(50 - 40) = 10$ pencils are at least 150 mm long.

(c) 'Below 95 mm' includes all pencils with lengths less than $x = 94.5$ mm. From Fig. 9.9, 94.5 on the x axis corresponds to a cumulative frequency of 20.5, approximately.

20.5 pencils out of the 50 are below 95 mm in length so a percentage $(20.5/50) \times 100 = 41\%$ are below 95 mm in length.

(d) '165 mm or more' includes all pencils with lengths greater than $x = 164.5$ mm. From Fig. 9.9, 164.5 on the x axis corresponds to a cumulative frequency of 44.5 approximately.

44.5 pencils are less than 165 mm in length so $(50 - 44.5) = 5.5$ pencils are 165 mm or more in length.

Hence a proportion $5.5/50 = 0.11$ are 165 mm or more in length.

The results obtained here are approximate since we can rarely achieve high precision with graphical methods.

Estimation of median and quartiles

The median is the value such that half the observations are less than or equal to it. We work out half the total frequency ($n/2$), find this value on the cumulative frequency axis and then find the corresponding value of the variable on the x axis.

For the pencil lengths, $n = 50$ so $n/2 = 25$. From Fig. 9.10, 25 on the cumulative frequency axis corresponds to $x = 106$ mm, approximately.

$$\text{median} = 106 \text{ mm}$$

To estimate the lower quartile, we find the value of x corresponding to $n/4$ on the cumulative frequency axis. In Fig. 9.10, $n/4 = 50/4 = 12.5$. This corresponds to $x = 76.5$ mm, approximately.

$$\text{lower quartile, } Q_1 = 76.5 \text{ mm}$$

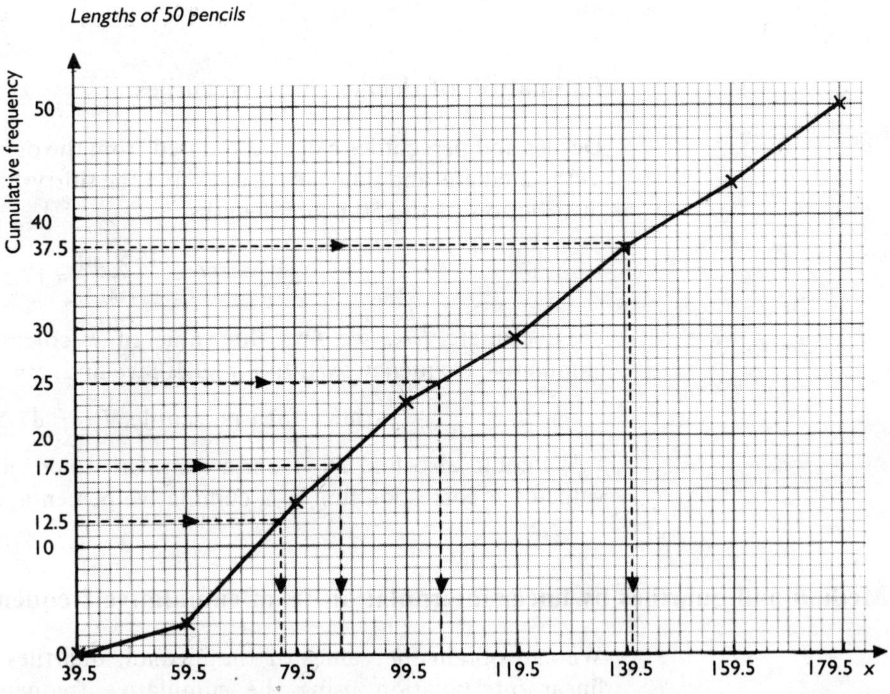

Fig. 9.10 *Estimation of median and quartiles*

To estimate the upper quartile, we find the value of x corresponding to $3n/4$ on the cumulative frequency axis. In Fig. 9.10, $3n/4 = 3 \times 50/4 = 37.5$. This corresponds to $x = 141$ mm, approximately.

$$\text{upper quartile, } Q_3 = 141 \text{ mm}$$

We can estimate the interquartile range using these results:

$$\begin{aligned}\text{interquartile range} &= Q_3 - Q_1 \\ &= 141 - 76.5 \text{ mm} \\ &= 64.5 \text{ mm}\end{aligned}$$

$$\begin{aligned}\text{semi-interquartile range} &= \text{quartile deviation} \\ &= \frac{64.5}{2} \text{ mm} \\ &= 32.25 \text{ mm} \\ &= 32 \text{ mm to nearest mm}\end{aligned}$$

Alternatively, if we draw the ogive using the cumulative percentage frequencies, we can estimate the median and quartiles directly.

The median is the value of x corresponding to a cumulative percentage frequency of 50%.

The lower quartile is the value of x corresponding to a cumulative percentage frequency of 25%.

The upper quartile is the value of x corresponding to a cumulative percentage frequency of 75%.

Estimation of deciles and percentiles

Deciles and percentiles can be estimated from the ogive in exactly the same way as the medians and quartiles. Let us find the thirty-fifth percentile, P_{35}, for the distribution of the 50 pencil lengths.

$$35\% \text{ of } 50 = \frac{35 \times 50}{100} = 17.5$$

To esimate P_{35}, we find the value of x corresponding to 17.5 on the cumulative frequency axis. In Fig. 9.10, we find, $x = 87.5$ mm, approximately.

$$\text{thirty-fifth percentile, } P_{35} = 87.5 \text{ mm}$$

We could also find P_{35} from a cumulative percentage ogive by finding the value of x corresponding to a cumulative percentage frequency of 35%.

Median and quartiles by linear interpolation from cumulative frequency distribution

We can obtain the values of the median, quartiles and other percentiles by linear interpolation using the cumulative frequency distribution, without needing to draw a graph.

To find the median of the distribution of the pencil lengths

We work out half the total frequency, $n/2 = 25$. We need to find the value of x corresponding to a cumulative frequency of 25 so we look at the cumulative frequency distribution to see where the value 25 lies. From Table 9.5, we see 25 lies between the cumulative frequencies 23 and 29 so the 25th observation is in the 100–119 mm class, i.e. the median pencil length is between 99.5 mm and 119.5 mm. There are 23 pencils with lengths less than 99.5 mm, so we require 2 of the 6 pencils in the 100–119 group to reach the 25th observation. We assume that the lengths of the 6 pencils are evenly spread out over the class interval so the 25th observation will be at the value 2/6 of the way across this class interval.

$$\begin{aligned}\text{median} &= 99.5 + \frac{2 \times 20}{6}\\ &= 99.5 + 6.7\\ &= 106.2 \text{ mm to 1 dec. pl.}\end{aligned}$$

You will see that this is exactly the same value that we obtained by estimation from the histogram and that the graphical estimate from the ogive is close to this value.

To find the quartiles

Lower quartile, Q_1

One quarter of the total frequency $= n/4 = 50/4 = 12.5$. 12.5 lies between 3 and 14 in the cumulative frequency distribution so Q_1 is in the 60–79 mm class. There are 11 pencils in this class so we need to consider $(12.5 - 3) = 9.5$ of them to reach Q_1.

$$\begin{aligned}Q_1 &= 59.5 + \frac{9.5 \times 20}{11}\\ &= 59.5 + 17.3\\ &= 76.8 \text{ mm}\end{aligned}$$

Upper quartile, Q_3

Three-quarters of the total frequency $= 3n/4 = 3 \times 50/4 = 37.5$. 37.5 lies between 37 and 43 so Q_3 is in the 140–159 mm class which contains 6 observations.

$$\begin{aligned}Q_3 &= 139.5 + \frac{37.5 - 37}{6} \times 20\\ &= 139.5 + \frac{0.5}{6} \times 20\\ &= 139.5 + 1.7\\ &= 141.2 \text{ mm to 1 dec. pl.}\end{aligned}$$

The values estimated from the ogive are in good agreement with the calculated values.

Exercise 9.3

1 The age last birthday of 240 Girl Guides in Ellbury was recorded. The results are tabulated overleaf. Determine the modal class.

Age (years)	Less than 10	Less than 11	Less than 12	Less than 13	Less than 14	Less than 15
Cumulative frequency	0	30	90	170	220	240

2 The weights of 100 cabbages were measured on electronic kitchen scales correct to the nearest 10 g. The frequency distribution of weights is as shown.

Weight (g)	Less than 300	300–390	400–490	500–590	600 or more
Number of cabbages	5	15	20	40	20

When plotting the cumulative frequency curve for these data, at what value of the variable would you plot a cumulative frequency of 20?

3 The weights of 100 professional footballers were recorded to the nearest kilogram as follows.

Weight (kg)	66–70	71–75	76–80	81–85	86–90	91–95	95–100
Frequency	5	11	14	21	23	17	9

(a) Construct a cumulative frequency distribution for the data.
(b) Draw a cumulative frequency curve for the data.
(c) Use your graph to estimate the median, the lower quartile and the upper quartile for this distribution. What is the value of the interquartile range?
(d) Use your graph to estimate the number of footballers weighing less than 73 kg.

4 The graph shows the ages in years of 80 motor cycles at a recent auction sale. Use the graph to estimate the fortieth percentile and the sixtieth percentile. What percentage of motor cycles were less than 18 months old? The six oldest motor cycles remained unsold. What was the age of the youngest bike that was not sold?

Ogive of ages of 80 motor cycles

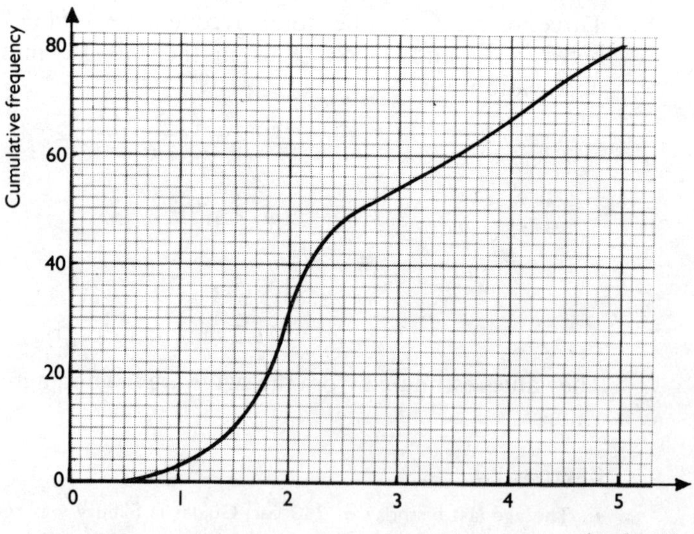

5 The manager of a busy filling station recorded the lengths of time that a sample of 200 customers had to wait before a petrol pump was free. His results are shown in the table.

Waiting time (minutes)	Number of customers	Cumulative frequency	Cumulative percentage frequency
		0	0
Less than $\frac{1}{2}$	8	8	4
$\frac{1}{2}$ but less than 1	11	19	9.5
1 but less than $1\frac{1}{2}$	15		
$1\frac{1}{2}$ but less than 2	22		
2 but less than $2\frac{1}{2}$	29		
$2\frac{1}{2}$ but less than 3	36		
3 but less than $3\frac{1}{2}$	28		
$3\frac{1}{2}$ but less than 4	20		
4 but less than 5	18		
5 but less than 6	13	200	100
Total	200		

(a) Copy out the table and complete the cumulative frequencies.
(b) Work out the cumulative percentage frequencies.
(c) Use your values to draw a cumulative percentage frequency curve for the data.
(d) From your graph find the median and the quartiles and estimate the semi-interquartile range.
(e) Estimate the percentage of customers kept waiting for at least 4 minutes.
(f) What proportion of customers are kept waiting for less than 2 minutes.

6 The cumulative frequency polygon below shows the distribution of lifetimes of 400 light bulbs.

Lifetimes of 400 light bulbs

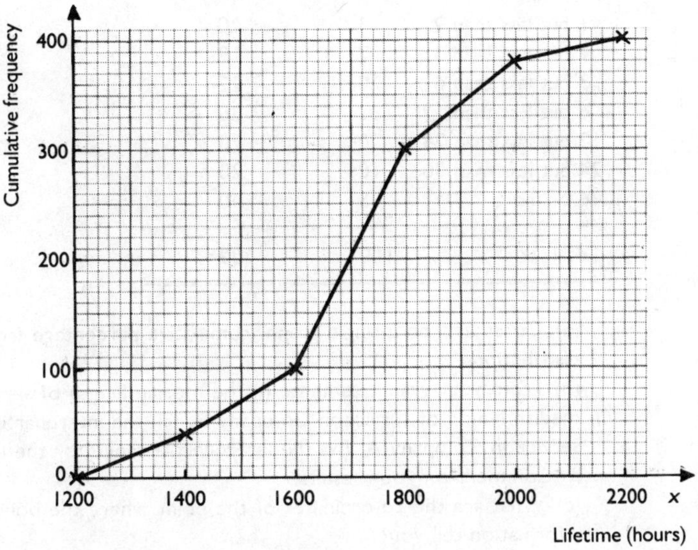

Use the graph to estimate
(a) the median lifetime of the bulbs;
(b) the time limits within which the lives of the middle 50% of the bulbs lie;
(c) how many of the bulbs lasted between 1500 and 1900 hours;
(d) the maximum lifetime of the worst 5% of the bulbs.

7 A manufacturer of components has to ensure that the lengths of one type of component are within the range 80.4 to 82.3 mm. A sample of 200 components had lengths, to the nearest tenth of a millimetre, as shown in the table.

Length (mm)	Frequency
80.0–80.4	10
80.5–80.9	38
81.0–81.4	70
81.5–81.9	54
82.0–82.4	16
82.5–82.9	12

(a) Draw a cumulative frequency diagram for the data.
(b) Use your graph to estimate the percentage of components that are less than 80.4 mm in length.
(c) Estimate the percentage of components that are more than 82.3 mm long.
(d) If the manufacturer rejects components outside the range 80.4 to 82.3 mm, use your graph to estimate the median length of acceptable components.

8 Two personnel managers in different companies want to compare the lengths of time that employees stay in their organisations before leaving. They consult their records and produce the following data.

Length of service (months)	Number of employees	
	Company A	Company B
Less than 1	2	40
1 but less than 2	3	20
2 but less than 3	7	18
3 but less than 6	20	22
6 but less than 12	33	20
12 but less than 24	20	20
24 but less than 36	10	20
36 or more	5	40
Total	100	200

(a) Construct, on a single graph, cumulative percentage frequency polygons for the two distributions.
(b) From your graph, estimate (i) the median length of service in Company A, (ii) the median length of service in Company B, (iii) the interquartile range for the length of service in Company A, (iv) the interquartile range for the length of service in Company B. Comment on your results.
(c) What are the co-ordinates of the point where the polygons cross? What does this information tell you?

9 The graph shows the cumulative percentage frequency distributions of marks, out of 100, in Mathematics and English of two large groups of pupils.

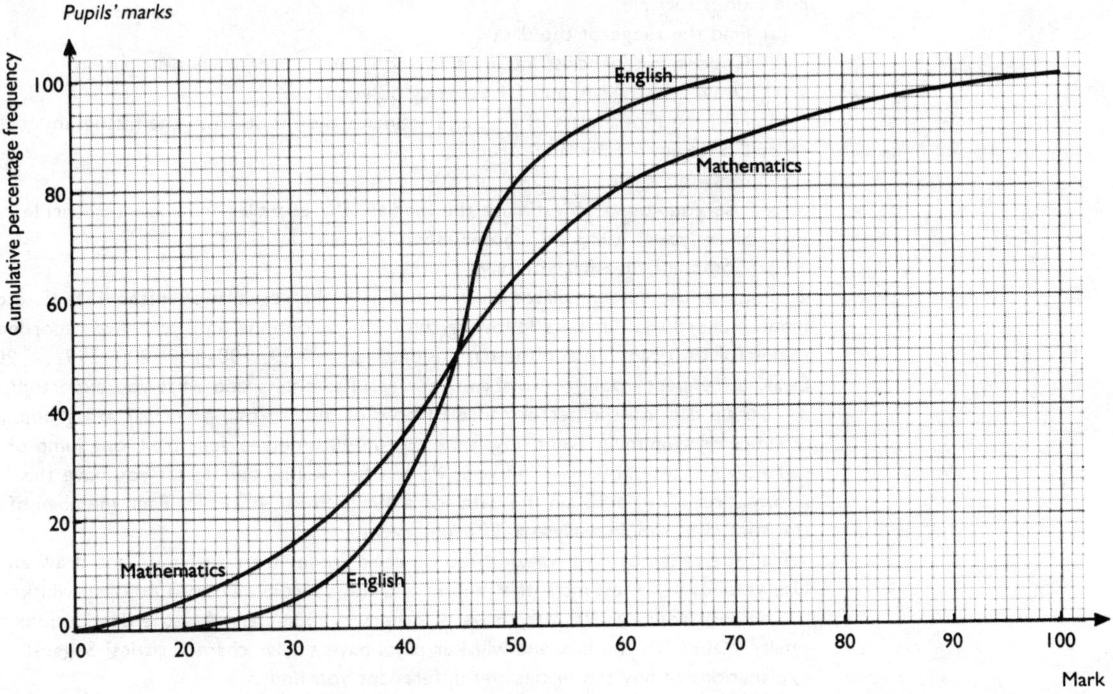

(a) Find the median mark for Mathematics and the median mark for English.

(b) Pupils fail if they get a mark below D_4, the fourth decile. What are the pass marks in the two subjects?

(c) If just the pass marks and the median marks were compared, what do these statistics fail to show about the two distributions? Suggest other statistics you could find from the graph that would show these differences.

(d) Find the eightieth percentile mark, P_{80}, in English. What percentage of mathematics marks are below this?

(e) Find the twentieth percentile mark P_{20}, in Mathematics. What percentage of English marks are below this?

10 The weights of 250 apples were measured correct to the nearest 10 grams.

Weight (g)	100–120	130–150	160–180	190–210	220–250
Number of apples	30	45	80	55	40

(a) Write down the boundaries of every class.

(b) Using linear interpolation, find (i) the median weight, (ii) the upper and lower quartiles, (iii) the third and seventh deciles.

(c) What is the smallest possible weight of one of these apples? What is the largest possible weight of one of these apples?

(d) Use your results to draw a box-and-whisker plot.

11 Use your results from Exercise 9.1, Question 8 to construct the cumulative frequency distribution for the variable 'number of complete letters on the casing'. Draw an ogive of the distribution and use it to estimate the median, the quartiles and the semi-interquartile range. Estimate, from the ogive, the values of the tenth and ninetieth percentiles and work out the $P_{90}—P_{10}$ range. How does this value compare with the range of the data? Comment on your results.

Practical exercise 9.4

1 Refer to the data you collected in Practical exercise 5.5 and look at data for a continuous variable.

(a) Find the range of the data.
(b) Choose suitable class intervals and construct a frequency distribution.
(c) Draw a histogram and a frequency polygon.
(d) Find the modal class, if any, and estimate the mode from the histogram.
(e) Construct a cumulative frequency distribution.
(f) Draw an ogive.
(g) Use your ogive to estimate the median, the quartiles and the interquartile range.
(h) Show your results on a box-and-whisker plot.
(i) Comment on what you have found.

2 Look at the number plates of cars that have the registration letter A, B, C, etc. at the front. Record the numbers following this letter. Continue until you have recorded the values for 200 cars. Group the data using classes 1–99, 100–199, 200–299, ..., 900–999. Draw a frequency polygon to show your results. Is its shape what you expected? Explain.

3 Obtain data on the performance of boys or girls of one particular age group in an athletics or swimming event, e.g. time to run 400 metres, length of long jump or time to swim 50 metres. You may find your PE teacher will be able to let you have this information. Try to obtain the data for a minimum of 40 pupils. Each member of the statistics class should analyse a different event.

Find the range of observations. Construct a frequency distribution and draw an ogive. Use your ogive to estimate the median and the quartiles. Draw a box-and-whisker plot.

Compare your results with those of others in your class. Are the distributions of a similar shape? Do the box-and-whisker plots have similar characteristics? Suggest explanations of any similarities and differences you find.

4 This is a practical that requires data collection over a number of months. Each week, note the date and make a list of the new entries in the top forty of the Hit Parade. In successive weeks note the date when these entries first drop out of the top forty. After you have collected data for at least 60 hits, work out the number of weeks each hit was in the charts. Construct a cumulative frequency distribution showing how many were in less than two weeks, less than three weeks, less than four weeks and so on. Draw an ogive and estimate the median time a hit is in the charts. Find the values of the twentieth percentile and the eightieth percentile. Is the median halfway between these values? What does your answer tell you about the distribution of times?

10 One variable analysis – quantitative data, grouped frequency distributions (2)

Arithmetic mean, mean deviation and standard deviation

Arithmetic mean

When data are presented in the form of a grouped frequency distribution, we can calculate the arithmetic mean, the mean deviation and the standard deviation using the same formulae we used for the frequency table. We have:

$$\text{arithmetic mean, } \bar{x} = \frac{\Sigma fx}{\Sigma f} \text{ or } \frac{\Sigma fx}{n}$$

where x is now the **class midpoint**. This assumes that the arithmetic mean of the observations in a particular class is at the midpoint of the class. In general, this assumption will not be true but the error involved is usually acceptably small.

Table 10.1 Calculation of $\bar{x}$

Length (mm)	Frequency f	Midpoint x	fx
40– 59	3	49.5	148.5
60– 79	11	69.5	764.5
80– 99	9	89.5	805.5
100–119	6	109.5	657.0
120–139	8	129.5	1036.0
140–159	6	149.5	897.0
160–179	7	169.5	1186.5
Totals	50		5495.0

Table 10.1 shows the calculation of the arithmetic mean of the 50 pencil lengths, using the grouped frequency distribution in Table 9.2.

$$\bar{x} = \frac{5495.0}{50} = 109.9 \text{ mm}$$

This compares to a value of 109.3 mm, if you add up the raw data and divide by 50, so the error is small.

Mean deviation

The formula is:

$$\text{mean deviation} = \frac{\Sigma f|x - \bar{x}|}{\Sigma f} \text{ or } \frac{\Sigma f|x - \bar{x}|}{n}$$

The calculation is shown in Table 10.2.

$$\text{mean deviation} = \frac{1623.2}{50} = 32.464 = 32.5 \text{ mm to 1 dec. pl.}$$

Table 10.2 Calculation of mean deviation

Length (mm)	Frequency f	Midpoint x	$x-\bar{x}$	$\|x-\bar{x}\|$	$f\|x-\bar{x}\|$
40– 59	3	49.5	−60.4	60.4	181.2
60– 79	11	69.5	−40.4	40.4	444.4
80– 99	9	89.5	−20.4	20.4	183.6
100–119	6	109.5	−0.4	0.4	2.4
120–139	8	129.5	19.6	19.6	156.8
140–159	6	149.5	39.6	39.6	237.6
160–179	7	169.5	59.6	59.6	417.2
Totals	50				1623.2

We have calculated the mean (absolute) deviation from the mean but we could have worked with deviations from the median instead.

Standard deviation and variance

The formulae are:

$$\text{variance} = \frac{\Sigma f(x - \bar{x})^2}{\Sigma f} \text{ or } \frac{\Sigma f(x - \bar{x})^2}{n}$$

$$\text{standard deviation} = \sqrt{\text{variance}}$$

The calculation is shown in Table 10.3.

$$\text{variance} = \frac{69\,992.00}{50} = 1\,399.84 \text{ mm}^2$$

$$\text{standard deviation} = \sqrt{1\,399.84}$$
$$= 37.4 \text{ mm to 1 dec. pl.}$$

Table 10.3 Calculation of the variance and standard deviation

Length (mm)	Frequency f	Midpoint x	$x-\bar{x}$	$\lvert x-\bar{x}\rvert^2$	$f\lvert x-\bar{x}\rvert^2$
40– 59	3	49.5	−60.4	3648.16	10 944.48
60– 79	11	69.5	−40.4	1632.16	17 953.76
80– 99	9	89.5	−20.4	416.16	3 745.44
100–119	6	109.5	−0.4	0.16	0.96
120–139	8	129.5	19.6	384.16	3 073.28
140–159	6	149.5	39.6	1568.16	9 408.96
160–179	7	169.5	59.6	3552.16	24 865.12
Totals	50				69 992.00

Using the ungrouped data, the standard deviation is 38.3 mm so the error is reasonably small. There are correction terms that can be applied to improve the accuracy of the approximation, if desired.

Exercise 10.1

1 The time taken by each of 40 mechanics to perform a routine car-servicing task was recorded correct to the nearest minute.

Time (minutes)	10–14	15–19	20–24	25–29
Frequency	3	12	16	9

(a) Write down the midpoint of each class.
(b) Estimate the mean time to do this routine task, correct to one decimal place.

2 At the last population count, the distribution of ages in country X was as shown in the table.

(a) Find the midpoint of each class.
(b) Estimate the mean age of a person in country X, correct to the nearest year.

Age last birthday (years)	Number of persons (000s)
0–19	1430
20–29	560
30–39	680
40–49	590
50–59	460
60–79	570
80–99	120
Total	4410

3 The marks obtained by 51 candidates in an examination had the distribution shown.

Marks	40–49	50–59	60–69	70–79	80–89
Frequency	4	6	30	8	3

(a) Estimate the mean mark obtained by a candidate in this examination.
(b) Estimate the mean deviation of the marks.
(c) Estimate the variance and the standard deviation of the marks.

4 Last term, Sam recorded the time, x minutes, correct to the nearest minute, that he spent each day waiting at the bus stop before the bus arrived to take him to school. His results are shown in the table.

Waiting times (minutes)

19	11	16	20	17	8	3	24	5	8
4	26	13	13	11	22	12	33	20	4
18	15	11	3	1	21	10	21	11	21
10	2	29	26	19	9	7	19	6	23
6	1	11	15	18	14	17	13	1	13

(a) Given that $\Sigma x = 680$ and $\Sigma x^2 = 12\,242$, calculate the mean and the standard deviation of his waiting times.
(b) Construct a grouped frequency distribution using classes 0–4, 5–9, 10–14 etc.
(c) Estimate the mean and the standard deviation of Sam's waiting times from this frequency distribution.
(d) Comment on your results.

Methods of simplifying calculations

Calculator

Some calculators with statistical functions (e.g. CASIO) can be used to find the arithmetic mean and the standard deviation directly for a grouped frequency distribution. The procedure is the same as that used with a frequency table, see Chapter 8, except that the midpoints of each class are used instead of the actual values.

Alternative formula for standard deviation

It may be quicker, particularly if the class midpoints, x, are small whole numbers and $\bar{x}$ is a decimal fraction, to use one of the alternative formulae:

$$\text{standard deviation} = \sqrt{\frac{\Sigma fx^2}{\Sigma f} - \left(\frac{\Sigma fx}{\Sigma f}\right)^2} \quad \text{or} \quad \sqrt{\frac{\Sigma fx^2}{\Sigma f} - \bar{x}^2}$$

Use of working zero and scaling

We can reduce the amount of arithmetic greatly by using a working zero and scaling. This is often referred to as **coding** the data. The greatest simplification occurs if we choose one of the class midpoints as the working zero, preferably the one nearest to where we think the mean might be. Scaling is achieved by dividing by the length of the class interval, if they are all the same, or by the smallest class interval length, if they are unequal. The new variable is usually denoted by d and we find its mean and standard deviation using:

$$\bar{d} = \frac{\Sigma fd}{\Sigma f}$$

$$\text{standard deviation, SD} = \sqrt{\frac{\Sigma fd^2}{\Sigma f} - \left(\frac{\Sigma fd}{\Sigma f}\right)^2}$$

For the distribution of pencil lengths, I would take the working zero,

Table 10.4 Calculation of mean and standard deviation, coding method

Length (mm)	Frequency f	Midpoint x	$x - x_0$	$d = \frac{x - x_0}{c}$	fd	fd^2
40– 59	3	49.5	−60	−3	−9	27
60– 79	11	69.5	−40	−2	−22	44
80– 99	9	89.5	−20	−1	−9	9
100–119	6	109.5	0	0	0	0
120–139	8	129.5	20	1	8	8
140–159	6	149.5	40	2	12	24
160–179	7	169.5	60	3	21	63
Total	50				1	175

denoted by x_0, to be 109.5 mm because this is the midpoint in the centre of the distribution. The length of the class interval, which will be the scaling factor, c, is 20 mm.

The procedure is shown in Table 10.4. You can see the numbers are smaller and the arithmetic is much easier.

$$\bar{d} = \frac{1}{50} = 0.02$$

$$\begin{aligned} \text{mean allowing for scaling factor} &= c \times 0.02 \\ &= 20 \times 0.02 \\ &= 0.4 \text{ mm} \end{aligned}$$

$$\begin{aligned} \text{mean allowing for working zero, } \bar{x} &= x_0 + 0.4 \\ &= 109.5 + 0.4 \\ &= 109.9 \text{ mm} \end{aligned}$$

Thus the formula for calculating $\bar{x}$ is:

$$\bar{x} = x_0 + c \times \frac{\Sigma fd}{\Sigma f}$$

$$\begin{aligned} \text{SD} &= \sqrt{\frac{175}{50} - 0.02^2} \\ &= \sqrt{3.50 - 0.0004} \\ &= \sqrt{3.4996} \\ &= 1.8707 \end{aligned}$$

$$\begin{aligned} \text{standard deviation allowing for the scaling factor} &= c \times 1.8707 \\ &= 20 \times 1.8707 \\ &= 37.414 \text{ mm} \\ \text{standard deviation allowing for working zero} &= 37.414 \text{ (no change)} \\ &= 37.4 \text{ mm to 1 dec. pl.} \end{aligned}$$

Thus the formula for calculating the standard deviation is:

$$\text{standard deviation} = c\sqrt{\frac{\Sigma fd^2}{\Sigma f} - \left(\frac{\Sigma fd}{\Sigma f}\right)^2}$$

We have, in fact, applied a **linear transformation** to the data, by putting $d = (x - x_0)/c$. We have chosen x_0 and c in such a way as to make the arithmetic as easy as possible. The calculation of the mean deviation cannot be simplified in this way and this is another reason why the mean deviation is used less often than the standard deviation.

Exercise 10.2

1 Use a working zero of 22 minutes and a scaling factor of 5 minutes to estimate the mean and the standard deviation of the distribution in Exercise 10.1 Question 1.

2 Using a suitable linear transformation of the ages in Exercise 10.1 Question 2, obtain estimates of the mean and the standard deviation of the ages of the population in country X.

3 The yields of 60 tomato plants were recorded correct to the nearest kilogram.

Yield (kg)	5–7	8–10	11–13	14–16
Number of plants	12	34	10	4

(a) By suitable coding of the data, estimate the mean and the standard deviation of the yields.

(b) Estimate the mean deviation of the yields.

4 The lengths of 60 rods of nominal length 100 mm were taken from the output of a production line. Their actual lengths correct to the nearest millimetre were:

Length (mm)	95–96	97–98	99–100	101–102	103–104	105–106	107–108
Number of rods	3	8	21	14	10	3	1

(a) Estimate the mean and the standard deviation of the lengths.

(b) Estimate the median length, correct to 1 decimal place.

(c) Estimate the mean deviation from the median.

Coefficient of variation

All the measures of dispersion we have calculated so far have been absolute measures and their values have the same units as the original data. It is convenient to have a measure of **relative dispersion** that is independent of the units of measurement. Such a measure is the coefficient of variation, CV. It expresses the standard deviation as a proportion of the mean and is usually put as a percentage.

For the pencil lengths:

$$\text{coefficient of variation, CV} = \frac{\text{standard deviation} \times 100\%}{\bar{x}}$$

$$= \frac{37.4}{109.9} \times 100\%$$

$$= 34.0\%$$

The main uses of the coefficient of variation are:

1 to compare variation in two distributions that have different units. For example:

UK company		US company	
mean wage	= £9000	mean wage	= \$30 000
standard deviation	= £1000	standard deviation	= \$ 2 500

$$CV = \frac{1000}{9000} \times 100\% \qquad CV = \frac{2\,500}{30\,000} \times 100\%$$

$$= 11.1\% \qquad = 8.3\%$$

From these results, we conclude that there is relatively less variation in the wages in the US company than in the UK company. Note that we did not need to convert the data to the same currency.

2 to compare variation when means differ greatly.
For example:
Data on lengths

	steel bolts	steel girders
mean	5 cm	25 m
standard deviation	0.5 cm	2 m

$$CV = \frac{0.5}{5} \times 100\% \qquad CV = \frac{2}{25} \times 100\%$$

$$= 10\% \qquad = 8\%$$

Two metres is a much greater length than the 0.5 cm, so in absolute terms, the variation in the lengths of the girders is greater than the variation in the lengths of the bolts. Comparing the coefficients of variation, however, we see that, relative to the mean lengths involved, the variation in the girders is less than the variation in the bolts.

Standardised scores

To compare individual observations taken from different distributions, we can use standardised scores. These allow us to make valid comparisons of relative positions in the two distributions, allowing for differences in the mean and the standard deviation.

The standardised score, z, corresponding to a value, x, of a variable is:

$$z = \frac{x - \bar{x}}{\text{standard deviation}}$$

Example

1 Compare the relative positions of an employee earning £10 500 per year in a UK company, where the mean wage is £9000 and the standard deviation is £1000, with one earning \$33 000 in a US company where the mean wage is \$30 000 and the standard deviation is \$2500.

UK: $$z = \frac{10\,500 - 9000}{1000} = \frac{1500}{1000} = 1.5$$

US: $$z = \frac{33\,000 - 30\,000}{2500} = \frac{3000}{2500} = 1.2$$

1.5 is greater than 1.2, so the employee earning £10 500 in the UK company is in a relatively higher position in the company than the one earning \$33 000 is in the US company.

2 For the same companies as in 1, compare employees earning £8400 in the UK company and $28 000 in the US company.

$$\text{UK:} \qquad z = \frac{8400 - 9000}{1000} = \frac{-600}{1000} = -0.6$$

$$\text{US:} \qquad z = \frac{28\,000 - 30\,000}{2500} = \frac{-2000}{2500} = -0.8$$

The z value in the US is more negative than the z value in the UK so the employee in the US company is doing relatively less well than the one earning £8400 in the UK company.

One of the most common uses of standardised scores is in the comparison of examination marks in different subjects.

Linear transformation of data to a given mean and standard deviation

An alternative approach to standardisation is to convert the data to a set having a specified mean and a specified standard deviation. We do this using a linear transformation of each value that makes its standardised scores equal in both the old and the new distributions.

The relationship is:

$$\frac{\text{new value} - \text{new mean}}{\text{new standard deviation}} = \frac{\text{old value} - \text{old mean}}{\text{old standard deviation}}$$

(Note: the z score is the special case of transformation to mean 0 and standard deviation 1.)

Example

The examination marks in mathematics for a fifth year class had a mean of 60 with a standard deviation of 12. The Head wants all examinations to have a mean of 50 with a standard deviation of 14.

1 Jane got 90 marks in the mathematics examination. What mark will she get on the Head's scale?

2 Adrian has scored 36 on the Head's scale, what mark did he get on the original scale?

The relationship between the scales is:

$$\frac{\text{new mark} - 50}{14} = \frac{\text{old mark} - 60}{12}$$

1 Jane

$$\text{old mark} = 90$$

$$\frac{\text{new mark} - 50}{14} = \frac{90 - 60}{12} = \frac{30}{12} = 2.5$$

$$\text{new mark} - 50 = 14 \times 2.5 = 35$$

$$\text{new mark} = 35 + 50 = 85$$

2 Adrian

$$\text{new mark} = 36$$

$$\frac{36 - 50}{14} = \frac{\text{old mark} - 60}{12}$$

$$\frac{\text{old mark} - 60}{12} = \frac{-14}{14} = -1$$

$$\text{old mark} - 60 = 12 \times (-1) = -12$$

$$\text{old mark} = 60 - 12 = 48$$

Exercise 10.3

1 The mean mark of 30 pupils in a mathematics test was 60 with a standard deviation of 12. The same pupils were given a test in English and the mean mark was 55 with a standard deviation of 8. Work out the coefficient of variation in each subject. Which subject shows the greater absolute dispersion? Which subject shows the greater relative dispersion?

2 The mean amount spent each month on travel by the Smith family is £75 with a standard deviation of £9.50. In West Germany the mean amount spent each month on travel by the Schmidt family is 300 DM with a standard deviation of 29 DM. Calculate the coefficient of variation for each family and state which has the greater relative variability in its monthly travel expenditure.

3 Jennifer sells computers and Joe sells shoes. Their monthly sales last year were as shown in the table.

	Value of sales (£000)	
Month	Jennifer	Joe
Jan	36.2	2.3
Feb	37.2	2.7
Mar	96.1	2.6
Apr	6.2	1.5
May	76.2	2.2
Jun	27.2	2.3
Jul	15.7	2.4
Aug	3.6	1.9
Sep	73.5	2.5
Oct	37.3	2.4
Nov	28.1	2.7
Dec	36.8	2.2

(a) Find the mean monthly sales and the standard deviation for Jennifer and for Joe.
(b) Calculate the coefficient of variation for Jennifer and for Joe.
(c) Comment on your results.

4 Use your results from Exercise 9.1 Question 8 to
(a) estimate the mean and the standard deviation for the variable 'number of complete letters on the casing';
(b) find the coefficient of variation of the number of complete letters on the pencils. How does this compare with the coefficient of variation for the lengths of the 50 pencils calculated in this chapter? Which characteristic of the pencils is relatively more variable, the number of letters or the length?

5 The mean mark of a class of pupils in a French test was 48.5 with a standard deviation of 12.2. The same class had a mean mark of 54.5 and a standard deviation of 10.1 in a German test.
(a) Sylvia had marks of 61 in French and 64 in German. In which subject did she do better, relative to the whole class?
(b) Maxine had marks of 35 in French and 37 in German. In which subject did she do better, relative to the whole class?

6 The mean and the standard deviation of a set of marks are 35 and 10 respectively. The marks are scaled linearly so that the mean and the standard deviation become 50 and 14 respectively. Find the adjusted mark corresponding to an original mark of 45.

7 The mean and the standard deviation of a set of raw marks are 40 and 8 respectively. The marks are scaled linearly so that a raw mark of 45 becomes a scaled mark of 60. If the mean of the scaled marks is 50, what is the standard deviation of the scaled marks? What is the raw mark corresponding to a scaled mark of 40?

8 Two students at a local college are comparing their examination results. Albert scored 85 in Business Mathematics and 75 in Statistics. Ahmed scored 80 in Business Mathematics and 81 in Statistics. The mean of all the Business Mathematics marks was 70 with a standard deviation of 8, whereas the mean of the Statistics marks was 65 with a standard deviation of 10.

(a) Work out the total marks of each student and state which student had the higher total.

(b) Scale the marks linearly so that each set has a mean of 50 and a standard deviation of 12. Find the scaled marks for each student in each subject. Work out the total scaled marks of each student and state which has the higher total.

(c) Which student has done better in the examinations? Why?

Shapes of frequency distributions

Frequency curves

From the stem-and-leaf diagrams, frequency bar charts, histograms, frequency polygons, ogives and box-and-whisker plots that you have drawn, you may have noticed that the shapes and characteristics of distributions fall into certain categories, for example, some are peaked near the centre of the range of values of the variable, whereas others are peaked nearer the extreme values. As mentioned earlier, when determining the mode of a grouped frequency distribution, if we could increase the number of observations without limit, taking progressively smaller class intervals, the histogram and the frequency polygon would tend to become a smooth curve called a **frequency curve**. This is a theoretical, mathematical curve that can only be attained approximately in a practical situation.

Symmetrical frequency curves

In symmetrical frequency curves, some examples of which are shown in Fig. 10.1, together with their box-and-whisker plots and ogives, the median and the mean coincide and are in the centre of the distribution.

The **uniform distribution**, sometimes called the **rectangular distribution**, has no mode since the frequency density is constant throughout the range.

In a symmetrical single-peaked distribution, such as the **normal distribution**, the mode also coincides with the median and the mean. The normal distribution is a very 'special' symmetrical distribution having a characteristic bell shape and long 'tails' extending without limit. For a normal distribution:

68.3% of the x values lie within 1 standard deviation of the mean;
95.5% of the x values lie within 2 standard deviations of the mean;
99.7% of the x values lie within 3 standard deviations of the mean.

In practice, variables that are often considered to have approximate normal distributions include:

- contents of packaged goods
  e.g. weight of baked beans in a can, volume of milk in a bottle;

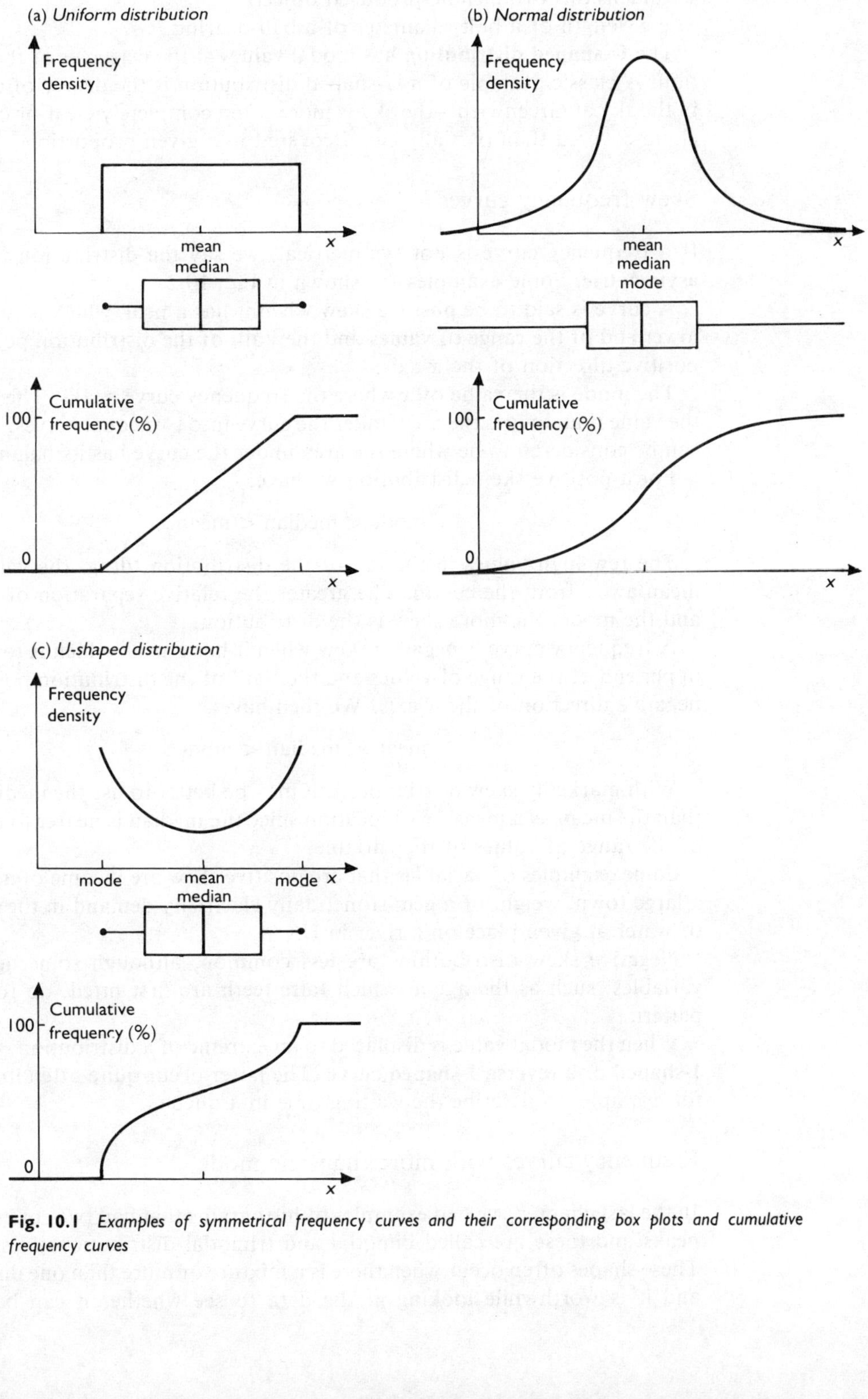

Fig. 10.1 *Examples of symmetrical frequency curves and their corresponding box plots and cumulative frequency curves*

- physical characteristics of living things
  e.g. head circumference of a new born baby, girths of 20-year old conifers;
- dimensions of machine-produced objects
  e.g. length of a bolt, diameter of a ball-bearing.

The **U-shaped distribution** has modal values at the extremes of the distribution. A classic example of a U-shaped distribution is the degree of cloudiness in the sky at Greenwich—the sky is more often completely clear or completely cloud-covered than partially cloud-covered in a given proportion.

Skew frequency curves

If a frequency curve is not symmetrical, we say the distribution is **skew** or **asymmetric**. Some examples are shown in Fig. 10.2.

A curve is said to be **positive skew** when it has a peak which is towards the lower end of the range of values and the 'tail' of the distribution points in the positive direction of the x-axis.

The mode is the value of x where the frequency curve peaks. The median is the value that divides the area under the curve into two equal halves. The mean can be considered to be where the area under the curve has its balancing axis.

For a positive skew distribution we have:

$$\text{mode} < \text{median} < \text{mean}$$

The few high values in the tail of the distribution 'drag' the value of the mean away from the centre. The greater the relative separation of the mean and the mode, the more skew is the distribution.

A frequency curve is **negative skew** when it has a peak which is towards the upper end of the range of values and the 'tail' of the distribution points in the negative direction of the x axis. We then have:

$$\text{mean} < \text{median} < \text{mode}$$

With markedly skew distributions, it may be better to use the median rather than the mean as a measure of location since the median is nearer to the centre of the range of values of the variable.

Some examples of variables that are positive skew are income of a family in a large town, weight of a gem stone, daily electricity demand in the UK, flow of water at given place on a river in UK.

Negative skew distributions are less common, although some age-related variables, such as the age at which false teeth are first fitted, do follow this pattern.

When the modal value is displaced to an extreme of a distribution, we have a **J-shaped** or a **reverse J-shaped** curve. The latter occur quite often in practice, for example, to describe the waiting time in a queue.

Frequency curves with more than one mode

In the last chapter, we had examples of histograms that had two, or even three, peaks and these are called bimodal and trimodal distributions, respectively. These shapes often occur when there is a mixture of more than one distribution and it is worthwhile looking at the data to see whether it can be usefully

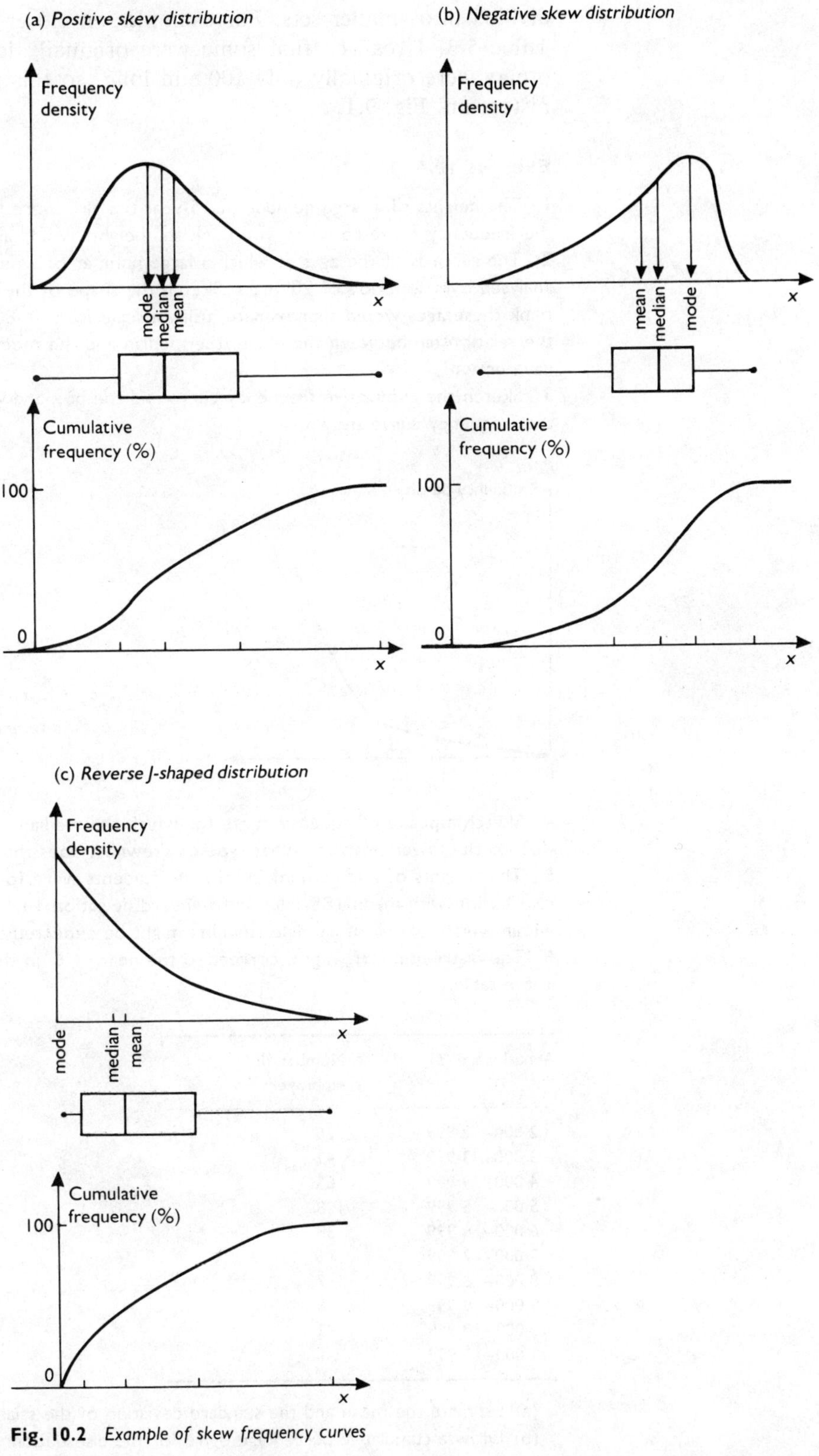

Fig. 10.2 *Example of skew frequency curves*

divided into smaller sets. For example, on closer inspection of my pencils, Table 5.3, I realised that some were originally long pencils (180 mm) and others were originally only 100 mm long, so this mixture is reflected in the histogram, Fig. 9.1.

Exercise 10.4

1 The heights of a large number of 15-year-old girls were measured. Sketch the shape of the frequency curve to which you think the heights would approximate.
2 The records of the ages at which a large number of women married in the UK were analysed over a period of 20 years. Sketch the shape of the frequency curve to which you think these ages would approximate, using a scale from 0–80 years on the *x* axis. What is the relationship between the mean, the median and the mode for the type of curve you have drawn?
3 Sketch the cumulative frequency curve and the box-and-whisker plot corresponding to the frequency curve shown.

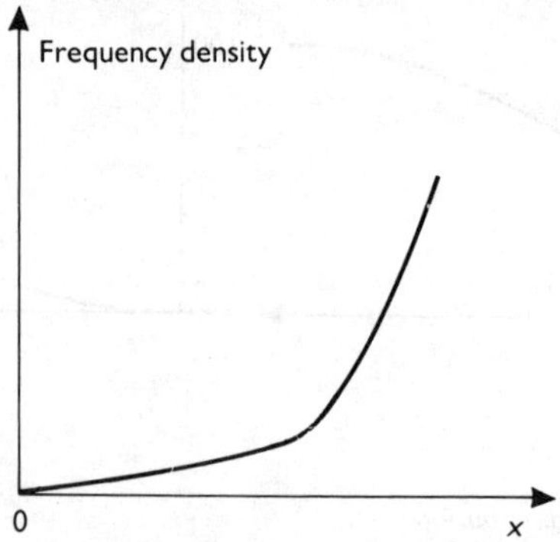

4 Sketch a peaked frequency curve for which the median is closer to the upper quartile than to the lower quartile. What type of skewness does this curve show?
5 The weights of a large number of male students were found to have a normal distribution with mean 185.1 lbs and standard deviation 14.1 lbs. Find the weight limits within which 99.7% of all male students might be expected to lie.
6 The distribution of wages, correct to the nearest £, in the Olbury company is shown in the table.

Annual wage (£)	Number of employees
2 000– 2 999	20
3 000– 3 999	42
4 000– 4 999	65
5 000– 5 999	108
6 000– 6 999	38
7 000– 7 999	11
8 000– 8 999	7
9 000– 9 999	5
10 000–10 999	3
11 000–11 999	1

(a) Estimate the mean and the standard deviation of the salaries.
(b) Draw a cumulative percentage ogive for the distribution.

(c) Use your ogive to estimate the percentages of salaries lying within
  (i) one standard deviation of the mean,
  (ii) two standard deviations of the mean,
  (iii) three standard deviations of the mean.

How do these compare with the corresponding percentages in a normal distribution?

Practical exercise 10.5

1 Refer to Practical exercise 9.4 Question 1. Using the frequency distribution you constructed, calculate the mean, the standard deviation and the mean deviation. Find the coefficient of variation.

Refer to Practical exercises 8.5, Question 1 and 7.7, Question 1, and calculate the coefficient of variation for the discrete variable you analysed there. Is its value greater than the coefficient of variation for the continuous variable? Does this surprise you? Explain.

2 You will need about 40 potatoes and a packet of dried peas. The aim is to investigate the relative variation in potato weights and in dried pea weights. You will need an accurate scientific balance to weigh a dried pea but ordinary kitchen scales will be suitable for weighing a potato. Decide what are suitable units and precision for the two types of weighing—they do not need to be the same in each case.

Weigh each potato and record its weight. Select the same number of dried peas from the packet, weigh each pea and record its weight.

For each data set
(a) construct a frequency distribution;
(b) draw a histogram;
(c) calculate the mean and the standard deviation;
(d) calculate the coefficient of variation.

Which set of weights has the larger relative variation? Is this what you expected?

Do the histograms have a similar shape? Do you think a normal distribution would be an appropriate description in either case?

3 Look back at all the data sets concerning numerical variables that you have collected and analysed by graphical methods. Classify each of the distributions of these variables under one or more of the following headings: symmetrical, skew, bimodal, positive skew, uniform, normal, U-shaped, J-shaped.

4 After your next set of school tests or examinations, ask each subject teacher to give you the mean mark and the standard deviation of the marks in that subject. (If the teacher has not worked them out, you will need to ask for all the marks and work the mean and its standard deviation out for yourself.) Look first at your actual marks and list the subjects in order of your performance. For each subject, scale your mark so that the mean scaled mark is 50 with standard deviation of 12. Look at your scaled marks and list the subjects in order of your performance. Is there agreement between the two lists? Can you explain any discrepancies that occur?

11 Two variable analysis

Contingency tables

The analyses in Chapters 6 to 10 have assumed that we are concerned with just one variable at a time. Often, however, we are interested in the relationship between **two** variables. For instance, we noticed after coding the data in Table 5.4 that only the graphite pencils in our data set had erasers. We can summarise the data about the two variables 'eraser' and 'graphite' in a two-way table called a **contingency table,** see Table 11.1.

The table has the different categories for one variable labelling the rows and the different categories for the other variable labelling the columns. Using the pencil data base, Table 5.3, or the coded data, Table 5.4, we record one tally mark for each pencil in the appropriate category or **cell** in Table 11.1(a). For example, the pencil with ID number 00 has no eraser and is not graphite so we put a tally mark in the (No, No) cell. Once all the pencils have been allocated to the correct cells, we add up the tally marks in each cell to obtain the frequencies shown in the final contingency table, Table 11.1(b). It is usual to put in the row and column totals as well as the total frequency.

Table 11.1 Construction of a 2 × 2 contingency table

(a) tally chart

Eraser \ Graphite	Yes	No
Yes	III	
No	𝍸 𝍸 𝍸 𝍸 𝍸	𝍸 𝍸 𝍸 𝍸 II

(b) final table

Eraser \ Graphite	Yes	No	Totals
Yes	3	0	3
No	25	22	47
Totals	28	22	50

Table 11.2 Construction of a 2 × 4 contingency table

(a) tally chart

Number of colours / Graphite	0	1	2	4
Yes	II	𝍸 III	𝍸 𝍸 𝍸	III
No		I	𝍸 𝍸 𝍸 𝍸 I	

(b) final table

Number of colours / Graphite	0	1	2	4	Totals
Yes	2	8	15	3	28
No	0	1	21	0	22
Totals	2	9	36	3	50

Similarly, we could investigate the relationship between the variables 'number of colours on the casing' and 'graphite' as shown in Table 11.2. In this table there are 2 row categories 'Yes' and 'No' and 4 column categories, 0, 1, 2 and 4, so this table is called a 2×4 contingency table. Table 11.1, with 2 rows and 2 columns, is a 2×2 table.

Proportions and expected frequencies

From Table 11.1, we can work out the proportions of pencils with and without an eraser by finding the ratios of the row totals to the total frequency:

$$\text{proportion of pencils with eraser} = \frac{\text{number of pencils with eraser}}{\text{total number of pencils}}$$

$$= \frac{3}{50}$$

$$= 0.06$$

$$\text{proportion of pencils with no eraser} = \frac{\text{number of pencils with no eraser}}{\text{total number of pencils}}$$

$$= \frac{47}{50}$$

$$= 0.94$$

If we assume there is no link, relationship or association between the two variables 'graphite' and 'eraser', we can use these proportions to work out how many of the graphite pencils we would expect to have an eraser:
expected number of graphite pencils with an eraser

$$= 0.06 \times \text{number of graphite pencils}$$
$$= 0.06 \times 28$$
$$= 1.68$$

Similarly:
expected number of graphite pencils with no eraser

$$= 0.94 \times \text{number of graphite pencils}$$
$$= 0.94 \times 28$$
$$= 26.32$$

For the non-graphite pencils, we have:
expected number of non-graphite pencils with an eraser

$$= 0.06 \times \text{number of non-graphite pencils}$$
$$= 0.06 \times 22$$
$$= 1.32$$

expected number of non-graphite pencils with no eraser

$$= 0.94 \times \text{number of non-graphite pencils}$$
$$= 0.94 \times 22$$
$$= 20.68$$

All the expected frequencies are shown in Table 11.3, rounded to one decimal place. In general, expected frequencies do not come out to be exact whole numbers but this does not matter.

You should check that you get the same values for the expected frequencies if you first work out the proportions of the total number of pencils that are graphite and non-graphite and then take these proportions of the total numbers of pencils with and without an eraser.

The following equivalent formula can also be used:

$$\text{expected frequency in cell} = \frac{\text{row total} \times \text{column total}}{\text{total frequency}}$$

Table 11.3 Expected frequencies assuming no association between variables 'graphite' and 'eraser'

Eraser \ Graphite	Yes	No	Totals
Yes	1.7	1.3	3
No	26.3	20.7	47
Totals	28	22	50

For example:

$$\text{expected frequency in (Yes, Yes) cell} = \frac{3 \times 28}{50} = 1.68$$

Comparing Table 11.3 with Table 11.1(b), we see that the expected frequencies are fairly close to the observed frequencies although not identical. It appears that, if there is no association between the variables, we should have had some non-graphite pencils with an eraser, whereas we observed none. We conclude that for our data set there **is** a relationship between the two variables.

If we want to generalise our findings, we can consider this set of 50 pencils to be a random sample from a much larger population of pencils. If you proceed to more advanced statistical work, you will learn about the chi-squared test that can be used to help decide when the expected frequencies are too far away from the observed frequencies. In order to apply this test to our data, we would have to make more observations. It could be that all pencils with erasers are graphite or it could be that we have observed so few pencils with erasers that we have not had the opportunity to find any that are non-graphite.

Other proportions and relative frequencies

To compare different data sets, we may find it useful to work out the proportion, or the relative frequency, of observations falling in a particular cell.

For example, from Table 11.1(b):
proportion of pencils that are graphite and have an eraser

$$= \frac{\text{number of pencils that are graphite and have an eraser}}{\text{total number of pencils}}$$

$$= \frac{3}{50}$$

$$= 0.06$$

proportion of pencils that are graphite and have no eraser

$$= \frac{\text{number of pencils that are graphite and have no eraser}}{\text{total number of pencils}}$$

$$= \frac{25}{50}$$

$$= 0.5$$

From the ratios of the cell frequencies to the row and column totals, we can work out other proportions of interest.

For example, from Table 11.1(b):
proportion of **graphite** pencils that have an eraser

$$= \frac{\text{number of pencils that are graphite and have an eraser}}{\text{total number of } \textbf{graphite} \text{ pencils}}$$

$$= \frac{3}{28}$$

$$= 0.11 \text{ to 2 dec. pl.}$$

proportion of pencils **with no eraser** that are graphite

$$= \frac{\text{number of pencils that have no eraser and are graphite}}{\text{total number of pencils } \textbf{with no eraser}}$$

$$= \frac{25}{47}$$

$$= 0.53 \text{ to 2 dec. pl.}$$

We can change these proportions to percentages, if desired, by multiplying by 100.

For example:

percentage of pencils that are graphite and have no eraser

$$= 0.5 \times 100$$

$$= 50\%$$

Exercise 11.1

1 Use Table 5.3 to construct a 2×11 contingency table for the variables 'graphite' and 'main colour of casing'. How many graphite pencils have a yellow casing?

How many pencils with a red casing are non-graphite?

2 Assuming there is no relationship between the two variables 'graphite' and 'number of colours on the casing', construct a table of expected frequencies to compare with the observed frequencies in Table 11.2(b). Comment on your findings.

3 The numbers of properties that an estate agent has on his books are shown in the table.

	For sale	For rent
Detached	20	5
Semi-detached	30	5
Terraced	10	10
Flats	15	40

(a) How many properties are for sale?
(b) How many properties are for rent?
(c) How many properties are there on the estate agent's books?
(d) What proportion of properties are for sale?
(e) What proportion of properties are flats to rent?
(f) What proportion of detached properties are for rent?
(g) What proportion of properties for rent are terraced?
(h) What percentage of properties for sale are semi-detached?

Practical exercise 11.2

1 Conduct a survey of at least 50 pupils in your school. For each one note down the natural colour of hair and the colour of eyes. (Suggested categories: fair, brown, auburn, black for hair; blue, brown, grey, green for eyes.) Put your results into a contingency table. If there is no relationship between hair colour and eye colour, what frequencies would you expect in each cell? Is there agreement between the observed and the expected frequencies? Comment on your findings. Mention any difficulties you had in carrying out the survey.

2 Conduct a survey of at least 50 pupils in your school to investigate whether there is a relationship between the main form of transport they use to get to school and the distance between home and school. Suggested categories of classification:
under 1 mile, 1 mile but under 3 miles, 3 miles or over; walking, cycle, car, public transport, coach, other.

3 From an ordinary pack of 52 playing cards, find the Ace, King, Queen and Jack of spades, the Ace, King and Queen of hearts, the Ace and King of diamonds and the Ace of clubs. Shuffle these 10 cards, select one card and note its suit and value in a table as shown. Replace the card, shuffle the 10 cards, select one card and note its suit and value. Repeat this procedure until you have the results for 80 cards. What frequencies did you expect in each cell? Do the expected and observed frequencies agree? Suggest reasons for any discrepancies you find.

Suit / Value	Spades	Hearts	Diamonds	Clubs	Tally of cards
Ace					
King					
Queen					
Jack					

Scatter diagrams

Construction

Contingency tables can be used with both quantitative and qualitative variables. If the two variables of interest are both quantitative, however, we can perform a more detailed analysis.

Referring to Table 5.3, consider only those pencils with letters on the casing. Let us investigate whether there is a relationship between the length of a pencil, which we will call x, and the number of letters on the pencil, which we will call y. We start by drawing a **scatter diagram** or **scattergraph**. The x values are represented on the horizontal axis of the graph, see Fig. 11.1. The range of x values, from Table 5.3, is from 43 mm to 175 mm so the horizontal scale has been drawn from 0 to 175 mm. The range of y values is from 2 to 100 so the vertical scale has been drawn from 0 to 100.

We put one point on the scatter diagram for each pencil.
For example,
Pencil ID number 01, Length $(x) = 132$ mm, Number of letters $(y) = 22$ so a cross is put at the point (132, 22), labelled A in Fig. 11.1.

Points for the other pencils are plotted in the same way. We do not attempt to join up the points but we look to see whether there is any pattern in the scatter of points.

From Fig. 11.1, you will notice that:
(a) there is some tendency for longer pencils to have more letters, i.e. as x increases, y also tends to increase;

Relationship between length and number of letters on casing for 39 pencils
(⊗ denotes two pencils)

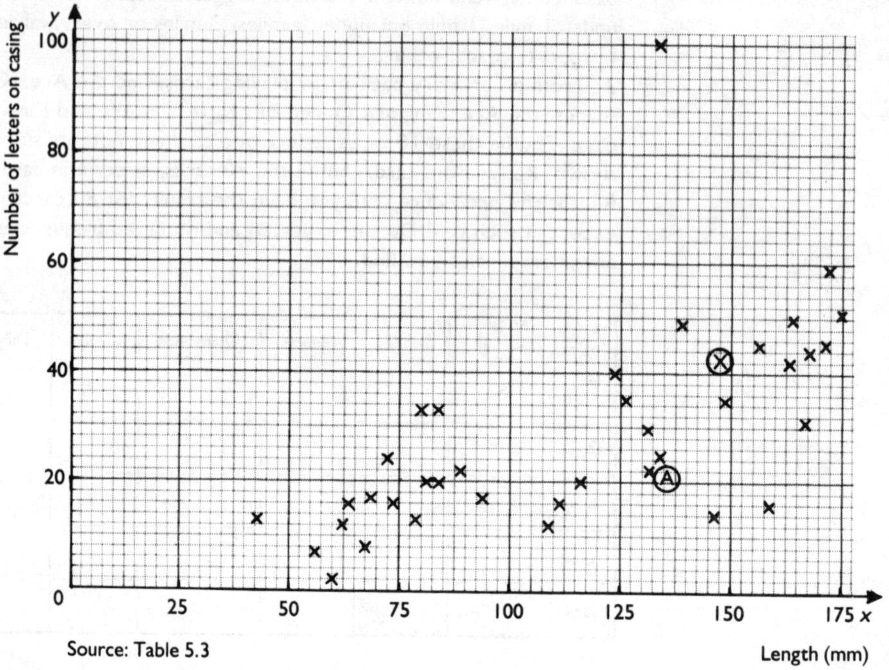

Source: Table 5.3

Fig. 11.1 *Scatter diagram*

(b) the pencil with ID number 32 appears to be an outlier because it is well away from the mass of points.

Types of scatter diagram

In a scatter diagram, we look first to see if there is a straight line relationship between the two variables. Some examples of scatter diagrams are shown in Fig. 11.2. If the points lie exactly on a straight line, as in Fig. 11.2(a) and (b), there is **perfect correlation** between the two variables. If the straight line slopes upwards from left to right, the correlation is **positive** or **direct** and, as the value of x increases, the value of y also increases. If the straight line slopes downwards from left to right, there is **negative** or **inverse** correlation and, as the value of x increases, the value of y decreases.

If the points lie close to a straight line, see Fig. 11.2(c), there is strong correlation. Otherwise we have little or no correlation, see Fig. 11.2(d), or perhaps a curved relationship, see Fig. 11.2(e), rather than a linear one.

Line of best fit

When there is perfect or strong correlation, it is useful to draw in a line of 'best' fit to the scatter points. We can use this line to predict the value of y for any value of x and be reasonably confident that the predictions will be reliable, at least within the range of sample data. If there is little or no correlation, we

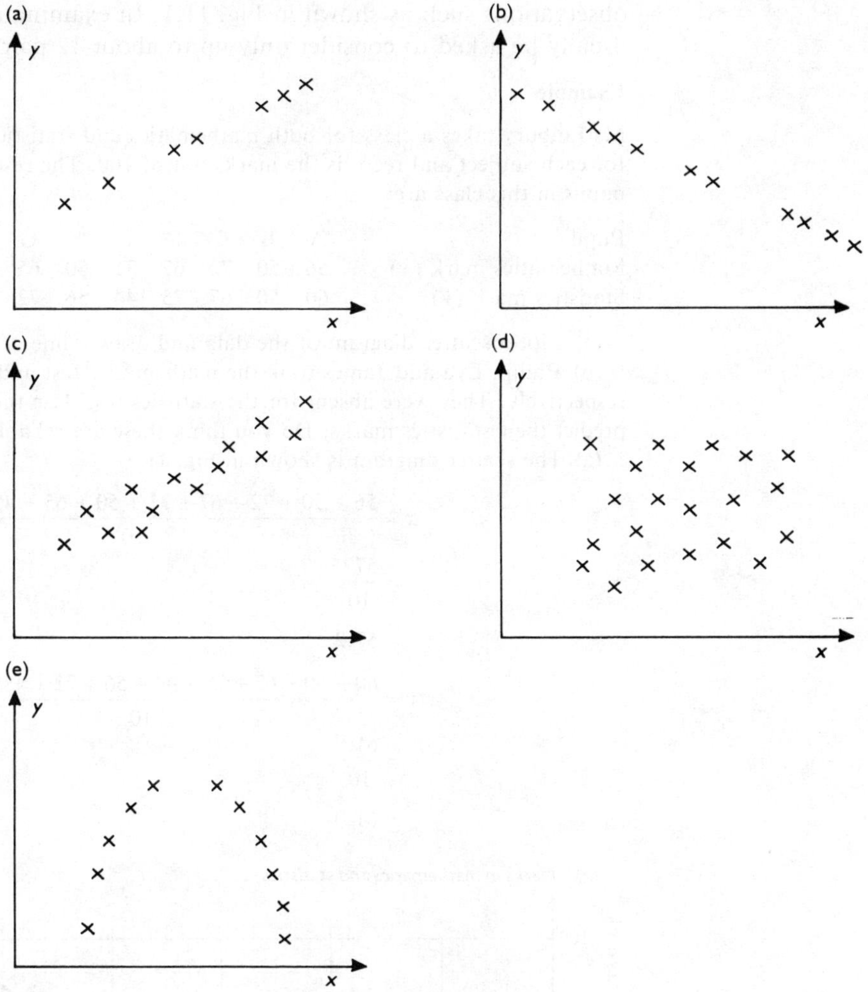

Fig. 11.2 *Types of scatter diagram (a) perfect positive correlation (b) perfect negative correlation (c) strong positive correlation (d) little or no correlation (e) curvilinear correlation*

could still draw a line of best fit but it would not be much use for prediction because of the wide scatter of the data about the line.

It can be shown that the line of best fit must pass through the point whose co-ordinates are $(\bar{x}, \bar{y})$ where $\bar{x}$ is the mean of the x values in the data set and $\bar{y}$ is the mean of the y values in the data set. Use a transparent ruler and place it on the scatter diagram so that it goes through $(\bar{x}, \bar{y})$. Adjust its position so that you balance the points on either side of the line. Then rule in the line.

Fitting a straight line 'by eye' in this way means that different people might draw different lines but the discrepancies are not large if the correlation is strong. The line of best fit is also called the **regression** line. There are other methods of finding a line of best fit but they require more advanced mathematics.

In practice, bivariate studies, i.e. studies of the way in which the values of two variables change together, should be based on a large number of observations such as shown in Fig. 11.1. In examinations, however, you will usually be asked to consider only up to about 12 pairs of observations.

Example

Ms Embury takes a class for both mathematics and statistics. She sets separate tests for each subject and records the marks out of 100. The results for a sample of 10 pupils in this class are:

Pupil	A	B	C	D	E	F	G	H	I	J
Mathematics mark (x)	56	50	72	67	31	50	65	40	80	61
Statistics mark (y)	60	50	67	75	44	56	72	48	76	62

(a) Plot a scatter diagram of the data and draw a line of best fit.

(b) Philip, Eva and James took the mathematics test and scored 60, 95 and 20 respectively. They were absent for the statistics test. Use the line of best fit to predict their statistics marks. Do you think these are reliable estimates?

(a) The scatter diagram is shown in Fig. 11.3.

$$\bar{x} = \frac{56 + 50 + 72 + 67 + 31 + 50 + 65 + 40 + 80 + 61}{10}$$

$$= \frac{572}{10}$$

$$= 57.2$$

$$\bar{y} = \frac{60 + 50 + 67 + 75 + 44 + 56 + 72 + 48 + 76 + 62}{10}$$

$$= \frac{610}{10}$$

$$= 61.0$$

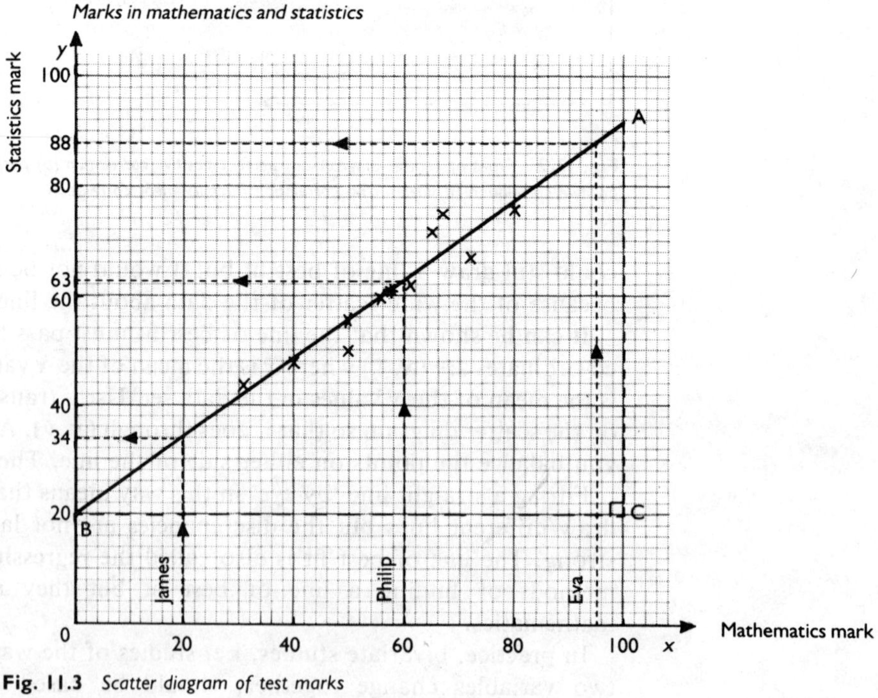

Fig. 11.3 *Scatter diagram of test marks*

The point $(\bar{x}, \bar{y})$ is marked by $*$ in Fig. 11.3. The line of best fit is drawn through this point in such a way that the points in the scatter diagram are as close to it as possible.

(b) Philip: mathematics mark = 60

Using Fig. 11.3, we find $x = 60$, draw a vertical line to meet the line of best fit and then find the y value for this point. We find $y = 63$.

predicted statistics mark = 63

Eva: mathematics mark = 95

From Fig. 11.3, $x = 95$ corresponds to $y = 88$.

predicted statistics mark = 88

James: mathematics mark = 20

From Fig. 11.3, $x = 20$ corresponds to $y = 34$.

predicted statistics mark = 34

The points in the scatter diagram are close to a straight line indicating strong correlation. Philip's mathematics mark, 60, is close to the mean mathematics mark, 57.2, so we can expect his predicted statistics mark, 63, to be close to the mark he would have obtained if he had taken the test. We cannot be so confident with the predictions for Eva and James. Their mathematics marks are well outside the range of marks on which we based our line. We cannot assume that a straight line relationship is still appropriate. When we make predictions outside the range of the sample data, we say we are **extrapolating.**

Exercise 11.3

1 Copy out and complete the following statements which refer to the figure shown.

Heights and weights of 15 fourteen-year old girls

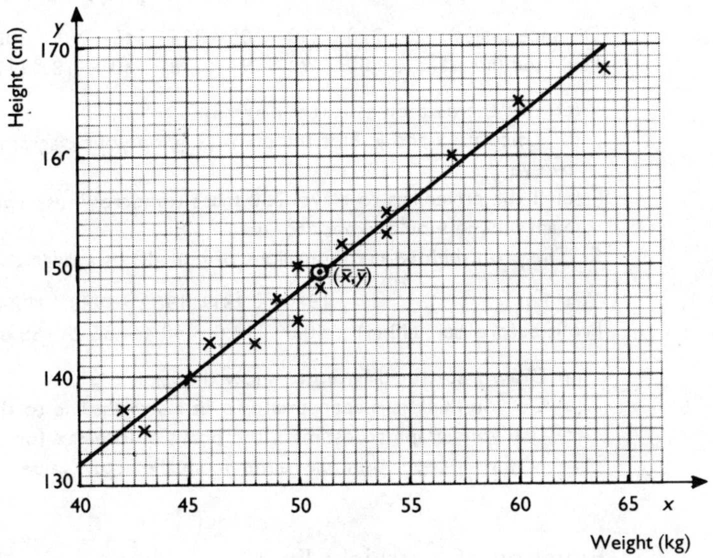

(a) The diagram is called a ....

(b) The line PQ is called ....

(c) The diagram shows .... correlation between height and weight.

2 Sketch a scatter diagram showing a scatter of points which indicate strong negative correlation.

3 Study the scatter diagram shown in the figure.

(a) The mean of the x values is 64, what is the mean of the y values?

(b) Predict the value of y when $x = 50$.

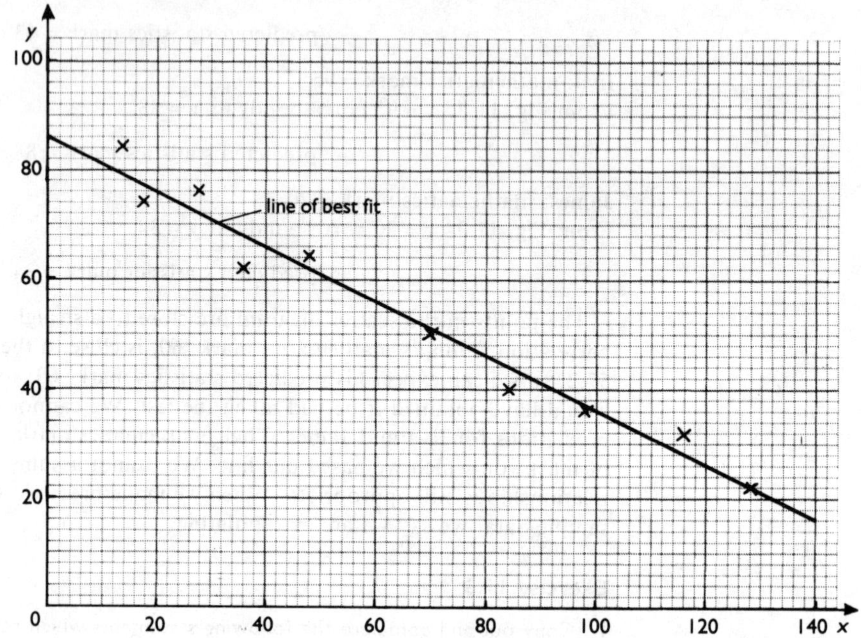

4 A heavy goods vehicle driver has to keep a record of miles travelled and fuel used each day. His record for the last eight working days is as shown.

Distance (miles)	220	250	205	205	345	285	300	320
Fuel used (litres)	80	94	94	78	130	118	112	142

(a) Plot the data on a scatter diagram.

(b) Calculate $\bar{x}$ and $\bar{y}$. Plot the point $(\bar{x}, \bar{y})$ on your diagram. Draw in the line of best fit 'by eye'.

(c) If the driver has to travel 250 miles tomorrow, use your graph to estimate how much fuel he would expect to use.

5 The profit before tax (in millions of pounds) of a large company is shown in the table.

Year (x)	1980	1981	1982	1983	1984	1985	1986	1987
Profit before tax, £M (y)	40.0	44.0	48.4	53.2	58.6	64.6	70.9	77.9

(a) Draw a scatter diagram to show the data.

(b) Do you think it is appropriate to fit a straight line to the data? Give reasons.

(c) Use your graph to estimate the profit before tax for this company in 1990. Suggest why your prediction may differ from the actual value.

Equation of a straight line

It is convenient to be able to write down the equation of the line of best fit so that we can make predictions for y without needing to refer to a graph.

It can be shown that the equation

$$y = mx + c$$

where m and c are constants, always represents a straight line graph.

Example 1

A taxi firm charges as follows:
fixed charge 75p
charge per mile 80p
The cost for a journey of 1 mile $= 80 + 75 = 155$ p.
The cost for a journey of 2 miles $= (2 \times 80) + 75 = 160 + 75 = 235$ p.
The cost for a journey of 3 miles $= (3 \times 80) + 75 = 240 + 75 = 315$ p.
We can work out the cost of longer journeys similarly.

When we plot a graph of cost against distance, see Fig. 11.4, we find the points lie on a straight line. If we extend the line so that it reaches the y axis, we find it cuts the y axis where $y = 75$.

The relationship between y and x is

$$y = 80x + 75$$

where x is the distance in miles and y is the cost in pence.

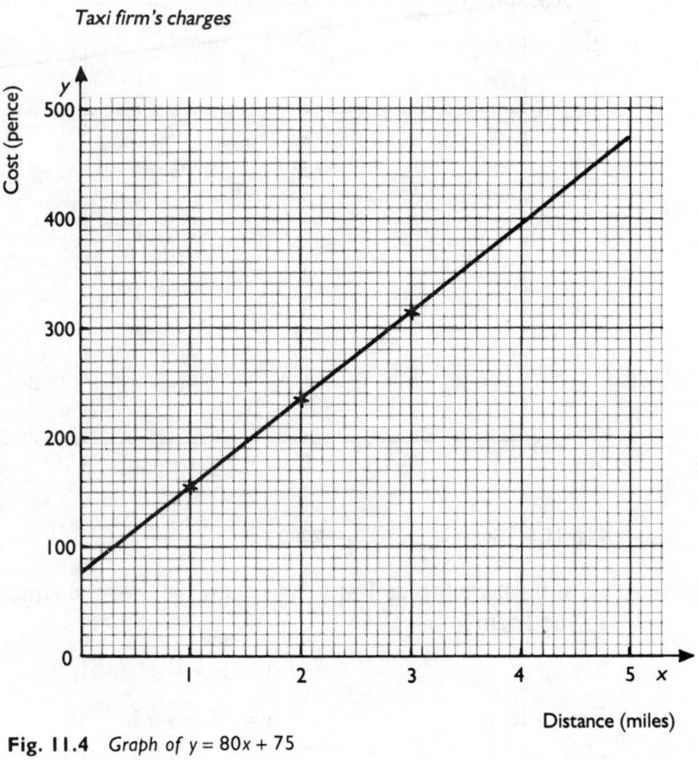

Fig. 11.4 *Graph of $y = 80x + 75$*

Example 2

There is a load of 2000 bricks at a building site. A bricklayer removes 60 bricks each hour.

number of bricks left after 1 hour $= 2000 - 60 = 1940$
number of bricks left after 2 hours $= 2000 - (2 \times 60)$.
$= 2000 - 120$
$= 1880$
number of bricks left after 3 hours $= 2000 - (3 \times 60)$
$= 2000 - 180$
$= 1820$

We can work out the number of bricks left at later times in the same way.

When we plot a graph of number of bricks left against time, see Fig. 11.5, we find the points lie on a straight line that cuts the y axis where $y = 2000$.

The relationship between y and x is

$$y = 2000 - 60x$$
$$\text{or } y = -60x + 2000$$

where y is the number of bricks left and x is the number of hours that the bricklayer has been working.

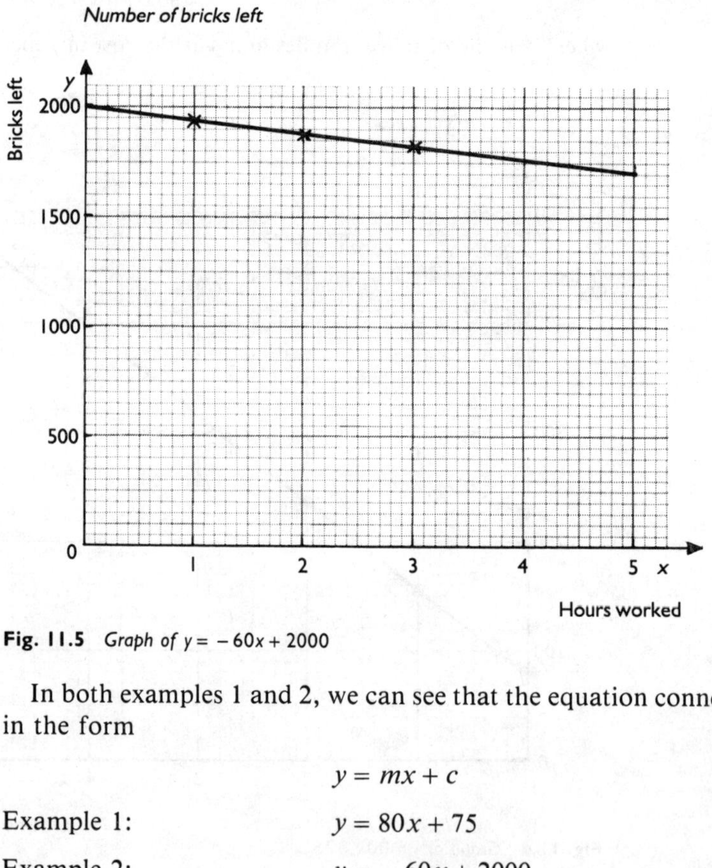

Fig. 11.5 *Graph of* $y = -60x + 2000$

In both examples 1 and 2, we can see that the equation connecting y and x is in the form

$$y = mx + c$$

Example 1: $y = 80x + 75$

Example 2: $y = -60x + 2000$

c is called the **intercept** on the y axis and is the value of y when $x = 0$. m is the **slope** or **gradient** of the line and is the amount by which y changes when the value of x increases by one.

In Example 1, the taxi fare increases by 80 p for every mile travelled so $m = 80$.

In Example 2, the number of bricks left decreases by 60 for every hour worked so $m = -60$.

m is positive for lines sloping upwards from left to right and m is negative for lines sloping downwards from left to right.

To estimate m and c

When we have the graph of a straight line, such as the line of best fit on a scatter diagram, we can estimate m and c.

The intercept, c, can be measured directly from the graph. It is the value of y when $x = 0$. In Fig. 11.6:

$$\text{(a) } c = 2 \qquad \text{(b) } c = -8 \qquad \text{(c) } c = 7$$

To estimate the slope m, we draw a large right angled triangle ABC, see Fig. 11.6. The slope is AC/BC. In Fig. 11.6:

$$\text{(a) } m = 15/5 = 3 \qquad \text{(b) } m = 20/5 = 4 \qquad \text{(c) } m = -20/5 = -4$$

The equations of the straight lines in Fig. 11.6 are:

$$\text{(a) } y = 3x + 2 \qquad \text{(b) } y = 4x - 8 \quad \text{(c) } y = -4x + 7$$

Alternatively, we can find m and c algebraically provided we know the co-ordinates of two points on the line. For example, from Fig. 11.5(a), we note that the line goes through the points (1, 5) and (4, 14).

If $y = mx + c$ for every point on the line, then:

$$5 = m + c$$
$$14 = 4m + c$$

This is a pair of simultaneous equations for m and c.

Subtracting, we find

$$14 - 5 = 4m - m$$
$$9 = 3m$$
$$m = 9/3 = 3$$

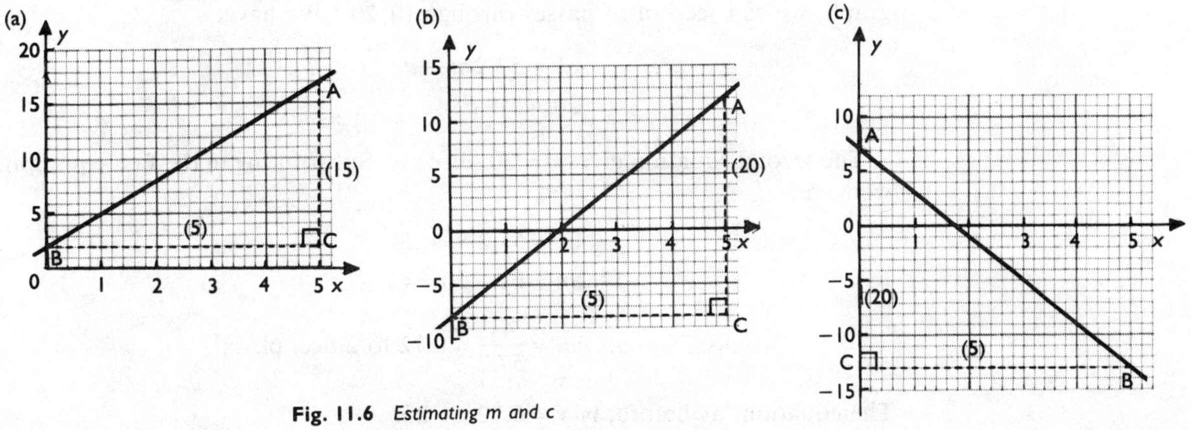

Fig. 11.6 *Estimating m and c*

Having found m, we substitute back into one of the equations to find c.

$$5 = 3 + c$$
$$c = 5 - 3 = 2$$

It is a good idea to check the values of m and c in the other equation. (Check: $(4 \times 3) + 2 = 12 + 2 = 14$.)

The equation for the straight line in Fig. 11.6(a) is $y = 3x + 2$, as before.

Equation of the line of best fit

We can now find the equation of the line of best fit for the test marks data in Fig. 11.3.

From the graph, the intercept, $c = 20$.

The slope, $m = AC/BC = 72/100 = 0.72$.

The equation is $y = 0.72x + 20$.

We can use this equation to check the graphical estimates we obtained previously.

Philip: $x = 60$, $y = (0.72 \times 60) + 20$
$= 43.2 + 20$
$= 63.2$
$= 63$ to nearest whole number

Eva: $x = 95$, $y = (0.72 \times 95) + 20$
$= 68.4 + 20$
$= 88.4$
$= 88$ to nearest whole number

James: $x = 20$, $y = (0.72 \times 20) + 20$
$= 14.4 + 20$
$= 34.4$
$= 34$ to nearest whole number

To find the equation algebraically, we need the co-ordinates of two points on the line. We know the line goes through $(\bar{x}, \bar{y})$ which is (57.2, 61). From the graph, we can see it also passes through (0, 20). We have:

$$61 = 57.2m + c$$
$$20 = 0 + c$$

The second equation gives $c = 20$, directly. Substituting in the first equation, we have:

$$61 = 57.2\,m + 20$$
$$57.2m = 61 - 20 = 41$$
$$m = \frac{41}{57.2} = 0.72 \text{ to 2 dec. pl.}$$

The equation, as before, is $y = 0.72x + 20$.

Exercise 11.4

1 The line of best fit on a scatter diagram has slope equal to -4. The line passes through the point (6, 2). Find the equation of the line and use it to estimate the value of y when $x = 3$.

2 Work out $\bar{x}$ and $\bar{y}$ for the following set of pairs of observations.

x	1	2	3	4
y	3	6	11	18

The line of best fit to these data goes through the point (0, -3). Find the equation of the line.

3 Pupils at Aitchbury school are given two English tests. One is written and one is oral. The marks, out of 100, obtained by 12 pupils are:

Pupil	1	2	3	4	5	6	7	8	9	10	11	12
Marks in written test (x)	66	88	82	84	90	80	82	68	78	82	67	72
Marks in oral test (y)	56	84	84	74	60	84	78	72	60	68	71	70

(a) Plot a scatter diagram of the oral test marks against written test marks.
(b) Draw the line of best fit 'by eye' on your diagram. If the equation of this line is $y = mx + c$, estimate m and c.
(c) Estimate the marks in an oral test for pupils who scored (i) 75, (ii) 45 in the written test. Comment on the reliability of your estimates.

4 The marks, out of 100, of eight pupils in Physics, Chemistry and Biology are:

Pupil	A	B	C	D	E	F	G	H
Physics	21	55	45	65	49	30	59	37
Chemistry	36	64	56	71	59	44	67	49
Biology	59	81	49	65	29	84	40	19

Plot three separate scatter diagrams of
(a) marks in Physics against marks in Chemistry,
(b) marks in Physics against marks in Biology,
(c) marks in Chemistry against marks in Biology.

Comment on the results.

Draw in the line of best fit on any diagram for which you think it is approriate.

Spearman's rank correlation coefficient

To measure how close the scatter points are to a straight line, we can calculate Spearman's rank correlation coefficient, r_s. This is a number whose value always lies between -1 and $+1$. A value of -1 indicates perfect negative correlation. A value of $+1$ indicates perfect positive correlation. Values close to -1 or $+1$ indicate strong linear correlation and suggest that the data set is a sample from a population in which there is a linear relationship between the two variables x and y. Values near zero indicate little linear relationship between x and y.

Strong correlation does not imply that there is a 'cause and effect' or **causal** relationship between x and y. That may be the case, particularly in scientific applications—for example, increasing the temperature of a metal rod does cause its length to increase. In general, however, all we can say is that the two variables concerned tend to change together. Statistics alone cannot provide the reasons why this should be so.

Calculation

Find the largest value of x in the data set and give it rank 1.
Find the next largest value of x and give it rank 2.
Continue until all the values have been ranked.
The smallest value of x has rank n, where n is the number of pairs of observations.
Rank the y values in the data set similarly.
For each pair of observations, work out d, the difference between its x rank and its y rank.
Calculate Spearman's coefficient using the formula:

$$r_s = 1 - \frac{6\Sigma d^2}{n(n^2-1)}$$

Table 11.4 Calculation of Spearman's coefficient

Pupil	Mathematics mark (x)	Statistics mark (y)	Rank of x	Rank of y	d	d^2
A	56	60	6	6	0	0
B	50	50	7.5	8	−0.5	0.25
C	72	67	2	4	−2	4
D	67	75	3	2	1	1
E	31	44	10	10	0	0
F	50	56	7.5	7	0.5	0.25
G	65	72	4	3	1	1
H	40	48	9	9	0	0
I	80	76	1	1	0	0
J	61	62	5	5	0	0
Totals				(check)	0	6.5

The calculation for the data set of mathematics and statistics test marks considered earlier, see Fig. 11.3, is shown in Table 11.4.

Students B and F had identical mathematics marks so we have **tied ranks.** In this situation, we give each the mean of the ranks they jointly occupy. Students B and F share seventh and eighth places, so we give each the rank:

$$\frac{7+8}{2} = \frac{15}{2} = 7.5$$

Substituting in the formula we find:

$$r_s = 1 - \frac{6 \times 6.5}{10(10^2-1)}$$

$$= 1 - \frac{39}{10(100-1)}$$

$$= 1 - \frac{39}{10 \times 99}$$

$$= 1 - \frac{39}{990}$$

$$= 1 - 0.039\ 39$$
$$= 0.961 \text{ to 3 dec.pl.}$$

It is usual to work out a correlation coefficient to three decimal places.

The value 0.961 is close to +1, confirming the strong positive correlation that is indicated in the scatter diagram.

To apply Spearman's correlation coefficient, we do not need to have numerical variables that are measured on a ratio or interval scale (see Chapter 2). So long as the variables are able to be measured on a rank scale, we can use this coefficient.

Exercise 11.5

1 Mrs A and Mrs B decide to compare their monthly expenditures on food for their families last month. Their expenditures are shown in the table.

Expenditure (£)

Food	Mrs A	Mrs B
Bread and cereals	20.52	25.19
Biscuits and cakes	14.03	16.35
Meat	25.12	33.14
Fish	0	10.23
Butter, oils and fats	6.73	9.51
Milk, eggs and cheese	32.44	27.19
Hot drinks	3.12	4.10
Soft drinks	5.81	8.37
Sugar and preserves	3.51	7.81
Sweets	4.73	6.42
Vegetables	12.43	12.72
Fruit	16.19	10.12
Other goods	5.43	6.50

Calculate Spearman's rank correlation coefficient for the data. What can you say about the spending patterns of the two mothers?

2 For one year a small investor kept a record of the share prices for the companies whose shares he owned. The highest and lowest prices for each share are shown in the table.

Share prices (pence)

Company	Highest value	Lowest value
British Telecom	278	178
Westland	112	50
Amstrad	168	36
ASDA	170	130
Hanson Trust	161	105
Irish Distillers	287	160
Coalite	313	246

Calculate Spearman's rank correlation coefficient between the highest and the lowest prices for each share. Do you think there is a relationship between the highest and the lowest prices of a share during the year? Why?

3 In an ice-skating competition, the competitors are given a mark out of six for technical merit by nine judges. The marks are to be ranked. Complete the table shown.

Judge	A	B	C	D	E	F	G	H	I
Mark	5.5	5.3	5.5	5.4	5.9	5.7	5.6	5.7	5.6
Rank					1				

4 Pupils at Ibury school are given marks out of 100 for achievement and letter grades, A being the best, for effort. A sample of pupils had the results shown for mathematics.

Student	1	2	3	4	5	6	7	8	9	10	11
Achievement mark	69	53	76	72	67	81	83	69	89	82	78
Effort grade	B+	C	A	C	B+	A−	A	B	B−	C+	A−

Calculate Spearman's rank correlation coefficient for these data. Comment on the value obtained.

5 Two fashion editors were asked to rank eight outfits in order of preference. The results are as shown.

Outfit	A	B	C	D	E	F	G	H
Editor 1	8	7	2	1	6	3	5	4
Editor 2	7	3	1	2	8	5	4	6

Calculate Spearman's rank correlation coefficient for the data. Do the editors agree in their preferences?

Practical exercise 11.6

1 Think of the make and model of a popular car. Look through the used-car advertisements in a newspaper and note the price and year of registration in any advertisements for this model.

Draw a scatter diagram with price on the y axis and year of registration on the x axis. What does your diagram suggest about the correlation between the age and the price of this model?

2 Visit a supermarket or shop selling different brands of orange drink to dilute. For each brand, note down the price, the volume of contents and the percentage of orange juice. Work out the price per litre of each brand.

Draw a scatter diagram with price per litre on the y axis and percentage of orange juice on the x axis. Calculate Spearman's rank correlation coefficient between price per litre and percentage of orange juice.

Which brand do you consider to be best buy? Why?

3 Roll a marble down an inclined plane on to a flat surface. Record the distance, x, measured along the plane, of the point of release from the foot of the plane and the distance, y, from the foot of the plane at which the marble comes to rest. Repeat for varying values of x until you have a minimum of 20 observations.

Draw a scatter diagram of your data. Do you think there is (a) a linear relationship between y and x, (b) a curvilinear relationship between y and x or (c) no relationship between y and x?

4 For this practical you will need at least 10 editions of a journal or magazine. For each copy, record the weight and number of pages. Construct a scatter diagram of weight against number of pages and draw in the line of best fit. If the equation of this line is $y = mx + c$, estimate m and c.

Use your findings to estimate (a) the weight of one page of the journal and (b) the weight of the cover of the journal.

12 Experimental design

In Chapters 2 and 3, we mentioned some of the problems of data collection. Now that you have some experience of collecting and analysing data we can consider further aspects of experimental design and sample survey methods (Chapter 13).

Preliminaries

In any investigation you have to define the variable of interest and decide how to measure or observe it. This variable is called the **response variable**. It is useful to make a list of anything that you think might affect the response variable. In a chemistry experiment, for example, these **factors** might include numerical variables, such as temperature, pressure or humidity, as well as qualitative variables, such as whether a solution is shaken or not. In general, you will not be able to take account of all conceivable factors so you select those which you feel are particularly important.

In an experiment, you deliberately design your collection of data so that at least some of the factors are within your control. For example, in a laboratory, you will usually be able to adjust the temperature and you can decide at what different temperatures you are going to make your observations. These temperatures are referred to as the different **levels** of the factor. When you have chosen the levels you are going to use for all the different factors, you can give a specification of a **treatment**, i.e. the levels that are to be used in one particular trial of an experiment. For example, in the following two-factor experiment, we might have:

	First factor	Second factor
Treatment 1	Temperature 15°C	Solution well shaken
Treatment 2	Temperature 20°C	Solution well shaken
Treatment 3	Temperature 20°C	Solution not shaken

Some factors, such as lapses of concentration by the experimenter or fluctuations in the power supply, may be uncontrollable. We want to design the experiment so as to separate the effects of interest from the uncontrollable variation. We also want to ensure that the effect of the uncontrollable variation is as small as possible.

Replication

Some uncontrollable variation gives rise to random errors (see Chapter 4) which, on any one occasion, are just as likely to result in a measurement being too high as too low. To allow for this, we use replication. We repeat the trial several times under as near identical conditions as possible. If we take the mean of the measurements, the low and the high values arising from random errors will tend to compensate and we should get a more precise estimate than from one single observation.

Precision is the degree to which measurements in a data set agree amongst themselves. It can be evaluated by calculating the standard deviation, for instance. A set of measurements with a smaller standard deviation is said to be more precise than a set with a larger standard deviation.

If we use the mean of measurements from replicated trials, it can be shown that the spread of values that this mean can take is smaller than the spread of values of individual measurements. Hence replication improves precision.

Randomisation

There is little point making precise measurements if they are not accurate. A set of measurements is said to be accurate if, in the long run, the mean of them equals the true value we are trying to measure.

For example, if apparatus is not correctly calibrated, such as a thermometer reading 1°C when it should read 0°C, then each measurement we make will be in error. However many observations are made, they will not be accurate because of this systematic error of 1°C.

Other systematic errors may not be so easy to identify.

Example 1

An experimenter is making observations on five different materials at eight different temperatures, 5°C, 10°C, 15°C, ... 40°C. Each day in one week she takes a material, starts at 5°C and then works up to 40°C.

When she analyses her results, she will not be able to separate the temperature effects from the other variables that change in the course of the day or the week such as her alertness or variation in the apparatus as it warms up.

Example 2

An agricultural scientist is assessing the yields of four varieties of wheat. He plants the different varieties in strips as shown in Fig. 12.1(a).

When he analyses his results, he cannot tell whether the differences between yields arise from the differences between varieties or whether variations in the fertility of the soil, the drainage or wind damage have also contributed.

To minimise the effects of such unknown systematic errors, it is important to use randomisation so that the order or layout of experiments is not predetermined by the experimenter but is chosen by some random process. We now consider some possible ways of achieving this in our two examples.

1 The experimenter could use eight playing cards, Ace, 2, 3, up to 8, to represent the eight different temperatures.

Card	Ace	2	3	4	5	6	7	8
Temperature °C	5	10	15	20	25	30	35	40

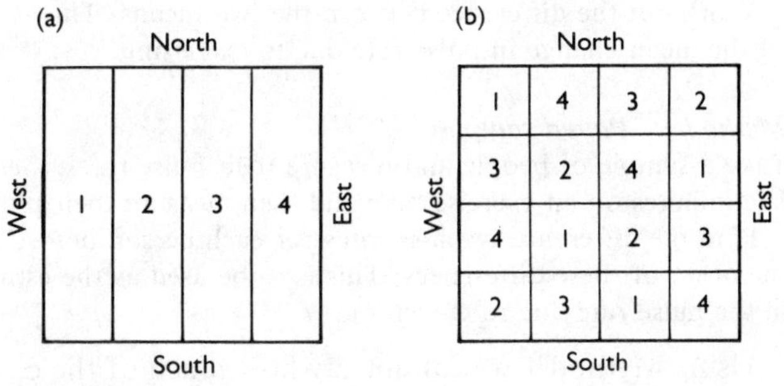

Fig. 12.1 *Allocation of four wheat varieties (a) not randomised (b) randomised*

She shuffles the cards and deals them out. Suppose the order is:

7 4 8 5 3 2 Ace 6

Her order of measurements on the first day should be, in °C:

35 20 40 25 15 10 5 30

On the following days, she shuffles the cards again to get the order for that day. Using this procedure she will have reduced any systematic errors that are related to time of day.

If she desired, she could also use a similar random process to decide which material she had to use in each measurement so as to reduce any systematic errors that are related to the day of the week.

Often, however, it is impracticable to attempt a fully randomised experiment. If she used a different material in each measurement and she had to clean the apparatus before changing the materials, it might mean she had insufficient time to complete all her measurements in five days. Using a random temperature order may also be unacceptable. It could take too long because of the time taken waiting for the apparatus to warm up or cool down. A material, if it were plastic, for example, might not resume its former state once it had been heated above a certain temperature so the measurements at low temperatures might **have** to be made first.

2 The scientist should design his layout so that each variety is subject to the different conditions that may exist in the different parts of the field. A possible layout, dividing the field into 16 plots, is shown in Fig. 12.1(b). Each variety appears once and only once in every East-West strip and every North-South strip. The order within the strip has been assigned randomly as in Example 1.

Again such a layout may impose practical difficulties. When it comes to harvesting the crops, it is likely to be much easier to use machines on the strip layout in Fig. 12.1(a) than on the smaller plots of Fig. 12.1(b).

Paired design

When just two treatments are to be compared, a **matched-pair** design can be used to reduce the effects of uncontrollable variation.

Example 1

To compare changes in pulse rates due to exercising

Method 1 Independent samples
Take a sample of people and measure their pulse rates. Find the mean of the pulse rates. Take another sample of people, get them to pedal for five minutes on an exercise bike and then measure their pulse rates. Find the mean of these pulse rates.

Work out the difference between the two means. This is to be used as the estimate of the mean change in pulse rate due to exercising.

Method 2 Paired samples
Take a sample of people and measure their pulse rates. Get these people to pedal for five minutes on an exercise bike and then measure their pulse rates.

Find the difference in pulse rates for each person before and after exercise. Find the mean of these differences. This is to be used as the estimate of the mean change in the pulse rate due to exercising.

Using Method 1 we cannot say how much of the change in pulse rate is due to exercise and how much is due to differences between the two groups of people. Using Method 2, we know that any change in pulse rate arises from the exercising and not from differences in the people.

The type of procedure described in Method 2 is sometimes called a **before/after** design because we observe the same sample before and after some treatment.

Example 2

Use of twins to assess the effectiveness of a new method of teaching keyboarding.

Identical twins are ideal subjects for matched-pair experiments because their genetic make-up is the same. A sample is taken of ten pairs of teenage twins with no previous experience of keyboarding. One twin from each pair is taught keyboarding by the traditional method and the other twin is taught by the new method. All the twins have the same amount of practice time. At the end of six months, they are asked to type out a standard piece and the number of mistakes each makes are counted. The difference between the numbers of mistakes made by each pair of twins is worked out. If, on average, a lot fewer mistakes are made by the twins using the new method, we would feel that the new method was more effective than the traditional method.

We are assuming that each twin in a pair has the same aptitude and ability and that any differences in the keyboarding test arise solely from the course. If we had selected two unrelated samples of teenagers and given one set the traditional course and the other set the new course, we would not have known whether differences in the performance of the two samples were due to the test or due to differences in the aptitude and abilities of the teenagers.

Example 3

Use of laboratory animals for drug tests.

Before new drugs are marketed, they have to be tested both to assess their effectiveness and to observe any side effects. In order to use a matched-pair design, genetically-identical animals from the same litter must be available. Pairs of such animals are selected and, typically, both are infected with the same disease. One of each pair is given the drug and one is not. The set of animals not given the drug is called the control group. All the animals are looked after in exactly the same way. At the end of a set time, for example, three months, the differences between the pairs can be observed, such as whether the infection has disappeared or the occurrence of any side effects. Once again, variation between the pairs of animals themselves has been reduced as much as possible so any difference between the animals in each pair is due to the drug.

Difficulties in experimentation

Unfortunately it is not always easy to set up a matched-pair design. Most people are not twins so testing drugs on humans cannot follow the pattern of Example 3. Even with matched pairs one of the animals might escape or injure itself, for example, or one of the twins in Example 2 might fall ill and miss some keyboarding tuition. If a matched-pair design cannot be used, then comparisons have to be made on the basis of independent samples such as in Example 1, Method 1.

Many difficulties can arise and we shall illustrate some of them in the context of drug testing in humans.

If people know they are trying out a new drug, they may make a better recovery purely because of the psychological effect of being part of the test programme rather than because the drug actually does any good. To counteract this, patients may not know whether they are getting the drug or some 'placebo', i.e. something that is harmless and ineffective. The group of patients on the placebo acts as a **control group** to be compared with those who are taking the new drug.

It may be important that the doctors and nurses attending the patients do not know who is taking the drug and who is taking the placebo. This is then called a 'double-blind' experiment. Doctors might otherwise be inclined only to put hopeless cases on a new drug and the test would not then be fair. Nurses may give more time and care to patients if they know they are on the new drug and it is because of this extra nursing that patients improve rather than because of the new drug.

It is not always necessary to have a control group. If the recovery rate from the standard treatment has been steady over a number of years for a wide variety of patients and hospitals, then the new treatment needs to be tried only in a random sample of patients to see whether it gives better results.

Drug testing in humans raises ethical issues. A doctor wants to give each individual patient what he or she feels is the best treatment at that time. The doctor may not feel justified in prescribing an untried product which, although it might give better results, may be detrimental to the recovery of the patient. Patients are usually asked to consent to be part of a trial but is is difficult for many to make a rational decision. If they agree and happen to receive a placebo, they may jeopardise their own recovery for the benefit, in the long term, of future patients.

Exercise 12.1

1 Four practical groups measured, several times, the mass in grams of a pebble with the following results:

Group 1	248	251	247	252	250	253	249
Group 2	251	249	248	252	253	254	250
Group 3	245	249	253	246	252	250	255
Group 4	244	254	255	248	252	253	254

(a) Represent the results for each group separately on a line.

(b) Find the mean and the standard deviation of the results for each group.

(c) Which groups had greatest precision in their measurements?

(d) The true weight of the pebble is in fact 250 g. Which groups were most accurate in their measurements?

(e) Find the mean and the standard deviation of the four means you have worked out in (b). How does the value of this standard deviation compare with the standard deviations you worked out in (b)?

2 You want to compare the yields of two different varieties of broad beans. You have a packet of seeds of each variety and a plot of land large enough to take all the beans. Decide how you are going to measure the yield. Design an experiment to make the comparison, showing how you would set out your plot. What practical difficulties can you foresee?

3 A large retail organisation has had complaints from customers about colour running from some fabrics when they are washed. It is particularly noticeable in blue and in purple tee-shirts. A dye manufacturer asserts that he has developed a new fixing solution which, when applied to the finished fabric will reduce the colour loss.

To demonstrate the new solution the manufacturer has been given 20 large pieces of the tee-shirt fabric in different colours.

List the factors that you think might affect the amount of colour loss in washing.

Suggest how the manufacturer should design his demonstration so that a valid comparison between treated and untreated materials can be made.

Practical exercise 12.2

1 You will need a stop watch and a skipping rope. Ask three groups of ten pupils to take part.

(a) *Group 1*. With the help of the stop watch, measure the pulse rate (pulses per minute) of each pupil. Find their mean pulse rate.

Group 2. Ask one pupil to skip 200 times and then measure his or her pulse rate. Repeat the procedure for the remaining pupils. Find their mean pulse rate. Work out the difference between the mean pulse rates of Groups 1 and 2.

(b) *Group 3*. Measure the pulse rate for one pupil, ask him or her to skip 200 times and then measure the pulse rate again. Repeat the procedure for the remaining nine pupils. Find the difference between the pulse rates for each pupil.

Work out the mean of all the differences.

(c) Compare your final answers in (a) and (b). If you had to estimate the mean change in pulse rate for any pupil as result of doing 200 skips, would you use method (a) or method (b) and why?

2 It has been suggested that adding sugar to the water in a vase extends the lifetime of cut flowers. Discuss how you would design an experiment using (a) independent samples, (b) paired samples, to test this suggestion. Carry out an experiment on 16 to 20 flowers using either design (a) or (b). Have you found any evidence to support the suggestion?

13 Sample survey methods

In Chapter 1 we defined the meaning of the terms 'sample' and 'population' and showed how to use a lottery method to select a random sample from a population. This simple lottery method is not suitable for all surveys and we shall now give some alternative procedures.

Sample frame

A sample frame is a list of the population to be surveyed. The data base in Table 5.3 provides a sample frame for the set of 50 pencils. Each pencil is identified by a number.

If you are surveying pupils in your school, you will be able to obtain a list from the school office. Of course, this list will change from time to time as pupils leave and new ones arrive. It may be in alphabetical order, in year order or simply a compilation of the individual form lists. You can be confident that every pupil is included on the list and that there are no duplications.

If you are conducting a survey within your town or locality, it becomes more difficult to find a list of individuals. The electoral register and the telephone directory are lists but they do not show all residents in an area.

The electoral register includes only those aged 18 and over who are entitled to vote, so it is no use for a survey that intends to cover children or aliens, for example. Although electoral registration is legally required, some individuals do not register. The list is compiled in October each year and is published in the following February. By the time the next register comes into effect, the list is 16 months out-of-date. With population movements and deaths, a register may have 10% of its entries incorrect.

The telephone directory lists the addresses of premises with telephones. Although the percentage of UK households with a telephone is growing—it was over 80% in 1986—there is not complete coverage. The name of only one person is given with each entry so no information is given about other individuals living there. Some people are ex-directory and are not included for security or personal reasons.

The Postcode Address File, the Post Office's list of addresses, is used as a sampling frame of households in some official surveys. It is, however, a list of addresses, some of which contain more than one household and some of which contain no households. Some households with more than one residence may be included twice, so again it is not entirely satisfactory.

Finding a suitable sample frame for a population may be impossible. For example, can you think of a list to use for a survey of smokers in your locality in order to discover how many cigarettes they smoke each day?

Random sampling

If a sample frame is available, then random sampling can be used. If we need a sample of n items from a population, we have to ensure that every set of n items in the population has the same chance of being selected.

Although the lottery method is adequate for small populations, a method based on the use of random numbers is usually easier to carry out for large populations. Random numbers can be generated by computers and are printed in books of statistical tables. They are strings of digits and each digit from 0, 1, up to 9 has the same chance in the long run of being at a particular position in the string. Just because the digit 3 appears at one position does not imply that 3 is more-likely or less-likely to occur as the next digit. You may find that your calculator will generate random digits for you. The appropriate button may be labelled RAN. You can generate them on a BBC micro, for example, using the RND function.

Table 13.1 Random digits

2117	1165	0022	7721	8316	2149
0832	3896	8122	5215	2573	8710
5825	4808	9172	1562	7329	2554
7192	1548	8239	7163	0766	1245
5862	5553	9402	4549	9675	0092

A series of random digits produced by my calculator is shown in Table 13.1. In a table of random digits, you will usually find the digits printed together in groups of four or five. This is to help you keep track of where you are in the table and does not mean that you have to use them in fours or fives.

Let us select a sample of five pencils from Table 5.3 using random digits. The ID numbers of the pencils go from 00 to 49 so each pencil is labelled by a two-digit number. Hence we read off digits from Table 13.1 in groups of two. Starting in the top left-hand corner, we have 21, 17, 11, 65, 00, 22, 77, and so on. We read systematically from the table. If we went on to another sample survey, we would either start at a different place in the table or use a completely different set of random digits. The five pencils to include in our random sample are those with ID number 21, 17, 11, 00 and 22. We cannot use the random number 65 because the highest ID number is 49.

To use this method to take a random sample of 30 pupils from your school, you would first have to number everyone on the list of pupils. Suppose there are 876 pupils in the school. To number everyone fairly we will have to use three-digit numbers, so the first person on the list is 000, the second 001, the third 002, the tenth 009, the hundredth 099, and so on up to the last person who is 875. Starting at the left-hand end of the second row in Table 13.1 and reading off in groups of three, we have 083, 238, 968, 122, 521, 525 and so on. We would include pupils with the numbers 083, 238, 122, 521, 525 in our sample. The number 968 cannot be used because 875 is the highest on the list. You continue in the same way until you have all the 30 pupils to be included in the sample.

If the same random number comes up twice, you must know what procedure to adopt. If you are sampling with replacement, for which the theory is slightly easier, you should include that item again. If you are sampling without replacement, then ignore that number when it occurs again and continue until you have the required number of different items.

Your sample must include those items selected. In school you may find some of the pupils chosen for your sample are unwilling to co-operate in your survey. You must encourage them to take part, as failure to cover the whole of the sample will introduce bias to your results. You must resist any temptation to substitute anyone else to replace a chosen pupil. This could also lead to bias because you have no guarantee that the new observation will be the same as for your original choice.

Errors in sampling

Estimation of population parameters

From the results of a sample survey, we are usually trying to do one of two things:

1 To estimate a population proportion.
For example,

proportion of the electorate supporting the Labour party,
proportion of pupils who watched a particular TV programme,
proportion of smokers who bought brand X cigarettes in the last month.

If we have taken a sample of size n, i.e. with n items in it, and x of these items had the particular attribute we were looking for, then the proportion, p, in the sample with the attribute is x/n. We use this value as our estimate of the unknown population proportion, P.

2 To estimate a population mean.
For example,

mean amount spent by pupils on sweets each week,
mean number of adults per household in a town.

If we have taken a sample of size n, with values $x_1, x_2, \ldots x_n$, then the mean, $\bar{x}$, of the sample is given by:

$$\bar{x} = \frac{x_1 + x_2 + \cdots + x_n}{n} = \frac{\Sigma x}{n}$$

We use this value as our estimate of the unknown population mean which is usually denoted by the Greek letter mu, μ.

Sampling errors

We do not expect that an estimate obtained from the sample will agree exactly with the true value of the parameter that we would have found if we had looked at the complete population. The difference between the estimate and the true value is called the **sampling error**. This error can be positive or negative and can be estimated provided we have used random sampling.

We first work out what is termed the standard error:

$$\text{standard error of a proportion} = \sqrt{\frac{P(1-P)}{n}}$$

$$\text{standard error of a mean} = \frac{\sigma}{\sqrt{n}}$$

where σ is the standard deviation of the parent population.

In both cases, you can see that n appears in the denominator so that, as the sample size increases, the standard error decreases and the precision of our estimate improves.

If sampling is with replacement or from an infinitely large population and provided the sample size, n, is large, it can be shown that for approximately 95% of samples we have:

$$\text{sample proportion} - 2\sqrt{\frac{P(1-P)}{n}} < \text{population proportion} < \text{sample proportion} + 2\sqrt{\frac{P(1-P)}{n}}$$

lower confidence limit **upper confidence limit**

$$\text{sample mean} - \frac{2\sigma}{\sqrt{n}} < \text{population mean} < \text{sample mean} + \frac{2\sigma}{\sqrt{n}}$$

These are referred to as 95% confidence intervals because, in 95% of samples, when we work out the lower and upper limits shown, the unknown population parameter lies between them.

To estimate the standard errors we need to have estimates of P and σ. If the sample size is large, we can get a good estimate of σ from the sample using the usual formula for a standard deviation but with $(n-1)$ replacing n in the denominator. This estimate is usually denoted by s or by σ_{n-1} on some calculators:

$$s = \sqrt{\frac{\Sigma(x-\bar{x})^2}{n-1}}$$

Sometimes σ may be known from past surveys.

Non-sampling errors

We noted earlier that other errors may occur when we use sampling methods. Non-response, failure to cover the whole sample, substitution of a chosen item and an incomplete or unsuitable sample frame can lead to biased errors. Poor interview techniques and badly-designed questionnaires, as mentioned in

Chapter 3, may also introduce bias. These errors tend to affect all the results in the same way. Usually, they do not cancel out in the long run and hence lead to inaccurate estimates. We expect the size of these errors to increase as the sample size increases but we have no mathematical way of estimating them. It is very important, therefore, to try to eliminate them if at all possible. These errors are sometimes called **non-sampling errors** because they are not an inevitable feature of sampling whereas the sampling errors are.

Purposive sampling

Often some individuals feel that they can select a sample more effectively than by using a random procedure.

For instance, when I ask pupils to choose a sample of five pencils from the box of 50 pencils, they tend to do one of two things:

1 they choose five pencils that appear to be of medium length;

2 they choose a very small pencil, a very long pencil, one of medium length, one between the smallest and medium length and one between medium length and the longest length.

When asked why they make their choice in this way, Group 1 say they are trying to select pencils to represent the average length. True, they will get a fair estimate of the mean or median length of the complete pencil set but their samples will tell them nothing about the variation in the lengths of the 50 pencils. Group 2 say they are trying to cover the whole range of lengths. True, they will have an estimate of the range of lengths in the complete pencil set and they may well get a fair estimate for the mean or median length. They will have learned nothing, however, about the clustering of values between the extremes, whether most pencils were close to the middle length and whether the pencils of extreme length were outliers.

Pupils tend to look at the length of the pencils when selecting their samples. If they are then asked to observe some other characteristic, such as the number of colours on the casing, they realise that, although they have tried to ensure that their samples are representative of length, they have ignored other characteristics completely.

Similarly, when sampling human populations, we might be tempted purposively to seek out either those that we think are average or try to ensure that a range from one extreme to the other is included. In the first case we will find less variation than is appropriate. In the second case, we may emphasise the extremes unfairly and not give sufficient weight to those in the centre.

Opportunity sampling

Sometimes we do not sample purposively but we include in our sample those items that are convenient or easy to select. With the 50 pencils, it would be easiest to choose the first five pencils at the top of the box as the sample. They may be representative of all the pencils in some respects but, on the whole, I have found that it is the smaller pencils that tend to be at the top. Using this method of sampling would underestimate the mean length of the complete set of pencils.

In school, you might decide to choose a sample by stopping people in the playground during the lunch hour. You will be able to find 30 people who are willing to take part in your survey but they might not be representative of the whole school. Some people might be at clubs or at games-practices, some may be off school premises for lunch. Once again you will tend to get biased results and less variation than might be expected.

This method could be used for a survey of smokers for which there is no sample frame. A market researcher could wait in a shopping centre, looking for people smoking. She could then approach them to ask her questions but she has no guarantee that these smokers are typical of all smokers in the locality. Alternatively, she might approach anyone and, if she discovers they smoke, ask them to take part in the survey.

Quota sampling

Opportunity sampling can be modified to provide a sampling method that is widely used by commercial research companies. It has the advantages over random sampling that no sample frame is required and that no named individual has to be contacted, just any individual that is of a given type.

When designing the survey, the organiser decides in what respects he wants it to be representative. For example, should it include both men and women, different age groups and different social groups. From information gained from the Census of Population, see Chapter 18, the organiser knows approximately the percentages of people in all these different categories. He tries to ensure that the sample will have a similar make-up by setting quotas for these categories.

An interviewer might be told to contact

25 men in the 25–44 age group who are unskilled manual workers

10 women in the 18–24 age group who are skilled manual workers and so on.

The interviewer approaches people to discover which category they are in and then asks them to take part in the survey. She continues until she has filled all her quotas. Non-response is not a problem because anyone with the appropriate characteristics can be approached. Those people, however, who do not wish to respond may have different opinions and spending habits, for example, from those willing to answer questions. Some quotas may be difficult to fill and the interviewer must be well-trained so that she is not tempted to try to fit people in the wrong category.

We could use this method with the pencil set. For instance, suppose that we want to ensure that both graphite and non-graphite pencils are included in the sample of five. From the data base we know there are 22 graphite and 28 non-graphite pencils. (If we did not know the number of graphite pencils, we could always assume that half were graphite and half not or estimate the proportion from a pilot survey.)

$$\text{number of graphite pencils in sample} = \frac{5}{50} \times 22 = 2.2$$

$$\text{number of non-graphite pencils in the sample} = \frac{5}{50} \times 28 = 2.8$$

We would choose two graphite and three non-graphite pencils for the sample. We can choose **any** two graphite pencils and **any** three non-graphite pencils.

Systematic sampling

To speed up the process of selecting a sample from a sample frame, systematic sampling can be used.

If we require a sample of five pencils from the set of 50, we need to select, on average, one pencil in evey ten. We say the **sampling fraction** is 1/10.

$$\text{sampling fraction} = \frac{\text{size of sample}}{\text{size of population}} = \frac{5}{50} = \frac{1}{10}$$

We consider just the first ten items in the sample frame, Table 5.3, and select one of them randomly, using random number tables for example. Suppose this is the pencil with ID number 7. Then we systematically include every tenth pencil after that in our sample so the chosen sample will be pencils with ID numbers

07 17 27 37 47

To choose a sample of 30 from the 876 pupils in a school, we find:

$$\text{sampling fraction} = \frac{30}{876} = \frac{1}{29.3}$$

We need to select on average every 29th pupil on the list. Using random number tables, I selected pupil labelled 016 as the one to be included out of the first 29, so the other pupils in the sample will be at intervals of 29 down the list. The sample of 30 will include the pupils numbered

016	045	074	103	132	161	190	219	248	277
306	335	364	393	422	451	480	509	538	567
596	625	654	683	712	741	770	799	828	857

Once the first item in a systematic sample is selected, the remaining items in the sample are automatically identified, so not as many different samples are possible as compared with random sampling.

We may also have problems if there is some order or pattern to the sample frame. For example, it might happen that every class in the school has 29 pupils and that the pupils are listed in decreasing order of age and class-by-class on the list. If we happened to select random number 001 to identify the first member of our sample, we would automatically include the oldest pupils in every class in our sample and this might introduce bias into the results.

Stratified sampling

In random sampling, we have no control over the sample chosen. Because we have removed the possibility of personal bias by using a random selection procedure, we cannot ensure that our sample is representative in any way. To ensure that a sample is representative in some respects, random sampling can be modified by using stratification.

If we want to ensure that a sample of five pencils from the set of 50 contains both graphite and non-graphite pencils in the same proportions as in the full set, we first divide the pencils into two strata, one containing all the graphite pencils and one containing all the non-graphite pencils. From Table 5.3 we know there are 22 pencils in the first stratum and 28 pencils in the second stratum.

$$\text{number of graphite pencils in sample} = \frac{5}{50} \times 22 = 2.2$$

$$\text{number of non-graphite pencils in sample} = \frac{5}{50} \times 28 = 2.8$$

We would choose two graphite and three non-graphite pencils for the sample. The two graphite pencils are selected from the 22 in that stratum using a random procedure such as the lottery method or random number tables. The three non-graphite pencils are selected randomly from that stratum. This method differs from quota sampling in that the final selection process is random, so a sample frame is needed. We must know before the start of a survey which stratum each item is in.

Stratified sampling is superior to unmodified random sampling because we can investigate each stratum separately and estimate the sampling errors, as well as obtaining information about the complete population from the full sample. The process of selecting the sample is also slightly quicker because we have to take smaller samples for each stratum and this is not as tedious as taking one large random sample.

Stratified sampling and quota sampling are the two methods most commonly used in market and opinion research. For example, in political opinion polls, the electoral rolls from each parliamentary constituency can be used to form the sample frame, with the constituencies being stratified by region, by size of Conservative majority or deficit, or by the order of the parties at the last election.

Comparisons of sampling procedures

Advantages

Random	*Purposive*	*Opportunity*	*Quota*	*Systematic*	*Stratified*
No personal bias in selection	No sample frame needed	Quick to carry out	No sample frame needed	Quicker than random sampling particularly for large populations	Representative in some respects
Sampling errors can be estimated mathematically	Usually quick to organise	No sample frame needed	Representative in some respects		Sampling errors can be estimated mathematically
	No difficulties with non-response	No difficulties with non-response	No difficulties with non-response		Gives information about each stratum as well as the complete population
					More efficient than random sampling

Disadvantages

Random	*Purposive*	*Opportunity*	*Quota*	*Systematic*	*Stratified*
Sample frame needed	Results may be biased	Results may be biased and may show too little variation	Need to have some estimate of proportions in each category to work out the quotas	Not as many different samples can be chosen as for random sampling	Sample frame needed
May not be representative	Sample may be representative in some respects but not in others		Results may be biased	Non-response may be a problem	Must know which stratum each member of the population is in
Tedious with large populations	Sampling errors cannot be estimated	Sampling errors cannot be estimated	Those who do not wish to respond might have given different answers from those in the same category who did respond	Sample frame needed	
Non-response may be a problem			Sampling errors cannot be estimated	Results may be biased if there is some order or pattern to the sample frame	Non-response may be a problem

Size of sample

If we are using random sampling, we can reduce the sampling error and increase the precision of our estimate to any desired amount at any given level of confidence by increasing the sample size, n. In order to work out how large a sample should be taken, we need to have an estimate of the unknown population proportion, P, or the population standard deviation, σ. The size of the population does not affect the calculation.

Example 1

A researcher wishes to estimate a population to within ± 0.02 using a random sample. Nothing is known about the likely value of this proportion. Using 95% confidence, what sample size should be used?

For 95% of random samples, we know that the sampling error is approximately 2 standard errors, so we require:

$$2\sqrt{\frac{P(1-P)}{n}} < 0.02$$

Since P is unknown, we assume P is 0.5, as this gives the largest value of $P(1-P)$ and ensures we are not underestimating the sample size.

$$2\sqrt{\frac{0.5(1-0.5)}{n}} < 0.02$$

$$2\sqrt{\frac{0.25}{n}} < 0.02$$

Squaring both sides

$$\frac{4 \times 0.25}{n} < 0.0004$$

$$\frac{1}{n} < 0.0004$$

$$n > \frac{1}{0.0004} = 2500$$

A sample size of at least 2501 is required.

Example 2

It is known from past records that the standard deviation of a population is 5 g. What is the minimum sample size needed, at the 95% confidence level, to estimate the mean of the population to within ±1 g?

With 95% confidence, the sampling error is approximately 2 standard errors, so we require:

$$\frac{2\sigma}{\sqrt{n}} < 1$$

$$2 \times \frac{5}{\sqrt{n}} < 1$$

$$\frac{10}{\sqrt{n}} < 1$$

Squaring both sides

$$\frac{100}{n} < 1$$

$$n > 100$$

The sample size must be at least 101.

Exercise 13.1

1 I have a novel whose pages are numbered from 7 to 249. I want a sample of 10 pages.
(a) Show how you would select a random sample of 10 pages using random numbers.
(b) Outline the procedure you would use to select a systematic sample of 10 pages.

2 In the fifth year at Arebury school, there are 200 pupils, of whom 110 are boys. You require a random sample of 20 pupils that is stratified so it contains both boys and girls. Describe in detail the procedure you would follow to select the sample.

3 Sampling errors in estimates of population parameters occur because we have looked at only part of a population. In sampling, other errors occur which can give rise to bias in the estimates. Give three different examples of how such errors due to bias might arise.

4 Suggest a suitable sample frame, if any, for each of the following surveys. Mention any difficulties you foresee in conducting the surveys.
(a) To estimate the mean amount of pocket money per week received by children in your locality.
(b) To estimate the mean girth of conifers in a plantation.
(c) To estimate the mean length of motorway per English county.
(d) To estimate the mean size of gas bill per household in your locality.

(e) To estimate the mean share price of shares listed on the London Stock Exchange.
(f) To estimate the proportion of the electorate intending to vote Conservative in the next general election.

5 Give two reasons why, in preference to a random sample, you might decide to use (a) a quota sample, (b) a systematic sample or (c) a stratified sample. Give one difficulty you might have in carrying out your sampling using (a), (b) or (c).

6 (a) Take $P = 0.5$ and work out $2\sqrt{P(1-P)/n}$ for $n = 5, 10, 20, 50, 100, 200, 500, 1000, 2000$, and 5000. If you want to estimate an unknown population proportion to within ± 0.04, state approximately what size of sample you need to take, using 95% confidence.
(b) A population standard deviation, σ, is known to be 1.00 cm. Work out $2\sigma/\sqrt{n}$ for $n = 5, 10, 20, 50, 100, 200, 500, 1000, 2000$ and 5000. If you want to estimate the mean of the population to within ± 0.05 cm, state approximately what size of sample you need to take using 95% confidence.

7 A school has 876 pupils in seven different year groups.

Year	1	2	3	4	5	6	7
Number	149	153	147	152	154	61	60

Describe in detail how you would select (a) a quota sample of 40 pupils, (b) a stratified sample of 40 pupils, so that your samples are representative of all the different year groups.

Practical exercise 13.2

1 Make a collection of 100 leaves, 20 from each of five different varieties of plants or trees. Put them in a shoe box or other similar size container. You must return all the leaves to the box after each stage of the practical.
(a) Ask someone who is not a member of your statistics group to select a sample of five leaves. Ask them why they chose the leaves in the way they did. Measure the length and note the variety of each of these five leaves. Work out the mean and the standard deviation of the sample lengths. How many different varieties are represented in the sample?
(b) Number every leaf in your collection with a small sticky label using digits 00 to 99. Select a random sample of five leaves using random number tables. Measure the length and note the variety of each of the five leaves. Work out the mean and the standard deviation of the sample lengths. How many different varieties are represented in the sample?
(c) Take a systematic sample of five leaves from your collection and analyse your sample in the same way.
(d) Take a quota sample of five leaves from your collection, ensuring each variety is represented. Analyse your sample as before.
(e) Take a stratified sample of five leaves from your collection ensuring each variety is represented. Analyse your sample as before.
(f) Take out the first five leaves that happen to be at the top of the box. Analyse this sample as before.
(g) Compare and comment on your results from the different samples.

2 You need a bag of uncooked rice or pearl barley. Colour some of the grains red or green by shaking them in a bag with a few drops of food colouring. When dry, mix the coloured and uncoloured grains in a container that has a lid. The proportion by weight of each type should be known, e.g. 500 g uncoloured to 50 g coloured.

Shake the container and, using a 5 ml measuring spoon, take out a spoonful of the cereal. Count the number of coloured grains and the number of uncoloured grains. Work out the proportion of coloured grains.

Return the sample to the container and shake well before taking another sample and repeating the observations. Continue until you have taken 40 samples in all.

Draw a graph of the proportion of coloured grains in a sample against the number of the sample. Draw in a line on the graph showing the true proportion (by weight) of coloured grains.

Repeat the experiment (a) using a different sized measuring spoon and (b) using a different proportion of coloured grains, e.g. 500 g uncoloured to 100 g coloured. Comment on the differences and similarities between your graphs in each case.

3 You need an Ordnance Survey Landranger (1 : 50 000) map of an inland area of Great Britain. Use random numbers to select a random sample of 100 of the 1 km squares marked on the map. Within each square measure the length of electricity transmission line. Work out the mean length of electricity transmission line per square kilometre from your sample and hence estimate the total length of electricity transmission line in the area covered by the map. Do you think you have obtained a reliable estimate? Give reasons for your answer.

14 Time series

Introduction

A time series is a series of observations of a variable taken at intervals in time. The intervals between consecutive observations may be of any length but usually we are dealing with annual, quarterly, monthly, weekly or daily observations.

By studying a time series over a sufficiently long period, we hope to be able to analyse its behaviour so that we can predict or forecast how the variable will change in the future. This is called a longitudinal study. (It is in contrast to a lateral or cross-sectional study where we take a 'snapshot' of several variables at one particular time and investigate the relationships between them.)

Some examples of time series that are published regularly are:

closing values of *Financial Times* share index numbers (daily),
numbers of births in each district of the UK (weekly),
numbers of unemployed persons in the UK (monthly),
operating profit of a public limited company (annually),
population of the UK (decennially, i.e. every ten years).

Graphs of a time series

The first stage in the analysis of a time series, such as those displayed in Tables 14.1 and 14.2, is to draw a graph, see Figs. 14.1 and 14.2. The values of the variable are plotted at the times to which they refer and the points are joined with ruled lines. This type of graph is called a line graph or a **historigram** (not to be confused with a histogram). The horizontal axis always shows the time.

Table 14.1 Annual turnover of Tebury plc (£M)

Year	1975	1976	1977	1978	1979	1980	1981	1982	1983	1984	1985	1986	1987
Turnover	14	10	13	14	15	19	11	15	16	16	21	13	17

Table 14.2 Quarterly sales of motor cycles by Essbury Garages

Year	1985				1986				1987			
Quarter	1	2	3	4	1	2	3	4	1	2	3	4
Number sold	235	202	203	192	231	199	195	180	220	193	190	172

Annual turnover of Tebury plc

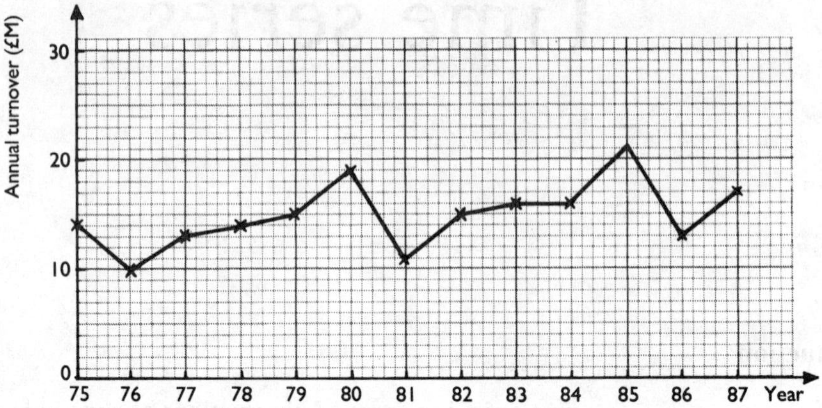

Source: Table 14.1

Fig. 14.1 *Historigram or line graph*

Sales of motor cycles by Essbury Garages

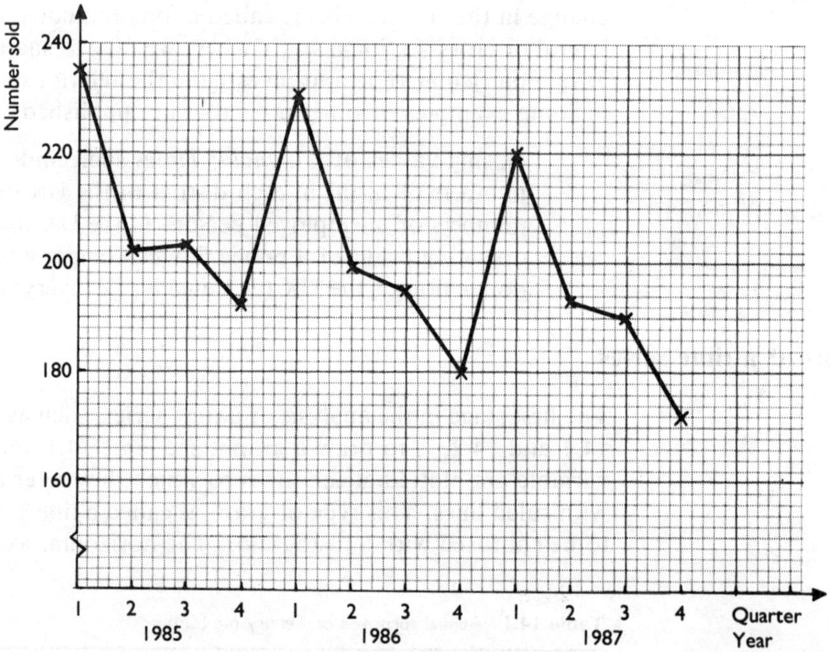

Source: Table 14.2

Fig. 14.2 *Historigram with broken vertical scale*

In Fig. 14.2, the **broken-scale convention** has been used on the vertical axis. Because all the observations are in the region of 200, I have chosen to start the vertical scale at 160. I can then show the quarterly variations clearly without having to use a large piece of graph paper. The zig-zag marking on the vertical axis indicates that the scale does not start from zero.

Use a broken scale only when it is absolutely necessary. It can result in a distorted impression of the data, as minor variations may be over-emphasised (see Chapter 16).

Alternatively, a time series can be represented by a vertical bar chart, see Fig. 14.3. This is adequate for presentation purposes but is less suitable for analytical purposes.

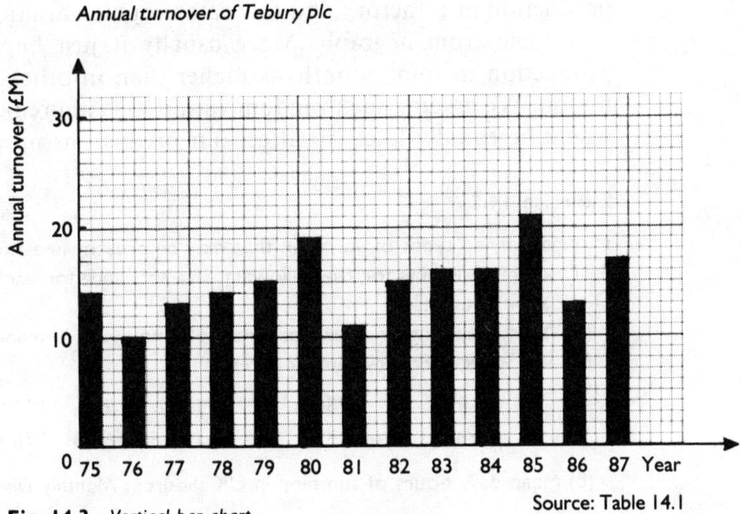

Fig. 14.3 *Vertical bar chart*

Components of a time series

There are some typical movements that we look for in a time series graph.

1 The **trend**, sometimes called the secular trend. This is the basic underlying long-term movement in the series with any other fluctuations smoothed out.

In Fig. 14.1 we see a slight upward trend since, taken overall, the turnover in later years is higher than in the earlier years. For example, the turnover peak in 1985 is higher than the peak in 1980 and the turnover trough in 1986 is not as low as the trough in 1981.

In Fig. 14.2 a downward trend is apparent with the sales in later years being less than the sales in corresponding quarters of earlier years.

2 **Seasonal variations**. These are short-term and regular fluctuations about the trend. Seasonal variations are present in Fig. 14.2. Every year, the highest sales are in the first quarter and the lowest sales are in the fourth quarter. Seasonal variations often occur in quarterly or monthly data when they do in fact coincide with the seasons of the year. Daily sales figures at a supermarket generally have a regular pattern from week to week with higher sales at the end of each week. Because this variation is regular and short-term it is still called seasonal variation although it coincides with the days of the week.

3 **Cyclical variations**. These are long-term fluctuations about the trend and, for economic variables, often reflect the general state of business activity within the country. In times of prosperity, we expect the sales of every

company to be higher than in times of depression. These fluctuations are not necessarily regular but the times between consecutive peaks and troughs can be estimated from the historigram.

Cyclical variations are apparent in Fig. 14.1. The peaks and troughs occur at five-year intervals.

4 **Residual variation**. This is any other variation that may be present. Occasionally, a 'catastrophe' such as a strike or fire may drastically cut the production at a factory and this catastrophic variation would be immediately noticeable from a graph. More usually it just happens that, for example, production in some months is higher than in other months for no apparent reason. We assume such random variation is unpredictable but in the long run would be equally likely to affect our predictions upward as downward.

Exercise 14.1

1 Name three types of variation that may be present in a time series.

2 Draw historigrams for the following data sets and, for each graph, identify the type(s) of variation present.

(a) Weekly earnings in April each year of employees in manufacturing industries in Great Britain (Source: *Employment Gazette*)

Year	1980	1981	1982	1983	1984	1985	1986
Earnings (£)	124.3	137.1	152.6	163.3	176.8	192.6	207.8

(b) Mean daily hours of sunshine in UK (Source: *Monthly Digest of Statistics*)

Month	Jan	Feb	Mar	Apr	May	Jun	Jul	Aug	Sep	Oct	Nov	Dec
1984	2.2	2.1	2.1	7.4	5.6	7.0	7.9	6.5	3.8	3.3	1.7	1.7
1985	1.7	2.9	3.8	4.5	5.5	5.7	6.3	5.2	4.4	3.4	2.7	1.2
1986	1.8	2.7	4.0	4.4	6.3	6.8	5.4	4.6	5.7	3.6	2.5	1.7

(c) Sales of gas (in millions of therms) to iron and steel industry (Source: *Monthly Digest of Statistics*)

Year	Quarter 1	2	3	4
1982	110	95	80	80
1983	91	86	77	88
1984	126	110	95	131
1985	124	118	99	124
1986	123	105	87	110

(d) Energy consumption (millions of tons of coal equivalent) in Ruritania

Year	1972	1973	1974	1975	1976	1977	1978	1979
Consumption	265	266	274	284	286	297	308	307

Year	1980	1981	1982	1983	1984	1985	1986	1987
Consumption	317	328	330	336	341	340	347	353

Estimation of trend

Freehand method

If there are no cyclical or seasonal variations in a time series, the simplest way to estimate the trend is to draw a freehand line (or curve) of best fit through the data points. This is the same procedure as we used to find the regression line in Chapter 11. To help you position the trend line you can work out the mean of the observations and plot this value at the mean of the times. The line of best fit should go through this point.

Moving average method

The moving average method can be used to estimate the trend when seasonal variations or regular cyclical variations are present. These variations are removed by finding the mean of an appropriate number of consecutive observations.

To remove cyclical variations

In Fig. 14.1, we have already noticed that cyclical variations are present and that peaks and troughs occur at five-year intervals. Therefore, if we average the observations in consecutive groups of five, we should remove the fluctuations. It is easiest to set out the calculation as in Table 14.3. It is usual to put a column for the totals as well as for the averages. Although we are using the mean as our average, we never refer to moving means, always to moving averages. The word moving is used because once we have found the total and the average of the first five observations (from 1975 to 1979), we move on by one observation to find the total and average for the next set of observations (from 1976 to 1980) and so on until we have used all the data. The totals and averages are put at the middle of the time period to which they refer so those for 1975 to 1979 are positioned at 1977, those for 1976 to 1980 at 1978 and so on.

$$\text{5-year moving total for 1975 to 1979} = 14 + 10 + 13 + 14 + 15 = 66$$

$$\text{5-year moving average} = \frac{66}{5} = 13.2$$

$$\text{5-year moving total for 1976 to 1980} = 10 + 13 + 14 + 15 + 19 = 71$$

$$\text{5-year moving average} = \frac{71}{5} = 14.2$$

A quick way to get the second moving total is to note that four of the numbers in the sum (10, 13, 14 and 15) remain the same, with 19 replacing 14 so:

$$\begin{aligned}\text{5-year moving total for 1976 to 1980} &= 66 + (19 - 14)\\ &= 66 + 5\\ &= 71\end{aligned}$$

Similarly,

$$\begin{aligned}\text{5-year moving total for 1977 to 1981} &= 71 + (11 - 10)\\ &= 71 + 1\\ &= 72\end{aligned}$$

Table 14.3 Calculation of moving average trend of annual turnover of Tebury plc (all figures in £M)

Year	Turnover	5-year moving total	5-year moving average
1975	14		
1976	10		
1977	13	66	13.2
1978	14	71	14.2
1979	15	72	14.4
1980	19	74	14.8
1981	11	76	15.2
1982	15	77	15.4
1983	16	79	15.8
1984	16	81	16.2
1985	21	83	16.6
1986	13		
1987	17		

All the totals and averages are shown in Table 14.3. Note that we have moving averages only for the period from 1977 to 1985 even though we know the turnover from 1975 to 1987. This is a disadvantage of the moving average method. The longer the time over which the moving average is taken, the more moving averages we 'lose' at each end of the series.

The data and the moving average trend are shown in Fig. 14.4. It is important to distinguish between the original data and the trend, so you should use either a dashed, dotted, bold or coloured line to join up the moving averages and give a key to the different lines at the side of the graph. You can see that the cyclical fluctuations have been satisfactorily removed and that the trend is increasing.

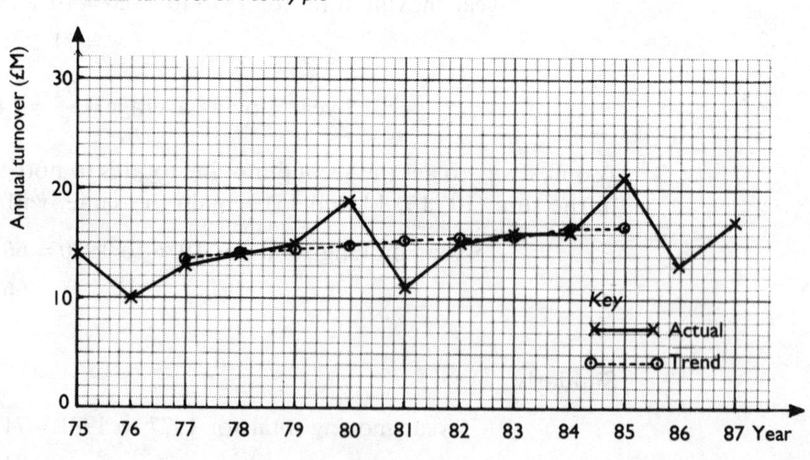

Fig. 14.4 *Moving average trend for cyclical data*

Table 14.4 Calculation of moving average trend of motor cycle sales

Year	Quarter	Sales	4-quarterly moving total	4-quarterly moving average (to 1 dec. pl.)
1985	1	235		
	2	202		
			832	208.0
	3	203		
			828	207.0
	4	192		
			825	206.3
1986	1	231		
			817	204.3
	2	199		
			805	201.3
	3	195		
			794	198.5
	4	180		
			788	197.0
1987	1	220		
			783	195.8
	2	193		
			775	193.8
	3	190		
	4	172		

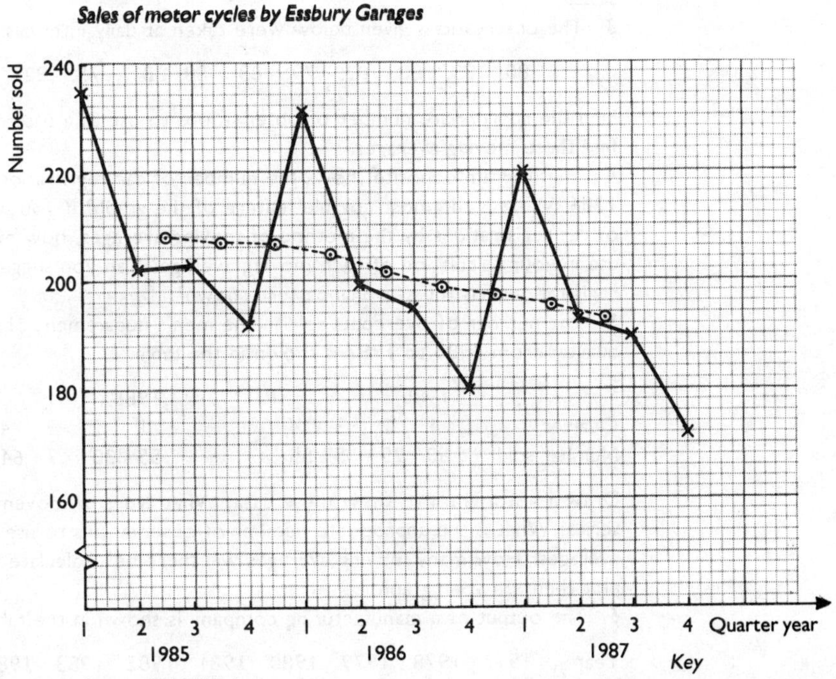

Source: Table 14.4

Key
×——× Actual
⊙- - - - -⊙ Trend

Fig. 14.5 *Moving average trend for quarterly data*

To remove seasonal variations

For the quarterly data in Fig. 14.2, we have noticed that there is a marked seasonal pattern each year. The appropriate moving average to take here is over four quarters. The calculations are set out in Table 14.4. The first moving total and moving average are positioned at the middle of the time period to which they refer, i.e. halfway between the second and third quarters of 1985. Whenever you take a moving average over an even number of points, such as four quarters or twelve months, your results will lie halfway between two of the given times, so you must take extra care, particularly when plotting the trend on a graph.

The data and the moving average trend are shown in Fig. 14.5. Once again you can see that the fluctuations have been removed to show that the trend of motor cycle sales is steadily downward.

Exercise 14.2

1 Explain the purpose of calculating moving averages.

2 The mean weekly sales of a shop during the period 1985 to 1987 are given in the table.

Sales (£)

	Jan–Apr	May–Aug	Sep–Dec
1985	8 000	7 500	8 500
1986	12 000	12 000	13 000
1987	17 000	16 500	17 500

Draw a historigram of the data. Calculate a suitable moving average to remove the seasonal variations. Plot the moving averages on your graph and comment on the trend of sales.

3 The observations given below were taken at daily intervals.

80, 85, 88, 82, 79, 83, 88, 81, 75, 82, 86, 81, 74, 78

Find the appropriate number of observations to use as a basis for moving averages and find these moving averages.

4 The diagram opposite shows the number of car registrations in the UK for 1985 and 1986. What is the most notable feature of the graph? If you were asked to find the trend of car registrations by the method of moving averages, how many observations would you use in your calculation of each moving average? Can you suggest why the number of car registrations has the seasonal pattern shown?

5 The number of overcoats sold in the men's department of a large store in each quarter from 1985 to 1987 is shown in the table.

Year	1985				1986				1987			
Quarter	1	2	3	4	1	2	3	4	1	2	3	4
Number sold	50	25	5	55	55	30	7	64	61	36	8	70

Draw a historigram to show these data. What types of movement are shown by this time series? What is the appropriate number of observations to use as a basis for moving averages? How many moving averages will there be? Calculate the moving averages and plot them on your graph.

6 The output of a manufacturing company is shown in the table.

Year	1977	1978	1979	1980	1981	1982	1983	1984	1985	1986	1987
Output (£000)	96	93	111	127	123	116	132	156	151	136	160

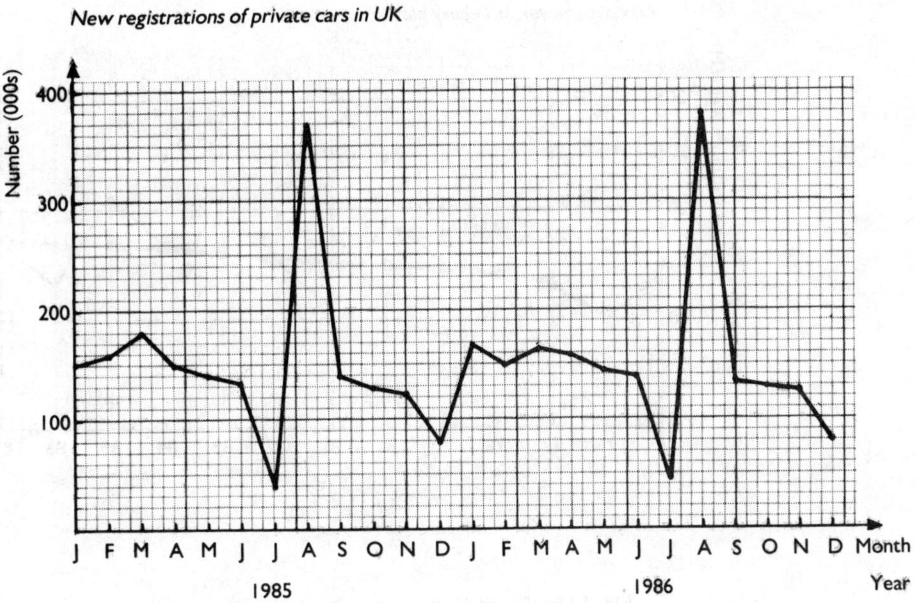

Source: *Monthly Digest of Statistics*

Plot the time series on a line graph. What is the appropriate number of observations to use as a basis for moving averages to remove the cyclical variations? Calculate these moving averages and plot them on your graph.

Forecasting

Extrapolation of trend

The first stage in forecasting is to predict the future trend. You will have noticed from your calculations and graphs that the moving averages are often close to a straight line, indicating a linear trend. We draw the line of best fit through these moving averages. It is usually satisfactory to do this 'by eye' but you can calculate the mean of the moving averages to help you if you wish.

The mean of the moving averages in Table 14.3 is 135.8/9 = 15.1 to 1 dec. pl. The mean of the times is 1981.

Figure 14.6 shows the time series, the moving averages and the line of best fit through the moving averages for the data in Table 14.3. To forecast the trend, we extend this line to the right. This is called **extrapolation**. We usually use a dotted line to show that it is a projection and not something that we are certain about. We are assuming that the trend is going to change in the future in the same way as it did in the past. Unforeseen circumstances, however, might completely invalidate the predictions.

From Fig. 14.6, we obtain the following forecasts of the trend:

Year	1986	1987	1988	1989	1990
Forecast of trend of annual turnover (£M)	17.0	17.4	17.8	18.2	18.5

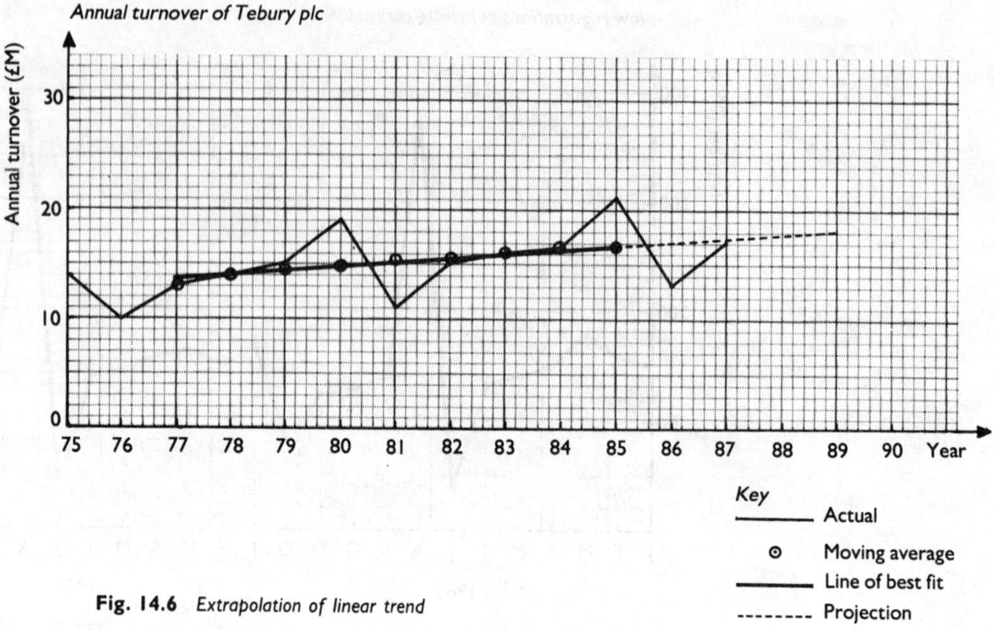

Fig. 14.6 *Extrapolation of linear trend*

Prediction of the next observation

In Table 14.3 and Fig. 14.6, the annual turnover is known from 1975 to 1987. The first turnover we do not know is for 1988. Let us call its value x (£M).

The five-year moving average from 1984 to 1988 is $(16 + 21 + 13 + 17 + x)/5$. This moving average is the trend value for 1986. We have an estimate for this trend (17.0) from our work in the previous section. Hence we know:

$$\frac{16 + 21 + 13 + 17 + x}{5} = 17.0$$

Solving for x:

$$16 + 21 + 13 + 17 + x = 5 \times 17.0 = 85$$
$$67 + x = 85$$
$$x = 85 - 67 = 18$$

We predict the annual turnover for 1988 to be £18M.

Estimating seasonal effects

When we analyse a time series, we can assume that the different types of variation are added together. For example, the sales of motor cycles in Table 14.2 can be modelled as:

$$\text{sales} = \text{trend} + \underset{\text{variation}}{\text{seasonal}} + \underset{\text{variation}}{\text{cyclical}} + \underset{\text{variation}}{\text{residual}}$$

This additive model is appropriate for short-term forecasting or when the trend is changing slowly. When we work out the difference between the observed sales and the trend at each time point, we obtain an estimate of the remaining variation.

$$\text{sales} - \text{trend} = \underset{\text{variation}}{\text{seasonal}} + \underset{\text{variation}}{\text{cyclical}} + \underset{\text{variation}}{\text{residual}}$$

If we are dealing with a short series with a marked seasonal pattern, as in Table 14.2, we can assume the cyclical component is negligible. In this case, the differences will give us an estimate of the seasonal variation at each time, together with any residual variation. If we average these differences for corresponding periods of each year, the effect of the residual variation should be removed and we will have an estimate of the average seasonal variation in each period of the year.

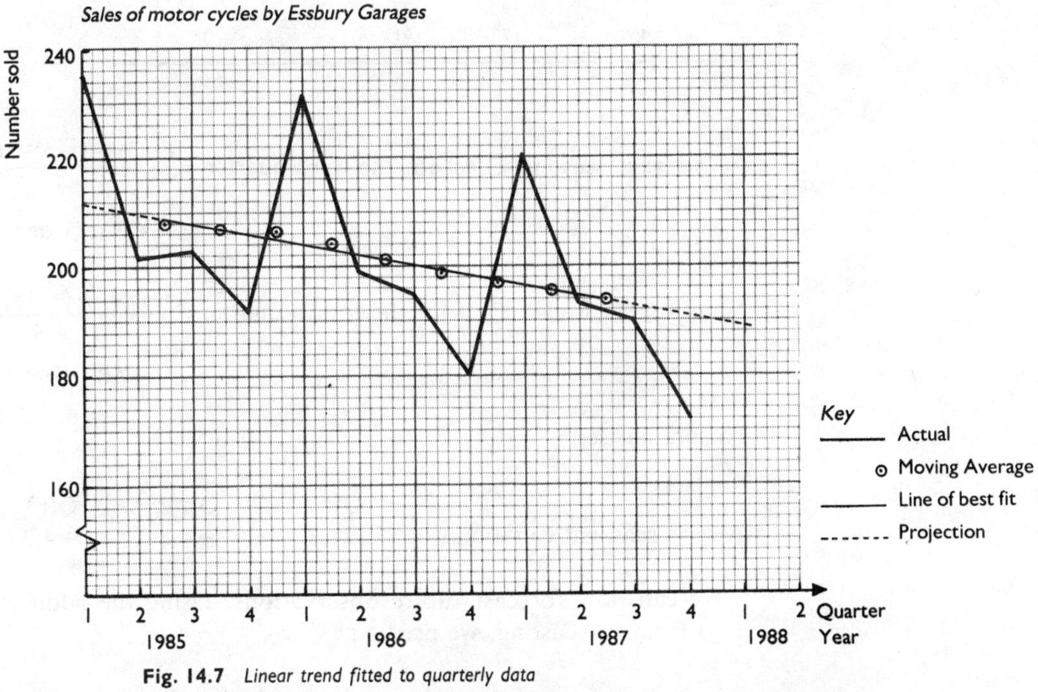

Fig. 14.7 *Linear trend fitted to quarterly data*

Figure 14.7 shows the time series, the moving averages and the line of best fit through the moving averages for the data in Table 14.4. From the line of best fit we can estimate the trend for each quarter. The values are given in Table 14.5. The differences between the actual sales and the trend are in the final column. A positive difference indicates a quarter when the actual sales were above the trend and a negative sign indicates when the actual sales were below the trend.

$$\text{average seasonal effect for the first quarter} = \frac{23 + 27 + 23}{3}$$

$$= 24.3 \text{ to 1 dec. pl.}$$

$$\text{average seasonal effect for the second quarter} = \frac{(-8) + (-3) + (-2)}{3}$$

$$= -4.3 \text{ to 1 dec. pl.}$$

Table 14.5 Estimation of the differences between the observed values and the trend

Year	Quarter	Sales	Estimated trend	Sales – trend
1985	1	235	212	23
	2	202	210	−8
	3	203	208	−5
	4	192	206	−14
1986	1	231	204	27
	2	199	202	−3
	3	195	200	−5
	4	180	198	−18
1987	1	220	197	23
	2	193	195	−2
	3	190	193	−3
	4	172	191	−19

$$\text{average seasonal effect for the third quarter} = \frac{(-5)+(-5)+(-3)}{3}$$

$$= -4.3 \text{ to 1 dec. pl.}$$

$$\text{average seasonal effect for the fourth quarter} = \frac{(-14)+(-18)+(-19)}{3}$$

$$= -17.0$$

To summarise:

	Qtr 1	Qtr 2	Qtr3	Qtr 4
average seasonal variation	24.3	−4.3	−4.3	−17.0

We can now forecast future observations. Using the additive model, for short-term forecasting, we predict:

$$\text{sales} = \text{trend} + \text{residual variation}$$

where we are ignoring cyclical and irregular variations.

From Fig. 14.7, the estimate of the trend in the first quarter of 1988 is 189. The average seasonal variation for a first quarter is 24.3.

Estimate of sales in the first quarter of 1988 = 189 + 24.3 = 213 motor cycles (to the nearest whole number).

Exercise 14.3

1 From Fig. 14.7, estimate the value of the trend of sales halfway between the third and the fourth quarters of 1987. By equating this to the four-quarter moving average for the period 1987 Qtr 2 to 1988 Qtr 1, estimate the sales of motor cycles in the first quarter of 1988. How does your estimate compare with the estimate found in the last section?

2 The table shows the number of marriages in the UK from 1983 to 1986.

Number of marriages (000s)

	Quarter	1	2	3	4
Year	1983	61.9	108.9	140.5	78.0
	1984	61.3	115.0	146.2	73.3
	1985	57.6	113.9	148.7	72.9
	1986	57.3	111.1	150.2	75.4

Source: *Monthly Digest of Statistics*

(a) Plot the data on a line graph.
(b) Comment briefly on the main features of the data.
(c) Calculate moving averages over an appropriate period to remove the seasonal variations. Plot the moving averages on your graph and draw, by eye, the line of best fit through these points.
(d) Estimate the average seasonal variation in each of the four quarters.
(e) Estimate the number of marriages in the first quarter of 1987. Refer to a copy of the *Monthly Digest* to see whether your estimate is close to the actual figure.

3 The following table shows the sales of a product during the years 1979–1987.

Year	1979	1980	1981	1982	1983	1984	1985	1986	1987
Sales (000s)	348	265	365	366	292	383	393	313	410

(a) Draw a historigram of the data.
(b) Comment briefly on the types of variation present in this time series.
(c) Calculate moving averages over an appropriate period and plot these on your graph. Draw in a trend line by eye.
(d) Estimate the trend value for 1987 and hence estimate the actual sales in 1988.

Practical exercise 14.4

1 Refer to a copy of the *Monthly Digest of Statistics*. Choose two time series that are of interest to you, e.g. balance of payments, numbers of road accidents. One series should be quarterly data and one series should be monthly data. Plot a historigram for each time series and comment on the main features of your graphs.

This practical can be extended, if desired. Estimate the trend for the quarterly data and forecast the values of the series for the next four quarters.

2 For a period of four weeks, note the exchange rate between £ sterling and a foreign currency such as US dollar, German mark or French franc. Plot a line graph of your data. Estimate the trend and predict the exchange rate for each day in the following week. Compare your estimates with the actual values when they become available.

15 Weighted means, Index numbers

Weighted mean

When we combine two or more data sets, we often need to be able to find the mean of the combined data from the means of the individual data sets.

For example, in Elbury plc, the mean wage of women workers is £50 per week and the mean wage of mean workers is £130 per week. What is the mean weekly wage of all the workers?

If there are **equal** numbers of men and women workers, the mean weekly wage of all the workers will be

$$\frac{£50 + £130}{2} = £90$$

If there are **unequal** numbers of men and women workers, we have to **weight** the individual means in proportion to the the number in each group.

Suppose there are 300 women and 1200 men:

$$\text{total weekly wages paid to all workers} = (300 \times £50) + (1200 \times £130)$$

$$\text{total number of workers} = 300 + 1200$$

$$\text{mean weekly wage of all workers} = \frac{(300 \times £50) + (1200 \times £130)}{300 + 1200}$$

$$= \frac{£15\,000 + £156\,000}{1\,500}$$

$$= \frac{£171\,000}{1\,500}$$

$$= £114$$

The numbers 300 and 1200 are referred to as weights and the final result is called a weighted mean. We can write the procedure using the summation sign, Σ.

$$\text{weighted mean} = \frac{\Sigma\,(\text{weight} \times \text{individual mean})}{\Sigma\ \text{weight}}$$

We do not need to know the actual number of men and women workers provided we know something about the relative numbers of each. Suppose we had been told that there were four times as many men as women. The wage for men needs to be given four times as much weight as the wage for women.

$$\text{mean weekly wage of all workers} = \frac{(1 \times £50) + (4 \times £130)}{1 + 4}$$

$$= \frac{£50 + £520}{5}$$

$$= \frac{£570}{5}$$

$$= £114, \text{ as before.}$$

Weighted means are often used to find an overall mark in studies that have marks for coursework, practical and written examination elements.

Example

Atiya's marks out of 100 in home economics were 85 in coursework, 75 in practical and 60 in the written examination. Her overall percentage mark for the subject has to be weighted so that coursework and practical count for 30% each and the written examination counts for 40%. What is her overall mark?

Element	Coursework	Practical	Written
Mark	85	75	60
Weight	30	30	40

$$\text{overall percentage mark} = \frac{(30 \times 85) + (30 \times 75) + (40 \times 60)}{30 + 30 + 40}$$

$$= \frac{2550 + 2250 + 2400}{100}$$

$$= \frac{7200}{100}$$

$$= 72$$

Her overall mark for home economics is 72%.

Exercise 15.1

1 An analysis of the 1500 staff at Elbury plc showed that the mean distance travelled to work by the 100 clerical and managerial staff is 12.8 miles. The 500 skilled manual workers travel a mean distance of 7.7 miles to work and the 900 unskilled manual workers travel a mean distance of 3.2 miles to work. What is the mean distance travelled to work by all the staff at Elbury plc?

2 Elbury plc uses three raw materials in its production process. The mean cost per tonne of each of the materials is

Material	A	B	C
Cost (£) per tonne	16.30	15.40	29.30

The materials A, B and C are used in the proportions 2 : 4 : 5, respectively. What is the overall mean cost per tonne of raw materials at Elbury plc?

3 A cake recipe uses the following ingredients:

300 g dried fruit	at 60 p per kg
200 g sugar	at 50 p per kg
400 g flour	at 35 p per kg
300 g eggs and milk	at 50 p per kg

What is the overall cost per kilogram of the ingredients of a cake made to this recipe?

4 Matthew and Tracey sat two examinations in statistics. Each examination was marked out of 100. The results were

	Matthew	Tracey
Exam 1	60	68
Exam 2	64	54

(a) Which pupil has the higher mean mark in the two examinations if the marks in both examinations carry equal weight?

(b) Which pupil has the higher mean mark in the two examinations if the marks for the first examination carry three times as much weight as the marks for the second?

Simple index number

When we look at changes in a variable over a period of time, it is often convenient to look at the **relative** changes, i.e. the proportional or percentage changes. One of the easiest ways to do this is to construct an index number.

For example, the average weekly earnings, in October, for UK male manual workers in the construction industry were:

Year	1983	1984	1985	1986
Earnings (£)	139.99	147.80	160.37	171.25

(Source: *Employment Gazette*)

Let us express each of these earnings as a percentage of the earnings in 1983.

Earnings as a percentage of 1983 earnings

1983 $\frac{£139.99}{£139.99} \times 100 = 100$

1984 $\frac{£147.80}{£139.99} \times 100 = 105.6$ to 1 dec. pl.

1985 $\frac{£160.37}{£139.99} \times 100 = 114.6$ to 1 dec. pl.

1986 $\frac{£171.25}{£139.99} \times 100 = 122.3$ to 1 dec. pl.

The results are an index number, or index, of earnings. It is usual to give the values of an index number correct to one decimal place. To indicate that our values are percentages of 1983 earnings, we put 1983 = 100 and we say that 1983 is the **base year** or **base period**. Index numbers are percentages but we never write in the % sign. If you are told a number is an index number, then you assume it is a percentage.

From the results we can see at once that earnings increased by:

5.6% from 1983 to 1984,
14.6% from 1983 to 1985,
22.3% from 1983 to 1986.

We make the comparisons with 1983 because that is the chosen base period.

An index above 100 indicates that the variable is greater at that time than in the base period. An index below 100 indicates that the variable is less at that time than in the base period.

Exercise 15.2

1 The price of a pint of milk in 1974 was 5 p. The price of a pint of milk in 1987 was 25 p. Taking 1974 as a base, calculate a price index for milk in 1987.

2 The sales of a company during the year were

Quarter	1	2	3	4
Sales (000s)	250	300	310	350

Work out an index number of sales for each quarter with Qtr 1 = 100.

3 In 1984 a washing machine cost £270 and a refrigerator cost £150. The equivalent models in 1987 cost £320 and £190 respectively.

(a) Using 1984 as base, calculate an index for 1987 for the price of the washing machine.

(b) Using 1984 as base, calculate an index for 1987 for the price of the refrigerator.

(c) Which item increased in price by the greater percentage from 1984 to 1987?

(d) Which item increased in price by the greater actual amount of money from 1984 to 1987?

4 The index number for the price of a colour TV in 1985 was 125, taking 1980 as a base year. The price in 1985 was £250, what was the price in 1980?

5 Last year Jill went on a school trip that cost £80. This year she is going on one costing £110. Using last year as base, calculate an index for Jill's costs this year.

Last year Jack's school trip cost £240 and, this year, his school trip will cost £280. Using last year as base, calculate an index of Jack's costs for this year. Comment on your results.

6 The number of stoppages of work due to industrial disputes in the UK in 1976 was 2034 and in 1986 was 1071. Figures for the construction industry show that 570 000 working days were lost for such stoppages in 1976 and 30 000 working days were lost in 1986.

(a) Calculate an index number of stoppages for all industrial disputes in 1986 using 1976 = 100.

(b) Calculate an index number of working days lost in the construction industry by industrial disputes in 1986 using 1976 = 100.

(c) By what percentage did stoppages in all industrial disputes fall from 1976 to 1986? By what percentage did working days lost in the construction industry by industrial disputes fall from 1976 to 1986?

Comment on your results.

Changing the base of an index number

The choice of base period is arbitrary. For our index of earnings in the previous section, we could just as easily have used any of the years as a base period. For example, if we take 1985 = 100:

Year	Earnings (£)	Index of earnings (1985 = 100)
1983	139.99	$\frac{£139.99}{£160.37} \times 100 = 87.3$
1984	147.80	$\frac{£147.80}{£160.37} \times 100 = 92.2$
1985	160.37	$\frac{£160.37}{£160.37} \times 100 = 100$
1986	171.25	$\frac{£171.25}{£160.37} \times 100 = 106.8$

From these results we can say that:

earnings in 1983 were (100 − 87.3)% = 12.7% less than in 1985,
earnings in 1984 were 7.8% less than in 1985,
earnings in 1986 were 6.8% more than in 1985.

We can change the base of the index number to 1985 using the series with 1983 = 100, without referring back to the actual earnings. We express each index (1983 = 100) as a percentage of the 1985 index (1983 = 100).

Year	Index of earnings (1983 = 100)	Index of earnings (1985 = 100)
1983	100	$\frac{100}{114.6} \times 100 = 87.3$
1984	105.6	$\frac{105.6}{114.6} \times 100 = 92.1$
1985	114.6	$\frac{114.6}{114.6} \times 100 = 100$
1986	122.3	$\frac{122.3}{114.6} \times 100 = 106.7$

The results are the same as we had before, apart from rounding errors.

Chain-base index number

If we want to compare the percentage increases from one period to the next, we can construct a chain-base index instead of using a fixed base. To do this we express the value of the variable as a percentage of its value in the previous period.

Year	Earnings (£)	Chain-base index
1983	139.99	—
1984	147.80	$\frac{£147.80}{£139.99} \times 100 = 105.6$

1985	160.37	$\frac{£160.37}{£147.80} \times 100 = 108.5$
1986	171.25	$\frac{£171.25}{£160.37} \times 100 = 106.8$

We cannot work out a chain-base index for 1983 without knowing the earnings in 1982. From the results we can see that the earnings increased by

5.6% from 1983 to 1984,
8.5% from 1984 to 1985,
6.8% from 1985 to 1986.

In a chain-base index, the percentages are worked out with a different denominator each period, so you must take great care when interpreting the results. Always ask yourself, percentage of what and when?

Exercise 15.3

1 The price of a commodity in each of the years 1984 to 1987 is as shown.

Year	1984	1985	1986	1987
Price (£)	1.40	2.10	3.30	3.70

(a) Using 1986 = 100, calculate price index numbers for each year from 1984 to 1987.
(b) Use the chain-base method to calculate price index numbers for 1985 to 1987.

2 An article cost £84 in 1980. By 1985 its price had increased by £10. From 1985 to 1987, its price increased by 10%.
(a) Calculate the price index for 1985 using 1980 as a base.
(b) Calculate the price index for 1987 using 1980 as a base.
(c) What is the price index for 1987 using 1985 as a base?

3 In 1985, the value of an index number with base year 1982 was 115. The same index number for 1986 with 1985 as base was 103. Find (a) the index for 1986 with 1982 as base, (b) the index for 1982 with 1985 as base.

4 In January 1986, the value of a house price index was 120 (1984 = 100). During 1986, house prices rose by 15%. Using 1984 as a base, what is the value of the house price index at the start of 1987?

5 The numbers of new orders received each year by merchant shipbuilders in the UK from 1981 to 1986 were as shown.

Year	1981	1982	1983	1984	1985	1986
Number	72	56	43	90	54	57

(a) Construct an index of orders for each year using 1981 as base.
(b) Change the base of the index number to 1983.
(c) Construct a chain-base index for each year from 1982 to 1986.

Comment on the results. What features of the data are emphasised by the different methods used in (a), (b) and (c)?

Composite index number

Price relative

The variables that are most commonly put into index number form are economic variables such as retail prices, earnings, share prices and industrial production. In general, such index numbers will combine information about many different items. An index of retail prices, for example, must be constructed from the prices of many commodities and services, not just one.

We shall consider a simplified situation where a family buys just three commodities, flour, instant coffee and sugar. The prices of these commodities in May 1983 and in May 1987 were as shown in Table 15.1.

Table 15.1 Commodity prices

Commodity	Price (pence)	
	May 1983	May 1987
Flour per 1.5 kg bag	34	47
Instant coffee per 100 g jar	115	143
Sugar per 1 kg bag	45	47

Our aim is to construct a single composite index number to measure the changes in the prices of these three items from May 1983 to May 1987.

If we consider each commodity separately and express its price in 1987 as a percentage of its price in 1983, the resulting index numbers are called **price relatives.**

$$\text{price relative for flour in 1987 } (1983 = 100) = \frac{47\text{ p}}{34\text{ p}} \times 100 = 138.2$$

$$\text{price relative for coffee in 1987 } (1983 = 100) = \frac{143\text{ p}}{115\text{ p}} \times 100 = 124.3$$

$$\text{price relative for sugar in 1987 } (1983 = 100) = \frac{47\text{ p}}{45\text{ p}} \times 100 = 104.4$$

From the price relatives, we can see that the price of flour rose by the greatest percentage (38.2%) from 1983 to 1987. The price of coffee, however, rose by the greatest actual amount (28 p).

To obtain an overall index number of prices we can find the mean of the price relatives.

$$\begin{aligned}\text{mean of price relatives index in 1987 } (1983 = 100) &= \frac{138.2 + 124.3 + 104.4}{3} \\ &= \frac{366.9}{3} \\ &= 122.3\end{aligned}$$

Weighted index number

We have assumed that price changes in the three products are of equal importance but this is usually not true. A small price change in a product we buy frequently will affect our spending much more than a large price change in a product we buy rarely. For example, the Olbury family buys four pints of milk each day, i.e. about 120 pints a month. A 1p increase in the price of milk implies increased expenditure of approximately £1.20 per month. The Olburys buy one bottle of tomato ketchup each month. A 15 p increase in the price of a bottle of ketchup implies increased spending of only 15 p per month.

To allow for differences such as this, we find a **weighted mean** of the price relatives so that the more important items have larger weights. The formula to use is:

$$\text{weighted mean of price relatives index} = \frac{\Sigma\,(\text{weight} \times \text{price relative})}{\Sigma\,\text{weight}}$$

We have to decide what to use as weights. The quantities bought in a given period can be used and we shall use this method in our calculations. Sometimes it is preferable to use weights proportional to the expenditure on each item, see the later section on the official Retail Prices Index.

Suppose a typical family buys two bags of flour, one jar of coffee and two bags of sugar each week.

weighted mean of price relatives index (1983 = 100)

$$= \frac{(2 \times 138.2) + (1 \times 124.3) + (2 \times 104.4)}{2 + 1 + 2}$$

$$= \frac{276.4 + 124.3 + 208.8}{5}$$

$$= \frac{609.5}{5}$$

$$= 121.9$$

We conclude that prices have risen by 21.9%, overall, from May 1983 to May 1987.

Exercise 15.4

1 The prices of a typical three-bedroomed semi-detached house in Yorkshire and of a similar property in Hertfordshire increased as shown from 1969 to 1987.

Price (£)

Year	Yorks	Herts
1969	3 000	6 400
1978	9 700	16 500
1987	29 800	75 000

Using 1969 as base calculate (a) Yorkshire house price relatives for 1978 and 1987, (b) Hertfordshire house price relatives for 1978 and 1987. Comment on your answers.

2 A shopper notes the prices of fruit she buys each week for her family's packed lunches.

Prices (p) per lb

Fruit	Oct 86	May 87
Apples	25	32
Oranges	50	62
Bananas	40	50
Pears	25	42

(a) Find the price relative for each variety of fruit using Oct 86 = 100.
(b) Calculate a mean of price relatives index (Oct 86 = 100).
(c) The shopper usually buys 2lbs of apples, 2lbs of oranges, 3lbs of bananas and 1lb of pears. Using these quantities as weights, construct a weighted mean of price relatives index (Oct 86 = 100).

3 The four items listed in the table had the given weights and price relatives in 1987.

Item	Weight	Price relative for 1987 (1980 = 100)
A	2	150
B	3	140
C	4	180
D	1	120

Calculate a weighted mean of price relatives index for 1987 with 1980 as base using the given weights. What does your result tell you about the overall change in prices of these items from 1980 to 1987?

4 Use a weighted mean of price relatives method to calculate a food price index number for 1987 (1985 = 100).

Food	Price (p) per kg		Mean weekly consumption
	1985	1987	(kg)
A	40	50	3
B	120	156	2

5 A company produces four items A, B, C and D.

Item	Number produced each week	Cost of production (£) per item 1980	1986
A	20	200	240
B	40	350	410
C	50	160	230
D	10	800	960

Calculate a weighted mean of price relatives index of production costs for 1986 (1980 = 100), using the numbers produced each week as weights.

6 In September last year a household with two schoolchildren set aside the following amounts each week to cover their expenditure on school items.

Travel to and from school	£5.00
School meals	£7.50
Uniform	£6.00
School trips	£7.00

In September this year, they know that the cost of travel has gone up by 10% and the price of school meals has increased by 5%. The price of uniform has remained unchanged and they expect the cost of school trips to be down by 5%.

Taking September last year as base, calculate for September this year
(a) the price relative for school meals,
(b) the price relative for school trips,
(c) a mean of price relatives index of expenditure on school items.

7 The records of a small investor show:

Company	Number of shares held	Market price (p) per share 1985	1987
Aybury plc	400	145	170
Bebury plc	600	236	292
Ceebury plc	750	62	75
Debury plc	1000	123	141
Ebury plc	500	95	102

(a) Calculate an index for the value of the Aybury plc shares in 1987, taking 1985 as base.

(b) Calculate an index for the total value of the investor's shares in 1987, taking 1985 as base.

Use of geometric mean

To avoid a sharp change in the price of just one commodity distorting the overall change in the value of a composite index number, a geometric mean of price relatives can be used instead of an arithmetic mean.

Using the flour, coffee and sugar data of the earlier section, we have price relatives (1983 = 100) of 138.2, 124.3 and 104.4, respectively.

$$\begin{aligned}&\text{geometric mean of price relatives index in 1987 (1983 = 100)}\\ &= \sqrt[3]{138.2 \times 124.3 \times 104.4}\\ &= \sqrt[3]{1\,793\,410}\\ &= 121.5 \text{ to 1 dec. pl.}\end{aligned}$$

This is slightly smaller than the arithmetic mean index (122.3) calculated before.

To calculate the weighted geometric mean of the numbers $x_1, x_2, \ldots, x_n$ with weights $w_1, w_2, \ldots, w_n$, we use:

$$\text{weighted geometric mean} = \sqrt[\Sigma w]{x_1^{w_1} \times x_2^{w_2} \times \cdots \times x_n^{w_n}}$$

To find the weighted index we take quantity weights as before.

	Flour	Coffee	Sugar
price relative (1983 = 100)	$x_1 = 138.2$	$x_2 = 124.3$	$x_3 = 104.4$
weight	$w_1 = 2$	$w_2 = 1$	$w_3 = 2$

sum of weights, $\Sigma w = 2 + 1 + 2 = 5$

$$\begin{aligned}&\text{weighted geometric mean of price relative index in 1987 (1983 = 100)}\\ &= \sqrt[5]{(138.2)^2 \times (124.3)^1 \times (104.4)^2}\\ &= \sqrt[5]{2.587\,546\,7 \times 10^{10}}\\ &= 120.9 \text{ directly by calculator}\end{aligned}$$

An alternative way to evaluate the weighted geometric mean is to take logarithms.

$$\log(\text{weighted geometric mean}) = \frac{w_1 \log x_1 + w_2 \log x_2 + \cdots + w_n \log x_n}{w_1 + w_2 + \cdots + w_n}$$

Using the values above:

$$\begin{aligned}\log(\text{weighted geometric mean}) &= \frac{(2 \times \log 138.2) + \log 124.3 + (2 \times \log 104.4)}{5} \\ &= \frac{4.2810 + 2.0945 + 4.0374}{5} \\ &= \frac{10.4129}{5} \\ &= 2.0826 \\ \text{weighted geometric mean} &= \text{antilog } (2.0826) \\ &= 120.9, \text{ as before}\end{aligned}$$

In an examination use a geometric mean only if you are told to do so, otherwise assume that a mean of price relatives index is to be worked out using an arithmetic mean.

Exercise 15.5

Rework Exercise 15.4 Questions 2 and 3 using geometric means. How do these index numbers differ from those you calculated before?

The Retail Prices Index

Background information

The Retail Prices Index is one of the most widely known index numbers in the UK. It measures the percentage changes month-by-month in the average level of prices of commodities and services purchased by the great majority of households in the UK.

Its value has been calculated regularly since the late 1950s, although alterations in its construction are made from time to time. In particular, the reference month is changed at about ten-year intervals. The present base is January 1987 which replaced the previous base, January 1974, in February 1987.

The Department of Employment is responsible for the collection of the necessary data and for the calculation of the index. The results are published in detail each month in *Employment Gazette* and in the *Monthly Digest of Statistics*. The index is weighted, so information on both prices and weights has to be collected.

Collection of prices

A representative 'basket' of approximately 600 commodities and services is priced each month, on a Tuesday close to the middle of the month. The basket contains items that are readily available throughout the country and are

Table 15.2 1987 weights for RPI subgroups

Main group	Subgroup	Weight
Food and catering	Food	167
	Catering	46
Alcohol and tobacco	Alcoholic drink	76
	Tobacco	38
Housing and household expenditure	Housing	157
	Fuel and light	61
	Household goods	73
	Household services	44
Personal expenditure	Clothing and footwear	74
	Personal goods and services	38
Travel and leisure	Motoring expenditure	127
	Fares and other travel costs	22
	Leisure goods	47
	Leisure services	30
Total		1000

Source: *Employment Gazette*

commonly bought by most households. The items are not restricted to basic necessities so the index is not a 'cost-of-living' index.

Each commodity and service is allocated to one of five main groups which are further divided into 14 subgroups as shown in Table 15.2. Each subgroup is divided into sections. For instance, the Catering subgroup comprises Restaurant meals, Canteen meals and Take-away meals and snacks.

Representative items are chosen for pricing in each section. For example, in the Bread section of the Food subgroup, the prices of large white loaves (sliced and unsliced), small loaves (white and brown), wholemeal loaves and bread rolls are the price indicators. The representative items remain the same throughout the year but from year to year the items may be changed. For example, in 1987 microwave ovens were included for the first time and TV tubes were dropped.

Officials from the Department of Employment collect prices of the representative items throughout the country from several different types of shop within each area. Hundreds of price quotations are obtained for each item. For example, in March 1987, 354 price quotations for a large white sliced loaf were obtained. Some items, such as the cost of posting a first class letter, are uniform throughout the country, so, in such cases, prices do not have to be collected from retail outlets.

The average percentage changes in price since January for all price indicators within one section, in each type of shop and for each region, can then be found. These are then combined to give an index number for each section for that month (Jan = 100).

Weighting system

The weights for each section are found each year from the Family Expenditure Survey. This is a sample survey conducted by the Office of Population

Censuses and Surveys for the Department of Employment. Approximately 7000 households, chosen by stratified sampling of the Postcode Address File, co-operate in the survey in the course of a year, although each individual household is involved for a two-week period only.

Each individual, aged 16 or over, in the household has to keep a diary of daily expenditure for two weeks. Information on longer-term expenditure such as fuel bills, season tickets etc. is obtained by interview.

Expenditure is defined as payment for goods and services received and consumed. Payments such as income tax, national insurance contributions, life assurance premiums, savings and investments are recorded in the survey but are not termed expenditure.

In calculating the weights for the Retail Prices Index, expenditure of high-income households is excluded. The actual income limit changes each year but it excludes the highest 3–4% of household incomes. Pensioner households are treated separately and have their own Retail Prices Indices. For the remaining households the total expenditure within each section of the Retail Prices Index subgroups is found. For example, all expenditure on any type of bread is included in the bread section, even though, when collecting price information, only the representative items are priced.

The expenditures within each section could be used directly as weights for the Retail Prices Index but, for convenience, they are scaled so that their total is 1000. The weights in 1987 for all 14 subgroups are given in Table 15.2. The weights for each section of the Catering subgroup are shown in Table 15.3. Revised weights come into use in January each year, based on the Family Expenditure Survey ending the previous June.

The weight of 46 for Catering tells us that 46/1000 or 4.6% of all household expenditure is on catering. The weight of 23 for Restaurant meals tells us that 23/1000 or 2.3% of household expenditure is on restaurant meals. Alternatively, we can say 23/46 or 50% of all catering expenditure is on restaurant meals.

The weights are an average and an individual household may have an expenditure pattern markedly different from this. For example, a teetotal, non-smoking household would not spend anything in the Alcohol and tobacco group.

Table 15.3 1987 weights for Catering subgroup of RPI

Restaurant meals	23
Canteen meals	7
Take-away meals and snacks	16
Catering	46

Source: *Employment Gazette*

Calculation of the Retail Prices Index

Each month, from the monthly collecton of prices, index numbers, based on January, are known for each section.

The weights, calculated from the Family Expenditure Survey, stay the same throughout the year, having been updated in January each year.

The 'All-items' Retail Prices Index is first worked out with January of the current year as base. It is a weighted mean of the index numbers for each section.

So that a long series of values of the Retail Prices Index (RPI) can be studied over a number of years, the calculated value is then chained back to a fixed reference date. For example,

$$\underset{(\text{Jan } 87 = 100)}{\text{RPI in May 1988}} = \frac{\underset{(\text{Jan } 88 = 100)}{\text{RPI in May 1988}} \times \underset{(\text{Jan } 87 = 100)}{\text{RPI in Jan 1988}}}{100}$$

$$\underset{(\text{Jan } 87 = 100)}{\text{RPI in Feb 1989}} = \frac{\underset{(\text{Jan } 89 = 100)}{\text{RPI in Feb 1989}} \times \underset{(\text{Jan } 87 = 100)}{\text{RPI in Jan 1989}}}{100}$$

As well as the All-items index, index numbers for each subgroup are calculated in a similar way.

Uses of the Retail Prices Index

To measure inflation

The annual rate of inflation, sometimes called the year-on-year rate of inflation, is worked out each month. It is the percentage increase in the value of the Retail Prices Index over the immediate past 12 months. For example,

$$\text{rate of inflation in May 1988} = \frac{\text{RPI in May 88} - \text{RPI in May 87}}{\text{RPI in May 87}} \times 100\%$$

$$= \frac{\text{RPI in May 88}}{\text{RPI in May 87}} \times 100\% - 100\%$$

Index-linking

The values of pensions, pay rises, investments and amounts insured are often index-linked, i.e. they change by the same proportion as the Retail Prices Index.

Example

I invested £500 in index-linked National Savings in January 1980 when the Retail Prices Index was 245.3 (Jan 74 = 100). In January 1987, when the Retail Prices Index was 394.5 (Jan 74 = 100), I withdrew my savings. How much money did I receive?

$$\text{RPI increased by the factor } \frac{394.5}{245.3}$$

$$\text{savings increased by the factor } \frac{394.5}{245.3}$$

$$\text{money received} = £500 \times \frac{394.5}{245.3}$$

$$= £804.12$$

Deflation

Sometimes we want to make comparisons that allow for the effect of inflation, i.e. we want to compare, for example, wages or value of output, in 'real terms'. This is called deflation. We have to decide on which month or year to base the comparison. Using the earnings data for the construction industry from the beginning of this chapter, let us deflate the earnings to 1983 prices.

Year	1983	1984	1985	1986
Earnings (£)	133.99	147.80	160.37	171.25
Annual average RPI (Jan 74 = 100)	335.1	351.8	373.2	385.7

Source: *Employment Gazette*

$$\text{Earnings at 1983 prices} = \frac{\text{Actual earnings in current year} \times \text{RPI for 1983}}{\text{RPI in current year}}$$

Hence:

$$\text{1983 earnings at 1983 prices} = £139.99$$

$$\text{1984 earnings at 1983 prices} = £147.80 \times \frac{335.1}{351.8} = £140.78$$

$$\text{1985 earnings at 1983 prices} = £160.37 \times \frac{335.1}{373.2} = £144.00$$

$$\text{1986 earnings at 1983 prices} = £171.25 \times \frac{335.1}{385.7} = £148.78$$

In 'real terms', earnings increased every year from 1983 to 1986, i.e., they went up at a greater rate than did the retail prices, particularly after 1984. If the deflated values in 1984, 1985 and 1986 had all been exactly £139.99, then earnings would have increased at exactly the same rate as retail prices.

Exercise 15.6

1 Answer the following questions about the UK Index of Retail Prices.
(a) How often is it calculated?
(b) Which government department is responsible for its compilation?
(c) Name two journals where details of its current value are published?
(d) Approximately how many different goods and services are priced each time it is calculated?
(e) Who collects the information on prices?
(f) How is the information collected to construct the weighting system?
(g) To what do the weights sum?
(h) What is the reference data of the index at present?

2 Suggest reasons why high-income households are excluded when the weights are calculated for the general Retail Prices Index.

3 (a) Construct an all-items index of retail prices for June (Jan = 100) by finding the weighted mean of the group index numbers shown.

Group	Group index for June (Jan = 100)	Weight	Percentage change in index from Jan to July
Food and catering	101.4	200	1.6
Alcohol and tobacco	100.6	100	0.9
Housing and household expenditure	101.0	350	1.1
Personal expenditure	100.8	100	1.0
Travel and leisure	100.6	250	0.8
All items		1000	

(b) Using the information given in the table, find the value of the all-items index in July (Jan = 100).

4 In Ruritania the Retail Prices Index for July 1988 was 101.6 (January 1988 = 100). The Retail Prices Index for January 1988 (January 1987 = 100) was 105.4. What is the value of the Retail Prices Index for July 1988 (January 1987 = 100)?

5 Separate Retail Price Indices are calculated for one-pensioner and two-pensioner households. They are calculated quarterly and exclude housing costs. The weights used for 1987 are shown in the table together with those for the general Retail Prices Index, excluding housing.

1987 Weights

Subgroup	One-pensioner household	Two-pensioner household	General household
Food	320	327	198
Catering	32	25	55
Alcoholic drink	29	45	90
Tobacco	35	51	45
Fuel and light	187	141	72
Household goods	83	87	86
Household services	69	44	52
Clothing and footwear	64	70	88
Personal goods and services	49	44	45
Motoring expenditure	20	73	151
Fares and other travel costs	22	18	26
Leisure goods	48	45	56
Leisure services	42	30	36
All items (except housing)	1000	1000	1000

Source: *Employment Gazette*

Draw a multiple bar chart to compare the different weights for each subgroup. Comment on what your chart reveals. Which type of household is most affected by (a) an increase in food prices, (b) an increase in the cost of fuel and light, (c) an increase in motoring costs?

6 A household contents insurance policy is index-linked by reference to the Consumer Durables Index within the Retail Prices Index. In March 1987, the Consumer Durables Index was 100.8 (Jan 1987 = 100). The contents of a house were insured for £10 500 when a policy was taken out in March 1986 and the index was then 99.9 (Jan 1987 = 100). What were the contents insured for in March 1987?

7 In April 1979 when the Retail Prices Index (RPI) was 214.2 (Jan 1974 = 100), the average weekly earnings for men in manual occupations was £93.00. In April 1986 when the RPI was 383.3 (Jan 1974 = 100), these earnings were £174.40.

(a) From April 1979 to April 1986, did earnings increase in the same proportion as prices, at a greater rate than prices or at a lesser rate than prices?
(b) A retired man received a pension of £50 per week in April 1979. What would he receive per week in April 1986, if his pension went up by the same proportion as wages? What would he receive per week in April 1986, if his pension went up by the same proportion as prices? Do you think pensions should be linked with wages or with prices? Why?

Practical exercise 15.7

1 Look at a recent copy of *Employment Gazette*. Find Table 6.2 and list the sections contained in the Leisure goods subgroup of the Retail Prices Index. What was the overall percentage change in prices of leisure goods (a) in the last month, (b) in the last year? Over the last year, which section showed the largest percentage change? Was it an increase or a decrease? Which section showed the smallest percentage change?
2 Look at a recent copy of the *Employment Gazette* and find Table 6.3. Note down the average prices of 10 food items that your household regularly buys. Also note the price ranges within which 80% of the Department of Employment quotations fell. Find out the prices that your household is currently paying for these items. Compare the two sets of prices. Do your prices fall within the 80% range? Note any differences that occur. Can you suggest reasons for the differences?
3 Write down the official definitions of the following:
(a) a household, (b) a pensioner household, (c) consumer durables, (d) expenditure (as used in the Family Expenditure Survey). You will need to refer to the *Employment Gazette* and the *Annual Supplement* to the *Monthly Digest of Statistics*.
4 Using Table 18.3 from a recent copy of the *Monthly Digest of Statistics*, calculate the annual rate of inflation for each month from January 1986 onwards. Draw a historigram of your results and comment on your graph.
5 The *Financial Times* publishes four different types of share price index numbers each day, FT-30, FT-SE 100, FT-Actuaries Share indices and FT-Actuaries World indices. Try to find out the following information about each index.
(a) How often is it calculated?
(b) How many share prices are used to calculate it?
(c) What is the base period?
(d) Is it a weighted index? If so, what are used as weights?
(e) Is an arithmetic mean or a geometric mean used?
(f) Who uses the index?
6 Refer to a copy of the *Monthly Digest of Statistics*. Make a table showing the names of ten different index numbers, together with their base periods. Note the current value of the index and its value a year ago. Work out the percentage change in the value of each index in the last year. Which variable showed (a) the greatest percentage increase, (b) the greatest percentage decrease, (c) the least change? Did any of the variables show similar-sized changes?

16 Misuse of statistics

Introduction

The words 'lies, damned lies and statistics' uttered by Disraeli are ones that members of the public still use when they are doubtful of the conclusions of some investigation. You often hear, 'Statistics can prove anything' and it is true that unscrupulous writers, on occasions, do select just those figures that either support their points of view or give rise to dramatic headlines. More usually, a distorted image arises because artists and graphic designers are more concerned with displaying their artistic skills than with giving a faithful presentation of data. It is not the statistics themselves that are at fault. It is the misuse of statistics that gives cause for concern. We shall look at various ways in which potentially misleading statements or presentations may arise.

Graphical presentations

If you look through the scrapbook that I suggested you made in Chapter 1, you will find examples of most of the following faults in presentation. Look out for them in others' work and make sure you do not make similar mistakes in your own.

Scales

Sometimes the scale of measurement is completely absent from a graph such as a vertical bar chart or a historigram, see Fig. 16.1(a). We have no idea of the size of a change in the vertical direction. All we can conclude is that cinema admissions went up between 1984 and 1986 but we do not know by how much.

Even when a scale is present, by making it smaller, Fig. 16.1(b), or larger, Fig. 16.1(c), we can either lessen the impact of variation or emphasise it.

The use of the **broken-scale convention,** Fig. 16.1(c), can also lead to a loss of sense of proportion in the size of variations. Its use should be confined to line graphs but you will see it used on bar charts in the press, Fig. 16.2(a). It is best if a complete scale running from zero is used on every graph, Figs. 16.1(b) and 16.2(b), although it is acceptable to have the base line at 100 for the graph of an index number.

Some presenters suppress the zero of a scale without even bothering to use the broken-scale convention. This over-emphasises changes. In Fig. 16.3, version (a) was the one used to display a company's results in a press

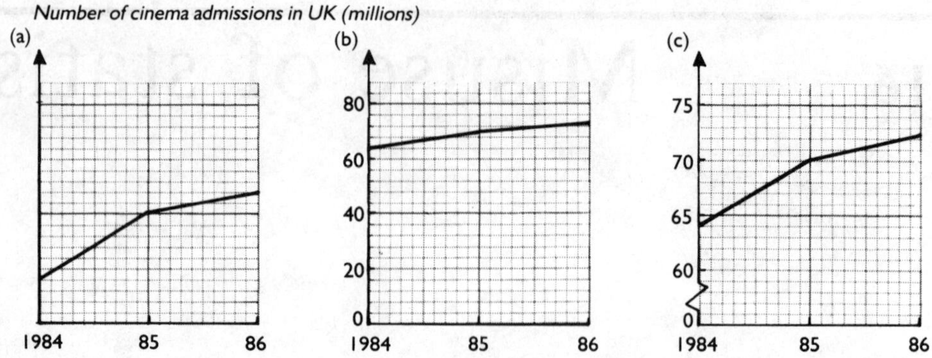

Fig. 16.1 *Graphs with (a) no vertical scale (b) complete vertical scale (c) larger scale and broken scale*

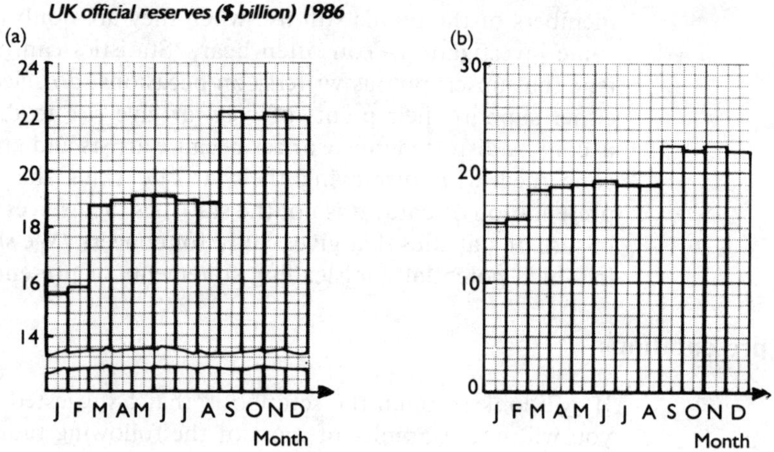

Fig. 16.2 *Bar chart (a) misleading, broken scale (b) complete scale*

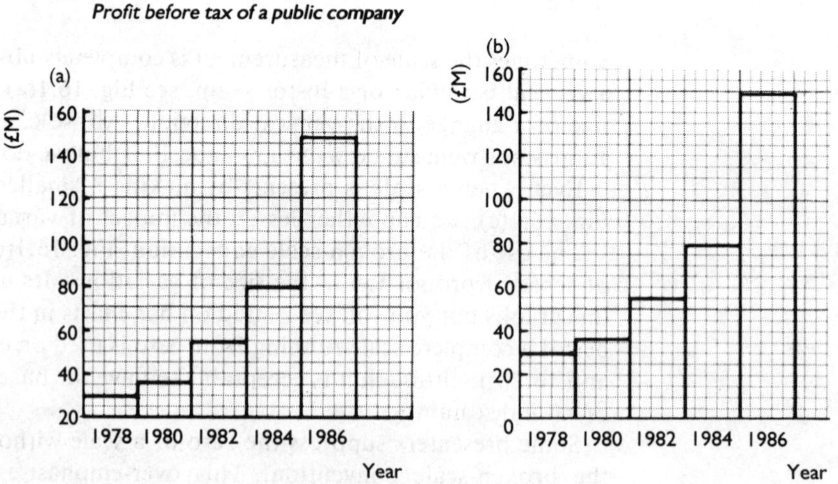

Fig. 16.3 *Bar chart (a) misleading, suppressed zero (b) complete scale*

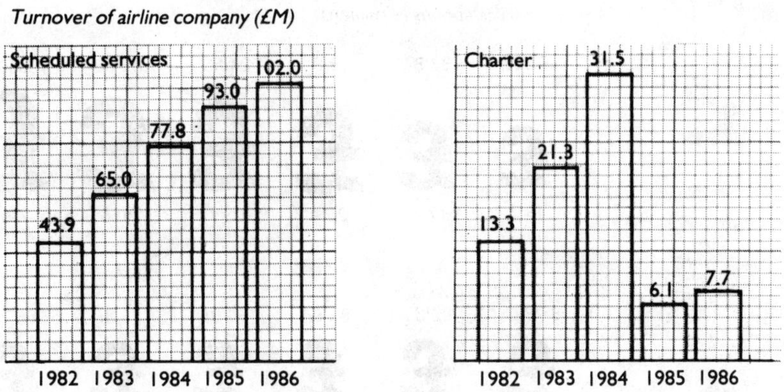

Fig. 16.4 *Related graphs but with different scales*

advertisement. Although the actual changes are correctly shown, a misleading impression is given of the proportional changes, so version (b) is preferable.

If two or more graphs on a related topic appear together, it is better if the same scale is used in each graph. The graphs in Fig. 16.4 appeared on the same page of an airline company report. At first glance, it appears that 1984 had by far the highest turnover because the total length of the bars is greatest in that year. If you look more closely, however, you will see that the charter turnover is measured on a larger scale. In fact the highest turnover, £109.7 M, occurred in 1986 as compared with £109.3 M in 1984.

Pictograms and three-dimensional effects

Pictograms are best drawn with a logo of a given size representing a stated amount and with the appropriate number of logos for each category. A favourite device of graphic designers is to use just one logo for each category and to change its size. To give a fair representation in two dimensions, as we noted with comparative pie charts, the **areas** of the logos should be in proportion to the amounts they represent. Often, however, a presentation changes both the width and the height of the logo in proportion to these amounts so that changes are overstated. Figure 16.5(a) presents the amount available in cash bonuses for the partners in a public company, as shown in a press advertisement. If you compare the logos for 81/82 and 86/87, their areas should be in the ratio 15.7 : 42.2, i.e. 1 : 2.7. In (a), both the height and the width of the £ symbol have been increased by approximately this ratio, giving a distorted impression. Worse still, the logos in the intervening years have been regularly sized to fit in neatly, and are not attempting to portray the bonuses in anything like the correct proportions. This is particularly noticeable when you compare 83/84 with 84/85. A simple bar chart of bonuses would have been easier to interpret, although not as eye-catching. A pictogram using a £ sign of fixed size as in Fig. 16.5(b) would be satisfactory. Alternatively, if just one logo is to be used for each year, it would be better to keep one dimension, e.g. the width, fixed and increase the other dimension in proportion to the amount represented, Fig. 16.5(c).

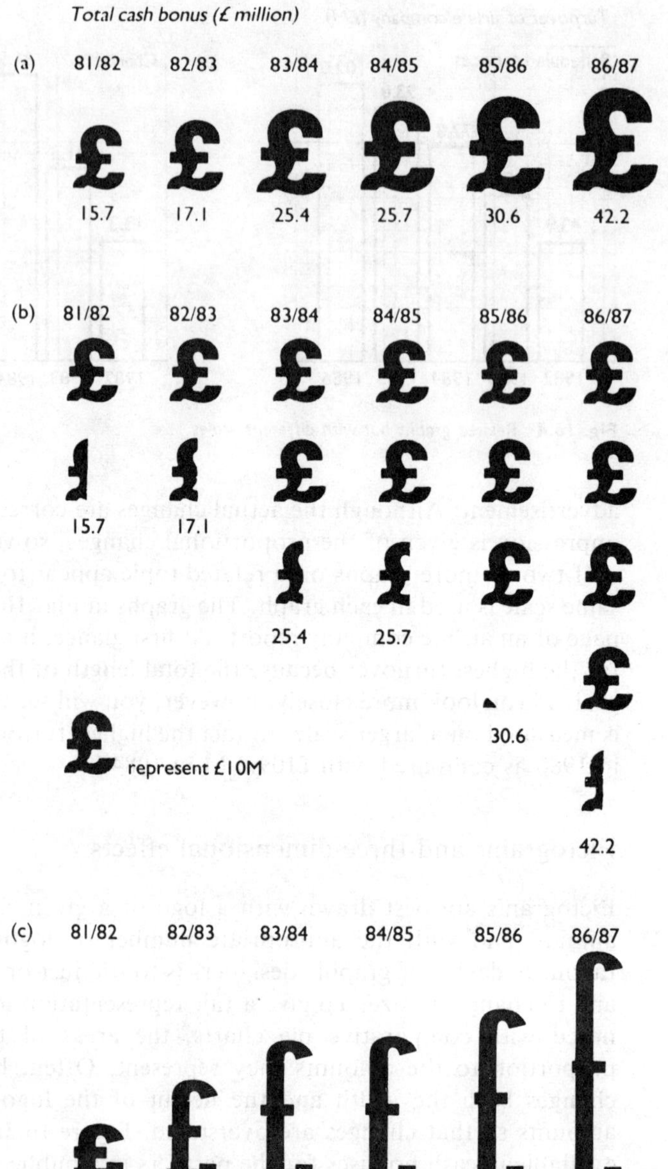

Fig. 16.5 *Pictograms (a) misleading, areas not in proportion (b) using logo of standard size (c) using logo of standard width*

It is becoming increasingly common to give a three-dimensional effect to pictograms. The volumes portrayed should be in proportion to the amounts they represent but artists are often tempted to change each of the three dimensions by this proportion, again resulting in a misleading chart. If a three-dimensional effect is specifically desired, it is best to keep the cross-sectional area fixed and just change one dimension in proportion to the quantity represented. This is easier to draw and to interpret.

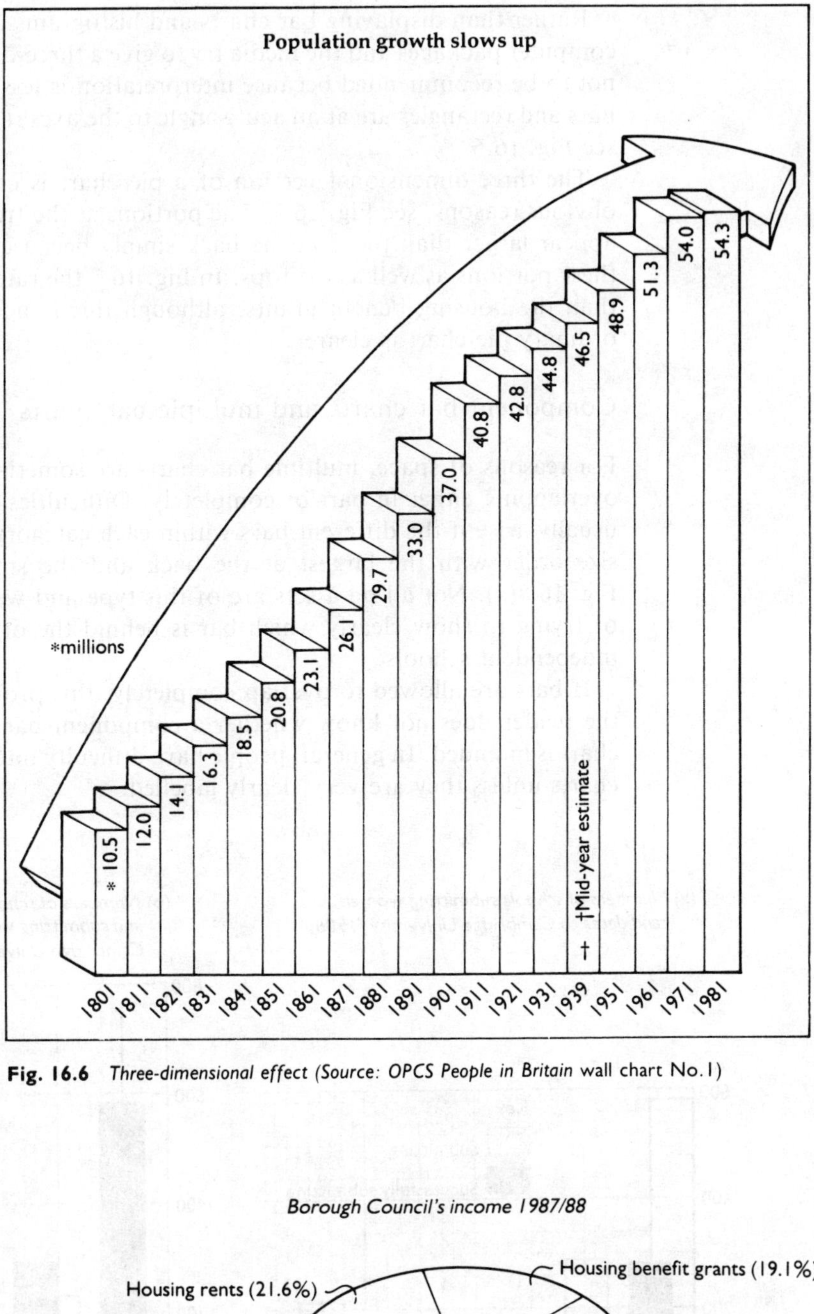

Fig. 16.6 *Three-dimensional effect (Source: OPCS People in Britain* wall chart No. 1)

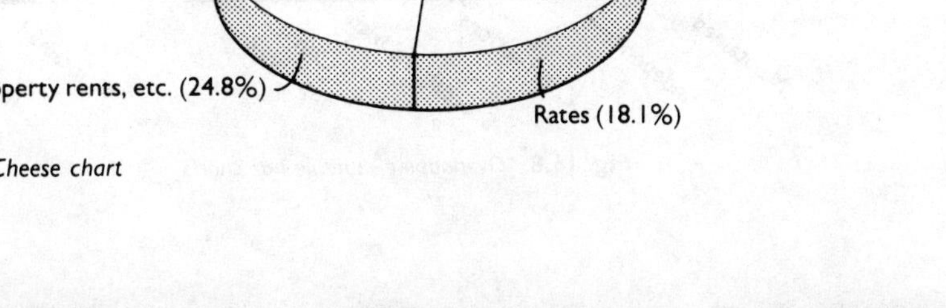

Fig. 16.7 *Cheese chart*

Rather than displaying bar charts and histograms in two-dimensions, some computer packages and the media try to give a three-dimensional effect. This is not to be recommended because interpretation is less easy. Some parts of the bars and rectangles are at an acute angle to the axes rather than at right angles, see Fig. 16.6.

The three-dimensional version of a pie chart is called a cheese chart, for obvious reasons, see Fig. 16.7. The portions at the front of the cheese tend to appear larger than those at the back simply because we can see the sides of these portions as well as the tops. In Fig. 16.7 the rates portion appears larger than the housing benefit grants, although this is not the true situation. An ordinary pie chart is clearer.

Component bar charts and multiple bar charts

For reasons of space, multiple bar charts are sometimes drawn with the bars overlapping either in part or completely. Difficulties in interpretation do not usually arise if the different bars within each category are always in the same size order with the largest at the back and the smallest at the front, see Fig. 16.8(a). Not all data sets are of this type and we then have the problem of trying to show clearly which bar is behind the other, see Fig. 16.8(b) for independent schools.

If bars are allowed to overlap completely, this problem is made worse and the reader does not know whether a component bar chart or a multiple bar chart is intended. In general, people have difficulty interpreting component bar charts unless they are very clearly labelled.

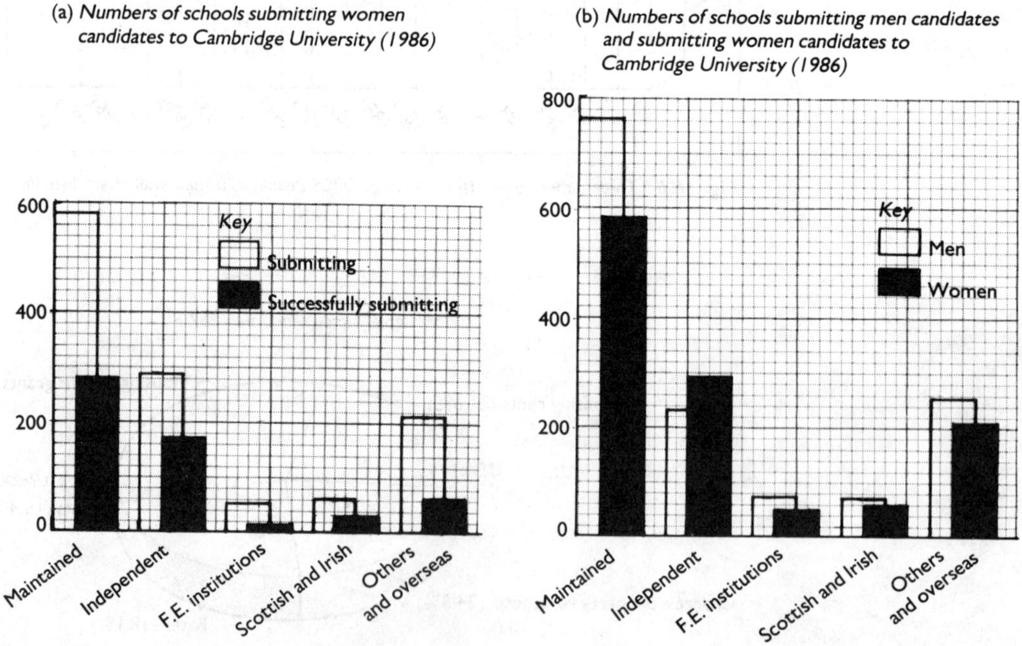

Fig. 16.8 *Overlapping multiple bar charts*

Averages

In earlier chapters we have seen that the term 'average' can be used for four different measures: the arithmetic mean, the median, the mode and the geometric mean. It is not always obvious in some published articles which of these measures have been used. Try to state clearly in your work which measure you are using. It is unfortunate that the word 'average' is conventionally used to stand for the arithmetic mean in many instances, particularly in sports performances such as football and cricket averages.

Example

The word 'average' has been used in each of the following statements. To which measure do you think it refers in each case?

1 'It is a deplorable fact that half the people in this country earn less than the average wage.'

2 'On average there are 2.2 children per family in Exbury.'

3 'The average family in Exbury has 2 children.'

1 average is median

In any data set, the median is halfway through the data when it is arranged in order of magnitude. Consequently half the data must lie below the median. There is nothing to be deplored about it. It is inevitable.

2 average is arithmetic mean

This is worked out by dividing the total number of children in Exbury by the total number of families. It is not surprising that the result is a decimal fraction rather than an exact whole number.

3 average is mode

This statement says that more families in Exbury have two children than any other number of children, i.e. there are fewer families that are without children or have just one child or three children etc.

Populations and samples

It is not always easy to tell whether assertions in the press and on television refer to results from a census, i.e. an investigation of a complete population, or from a sample.

For instance, statements such as the following appear:
'one in 4000 men refuses murder test'
'eight out of ten dog owners say their dogs prefer Barkbury dog food'.

From these assertions, we do not know whether 4000 men and ten dog owners were the total numbers involved or whether the statements are implying that one in every 4000 men and eight in every ten dog owners throughout some region are involved.

Reading the murder-test article in detail revealed that almost exactly 4000 men had been asked to give blood samples to enable them to be eliminated from a murder enquiry. One man had refused to co-operate. A clearer statement would be, 'Only one man out of 4000 refuses murder test'.

Further clarification of the dog food claim is more difficult. Advertisers tend not to give full details of the basis of their assertions. We really need to know how many dog-owners were approached, how they were chosen, what choice was offered to the dogs (they may just prefer Barkbury dog food to water) before we can make reliable conclusions.

Percentages

Percentages can easily be misinterpreted. As mentioned in the chapters on index numbers, always ask yourself, 'Percentage of what, when?'

Example 1

Is the following assertion correct? 'Earnings went up by 5% from 1985 to 1986 and by 6% from 1986 to 1987. Therefore, earnings went up by 11% from 1985 to 1987.' Let us consider weekly earnings of £100 in 1985.

$$5\% \text{ of } £100 = \frac{5}{100} \times £100 = £5$$

weekly earnings in 1986 = £100 + £5 = £105

$$6\% \text{ of } £105 = \frac{6}{100} \times £105 = £6.30$$

weekly earnings in 1987 = £105 + £6.30 = £111.30

increase in earnings from 1985 to 1987 = £11.30

$$\text{percentage increase in earnings from 1985 to 1987} = \frac{£11.30}{£100} \times 100$$

$$= 11.3\%$$

This is greater than the value asserted. The 6% must be worked out with reference to the 1986 earnings not the 1985 earnings.

Example 2

'The annual rate of inflation decreased from 3.0% last month to 2.8% this month, so prices are coming down.' Is this statement true?

This statement is not true. The annual rate of inflation is the percentage change in the Retail Prices Index over the past 12 months. Although this fell from 3.0% to 2.8%, prices have still risen by 2.8% in the past year. It is the rate of change that is decreasing. If inflation is 0%, prices are steady. It is only if negative inflation is achieved, that prices are actually decreasing.

Even when the percentage change is reduced, the actual amount in money terms can still be increasing.

Example 3

Consider the following statement. 'A bookcase cost £100 in 1980. The price went up by 100% between 1980 and 1983. It increased by "only" 75% from 1983 to 1986 so the price did not go up as much in the three later years.'

$$\text{price in 1980} = £100$$

$$\text{increase in price 1980 to 1983} = 100\% \text{ of } £100 = £100$$

$$\text{price in 1983} = £100 + £100 = £200$$

$$\text{increase in price 1983 to 1986} = 75\% \text{ of } £200$$

$$= \frac{75}{100} \times £200 = £150$$

Hence the increase in price (£150) between 1983 and 1986 is greater than the increase in price (£100) between 1980 and 1983, even though the percentage increase is smaller, 75% as compared with 100%.

Exercise 16.1

1 Consider each of the following diagrams and state why they may be misleading.

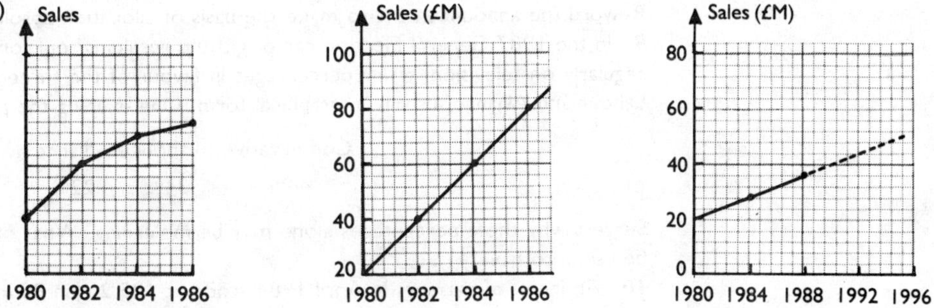

2 Number of new houses completed in Teebury

Year	1980	1983	1986
Number	50	40	25

Draw three different pictograms of these data using

(a) a logo of a brick to represent 10 houses;

(b) a two-dimensional logo of a house whose height changes in correct proportion, the width remains constant;

(c) a 'three dimensional' logo of a brick whose length changes, in correct proportion, the cross-section remaining of constant size. Which presentation do you prefer?

3 The following categories of classification were used on a graph showing the distance travelled to work:

Working at home, >5 km, 6–9 km, 10–14 km, <15 km

Criticise these categories and suggest what the appropriate categories might be.

4 In February 1987, the percentage unemployed in Belgium was 16.5% and in Japan was 2.7%. Therefore the number without a job in Belgium is greater than the number without a job in Japan.'

Give two reasons why the second sentence is not necessarily true. (If you consult Table 2.18 in *Employment Gazette*, you will see that the assertion is not true.)

5 Which measure would you use as an average in the following situations and why?

(a) To quote an average weekly wage to use in wage negotiations in Yewbury Company. The company employs 500 people, just a few of whom are highly-paid specialists.

(b) To quote an average weekly wage to use to attract new employees to Yewbury Company.

(c) So that shareholders know what is paid on average each week to workers in Yewbury Company.

(d) To quote the average size of boiler suit worn by male employees at Yewbury Company.

6 'The number of new vehicles registered in the UK last year was 3 million and the number of vehicle licences renewed was 24 million. Hence there are 27 million vehicles in the UK.'

Suggest reasons why this conclusion may not be true.

7 'In Kaybury, the correlation coefficient between the ages of men and women at marriage is 0.95. Hence a man is likely to marry a woman of about his own age.'

Explain what is wrong with this assertion.

8 XYZ company shares were offered for sale at £1 each. The issue was oversubscribed and the basis for allocation was announced as follows: 'Those applying for more than 1000 shares are allocated 12% of their application. Those applying for less than 1000 shares are allocated 100 shares.'

If you applied for exactly 1000 shares, how many do you think you were allocated? Reword the announcement to make the basis of allocation absolutely clear.

9 In the 1987 General Election campaign, the results of opinion polls were presented regularly on television, giving percentages in favour of the three parties, Conservative, Labour and Alliance, usually in graphical form. One evening the percentages shown were:

Conservative	Labour	Alliance
44%	34%	22%

Suggest why these percentages alone may be misleading. What other information would it be useful to have?

10 An index of earnings in April 1984 stood at 125.2 (Jan 80 = 100). In April 1987 the value of the index was 160.3 (Jan 80 = 100). The index had increased by 35.1 percentage points. Does this mean that wages had gone up by 35.1% between April 1984 and April 1987? Explain.

Practical exercise 16.2

1 Look through the scrapbook of charts and graphs you have made during your course. Count up how many of the charts were badly drawn or misleading in some way. Count up how many of the charts were well drawn. Comment on your results.

2 Each night for a fortnight, watch a televison news programme. Look carefully at any charts or diagrams that appear on the screen and note down any defects of presentation such as an absence of units, incorrect scale. Discuss your results with your classmates and summarise the major ways in which you think graphical presentations on TV could be improved.

17 Probability

Introduction

We use words such as 'certainty', 'probability' and 'impossibility' in everyday speech. In the study of statistics, however, we have to use these terms with more care. We shall consider how to evaluate probabilities. You will find it helpful to refer back to earlier practical exercises where you tossed coins or dice and selected cards from a pack.

Sample space

When we roll a six-sided die on a flat surface, we know that it will stop with one of its faces uppermost and that the score on this face can be 1, 2, 3, 4, 5 or 6. In formal language we say that we are conducting a **statistical experiment** with a die. Each time we roll the die we are making one **trial** of the experiment. The result of a trial is called an **outcome**. The list or set of all possible outcomes is termed the **sample space** and, for convenience, we can refer to it by the letter S.

For the die experiment we have:

$$\text{sample space } S = \{1, 2, 3, 4, 5, 6\}$$

The outcomes are enclosed in curly brackets as is customary in set notation.

The particular outcome or outcomes of interest to us are termed an **event**. Events are usually referred to by capital letters such as A, B or E. For example:

$$A = \{\text{score on die is even number}\} = \{2, 4, 6\}$$

$$B = \{\text{score on die is less than 2}\} = \{1\}$$

Events are subsets of the sample space S.

We want to be able to assess how likely it is that a particular event occurs, i.e. we want to know the **probability** that the event occurs.

Exercise 17.1

1 What is the sample space when a coin is tossed once?

2 List all possible outcomes when a 5p coin and a 20p coin are tossed at the same time. How many outcomes are in the event $A = \{\text{exactly one head can be seen}\}$?

3 The ten cards, Ace, King, Queen and Jack of spades, Ace, King and Queen of hearts, the Ace and King of diamonds and the Ace of clubs, are well shuffled and one card is selected at random. List all the different outcomes that can occur. How many outcomes are in the event $B = \{\text{card is a King}\}$?

4 A red die and a green die are shaken together. List all the different ways in which the two dice can land, giving the score on the red die first, e.g. (2, 4) means the red die shows 2 and the green die shows 4. How many outcomes are there in this sample space? How many of them are in the event $E = \{\text{total score is 8}\}$?

Equally likely outcomes

In some experiments we may think it is reasonable to assume that all outcomes are equally likely. For instance, if we believe we have a fair die and shake it well, then it seems that each of the different faces should have the same chance of appearing uppermost. When we can make this assumption that all outcomes in the sample space are **equally likely**, we find the probability of an event E occurring from the formula:

$$\text{probability of event } E = \mathrm{P}(E) = \frac{\text{number of outcomes in } E}{\text{number of outcomes in } S}$$

P(E) is the notation used to stand for the 'probability of event E'. Referring to the examples in the previous section and assuming we have a fair die:

$$\text{probability that score on die is an even number} = \mathrm{P}(A)$$

$$= \frac{\text{number of outcomes in } A}{\text{number of outcomes in } S}$$

$$= \frac{3}{6} = \frac{1}{2}, \text{ in lowest terms}$$

We can also express P(A) as the decimal fraction 0.5 (or as the corresponding percentage 50%).

$$\text{probability that score on die is less than } 2 = \mathrm{P}(B)$$

$$= \frac{\text{number of outcomes in } B}{\text{number of outcomes in } S}$$

$$= \frac{1}{6}$$

When you are told that a coin or die is fair or unbiased, you may assume that you can use the equal likelihood formula to find probabilities. You can also make this assumption if you are told that an object or person is selected at random from a set.

Exercise 17.2

1 What is the probability of obtaining a head when a fair coin is tossed once?

2 What is the probability of obtaining exactly one head when two fair coins are tossed at the same time?

3 Find P(B) for Exercise 17.1 Question 3.

4 What is the value of P(E) in Exercise 17.1 Question 4?

5 There are 14 boys and 16 girls in a classroom. The teacher selects a pupil at random. What is the probability that the chosen pupil is a girl?

6 One hundred raffle tickets numbered from 001 to 100 are well mixed and one ticket is drawn at random. Find the probability that the number on the selected ticket is (a) greater than 090; (b) a multiple of 5; (c) 050.

7 Refer to Table 6.3. If you select one of the 50 pencils at random, what is the probability that it is purple?

8 (a) List all the different ways in which the three letters A, B and C can be written down in any order, without repetition. If you choose one of these sequences at random, what is the probability that it spells the word CAB?

(b) List all the different ways in which the three letters A, B, A can be written down. If you choose one of these sequences at random, what is the probability that it spells the word BAA?

(c) List all the different ways in which the letters A, B, C can be written down in a sequence of three letters when repetition of the same letter is allowed, i.e. AAA and AAB are possible. If you choose one of these sequences at random what is the probability that it spells (i) CAB, (ii) BAA?

9 A bag contains 20 sweets. A fifth are liquorice, half are fruit pastilles and the rest are toffees. How many are toffees? Jim chooses a sweet at random from the bag. What is the probability that it is a toffee?

10 The numbers of properties that an estate agent has on his books are shown in the table.

(a) How many properties are (i) for sale, (ii) for rent, (iii) on the estate agent's books?

(b) One of the properties is selected at random. What is the probability that it is (i) for sale, (ii) a flat to rent?

(c) A detached property is selected at random. What is the probability that it is for rent?

(d) A property is selected at random from those to rent. What is the probability that it is terraced?

(e) A property is selected at random from those for sale. What is the probability that it is semi-detached?

(Compare your answers with those of Exercise 11.1 Question 3).

	For sale	For rent
Detached	20	5
Semi-detached	30	5
Terraced	10	10
Flats	15	40

Relative frequency

We cannot always assume that we have equally likely outcomes. It seems reasonable to think, when we toss a coin, that it will be equally likely to come down heads or tails. When we toss some obviously asymmetrical object such as a drawing pin, however, we cannot assume that it is just as likely to land with the point up as with the point down, see Fig. 17.1. In such cases we perform a series of trials of the experiment and note the number of trials in which the event of interest occurs.

We use:

$$\text{probability of event } E = \mathrm{P}(E) \approx \frac{\text{number of trials in which } E \text{ occurs}}{\text{total number of trials performed}}$$

Thus, if we toss a drawing pin 100 times and find that it lands with its point

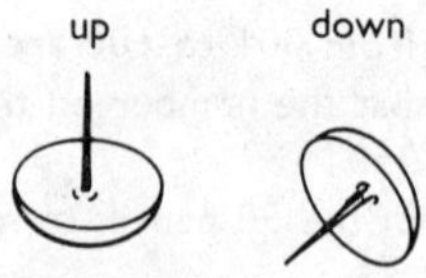

Fig. 17.1 *Tossing a drawing pin*

upwards 80 times, we would estimate the probability of it landing point upwards as 80/100 = 4/5 or 0.8.

This is only an estimate or approximation of P(E) because, if we performed more trials, the value would change. The greater the number of trials, the closer we expect the value to approach the required probability.

This method is referred to as the **relative frequency method** of finding probabilities because we have worked out the proportion or relative frequency of trials in which event E occurred. This estimate of a probability is also called an **empirical probability** because it has been found from an experiment.

Important note

Whether we use the equal likelihood method or the relative frequency method to estimate probabilities, we can see that P(E) must be a value between 0 and 1.

If event E never occurs in any trial, then P(E) = 0 and we say event E is an **impossibility**.

If event E occurs in every trial, P(E) = 1 and we say the event is a **certainty**.

Exercise 17.3

1 Refer to your results from Practical exercise 7.7 Question 2 and use them to estimate the probabilities of obtaining scores 1, 2, 3, 4, 5 and 6. Do you think your die was fair? Explain.
2 Refer to your results from Practical exercise 6.6 Question 3. Estimate the probabilities of the coin landing heads and tails after (i) 30 tosses, (ii) 60 tosses, (iii) 90 tosses and (iv) 120 tosses. Comment on your answers.
3 Refer to your results from Practical exercise 7.7 Question 3. Estimate the probabilities that a selected card is a heart, a club, a diamond and a spade after (i) 36 cards, (ii) 72 cards, (iii) 108 cards and (iv) 144 cards. Comment on your answers.

Complementary events

The **complement** of event E is the event 'not E' and this is denoted by E'. For example

Experiment: rolling a fair die

$$A = \{\text{score on die is an even number}\} = \{2, 4, 6\}$$
$$A' = \{\text{score on die is not an even number}\} = \{1, 3, 5\}$$
$$B = \{\text{score on die is less than 2}\} = \{1\}$$
$$B' = \{\text{score on die is not less than 2}\} = \{2, 3, 4, 5, 6\}$$

Using the equal likelihood method for finding probability we have:

$$P(A) = \frac{3}{6} = \frac{1}{2} \qquad P(A') = \frac{3}{6} = \frac{1}{2}$$

$$P(B) = \frac{1}{6} \qquad P(B') = \frac{5}{6}$$

Hence:

$$P(A) + P(A') = \frac{1}{2} + \frac{1}{2} = 1$$

$$P(B) + P(B') = \frac{1}{6} + \frac{5}{6} = 1$$

In general, for any event E:

$$P(E) + P(\text{not } E) = 1$$

i.e.
$$P(E) + P(E') = 1$$

This relationship may seem trivial but it can be very useful. In some instances it is easier to find the probability that an event does not occur than to find the probability that it does occur.

Odds

Stating the odds for or against the occurrence of an event is an alternative method of presenting a probability. Instead of using a vulgar or a decimal fraction, we express a probability as a ratio in lowest terms. With equally likely outcomes, the odds **against** an event E are:

number of outcomes in E' : number of outcomes in E

For event B, {score on a fair die is less than 2}, the **odds against** B are 5 : 1 or 5 to 1. We could say the odds **on** B happening are 1 to 5 but it is only usual to use this form when $P(E)$ is greater than 0.5.

For empirical probabilities, the odds against an event E are:

number of trials in which E' occurs : number of trials in which E occurs

If we toss a drawing pin 100 times and it lands point upward 80 times, the odds against it landing point upwards are:

$$20:80 = 1:4$$

In this case it is more likely to land point upwards than point downwards, so we would say that the odds **on** it landing point upwards are 4 : 1 or 4 to 1.

For event A, {score on a fair die is an even number}, the odds **against** A are 3 : 3 or 1 : 1 and the odds **on** A are also 1 : 1. In this situation we say the odds on or against A occurring are **evens** or **fifty-fifty**!

We can always rewrite odds as probabilities if we wish. For example, we are told that the odds of getting a red sweet from a bag containing different colours of sweets are 7 to 1 against. This implies that for every red sweet there are 7 that are not red. Hence,

$$\text{P(getting a red sweet)} = \frac{1}{1+7} = \frac{1}{8}$$

$$\text{P(getting a non-red sweet)} = \frac{7}{1+7} = \frac{7}{8}$$

$$\text{check: P(red) + P(not red)} = \frac{1}{8} + \frac{7}{8} = 1$$

Betting odds

Betting odds are different from the 'true' odds defined above. Betting odds indicate how much money a gambler stands to win, ignoring betting tax, if any, for a given stake.

For example, if the odds for a horse are quoted as 5 to 1, this indicates that, if the horse wins, gamblers will gain £5 for every £1 they have staked on this horse. If the odds are 4 to 1, they will gain only £4 for a £1 stake and we say the odds are **shorter**. It is usual to assume that the odds quoted are against the horse winning. If the odds are in favour of the horse winning, this is specifically stated. If a horse is 2 to 1 **on** then gamblers will gain £1 for every £2 staked, i.e. 50p for every £1 staked, assuming the horse wins.

Betting odds are not based on probabilities such as we have evaluated earlier. We cannot assume, for example, that each horse is equally likely to win nor do the horses keep running the same race under identical conditions.

In a totaliser or pool betting system, a percentage (e.g. 30%) of the money staked is set aside for administration costs and profit. The remaining money goes into the win pool and a place pool (if there are more than six horses running) and the odds are determined in relation to the money staked on each horse.

A bookmaker can give whatever odds he chooses but he tries to ensure that he makes a profit whichever horse wins or at least that he minimises his loss. Punters also expect a bookmaker's odds to be fair in the sense that the bookmaker is not guaranteed an unduly large profit.

Exercise 17.4

1 A fair six-sided die is tossed. Write down the complements of the following events.
(a) A = {score is an odd number}
(b) B = {score is at least 3}
(c) C = {score is not more than 1}
(d) D = {score is greater than 4}
(e) E = {score is 2 or more}

2 A bag contains 8 red sweets, 10 yellow sweets and 14 green sweets. Gina selects a sweet at random. What is the probability that it is not red?

3 Two fair coins are tossed together. What is the probability that not more than one head results?

4 Tom bought 60 hyacinth bulbs, 10 were pink, 20 were blue and 30 were white. If he selects a bulb at random, what are the odds that it is (a) pink, (b) blue, (c) white?

5 A patient is told that the odds on his recovery after major surgery are 2 to 1. What is the probability that he will recover?

6 A retailer tells a customer that the odds are 3 to 1 against a three-piece suite being delivered within two weeks. What is the probability that the suite will be delivered within two weeks?

7 Joe goes to a race meeting. He stakes £5 on the horse Speedy to win the first race at odds of 3 to 1 against. He puts £10 on Allegro to win the second race at evens. At the end of these two races, list the different sums of money he could have won or lost.

8 At a race meeting, Lucy puts a £1 stake on Stagecoach which wins the first race at 8 to 1 against. She stakes her winnings plus her original £1 stake on Express which wins the second race at 2 to 1 on. How much money has she gained at the end of these two races?

9 Four horses A, B, C and D are the only runners in a race. A bookmaker gives the following odds:

A 4 to 1, B 5 to 1, C 3 to 1, D evens.

Work out how much the bookmaker gains or loses if (i) A wins, (ii) B wins, (iii) C wins, (iv) D wins,

when (a) £100 is staked on each horse;
(b) £50 is staked on each of A and B and £100 is staked on each of C and D;
(c) £150 is staked on A, £100 on B, £200 on C and £1000 on D.

Venn diagram

We can use a Venn diagram to represent a sample space and events. We draw a rectangle to enclose all the outcomes in the sample space S. A closed curve is used to surround those outcomes in the event of interest. Figure 17.2 shows a Venn diagram for the sample space S, the score on a die, and the event A, the score is an even number. The size of A is unimportant, although it must be entirely within S, and the shape of A does not matter.

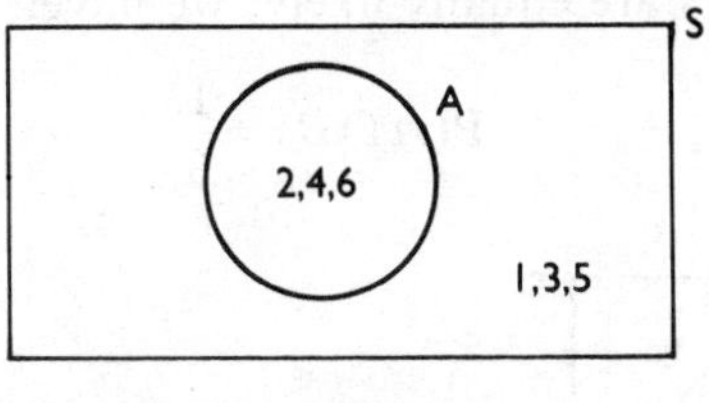

Fig. 17.2 *Venn diagram*

Union of events

If we have two events, A and B, in a sample space, we represent them by overlapping closed curves, in general, as in Fig. 17.3. The shaded area represents the union of events A and B and is denoted by $A \cup B$. It contains all outcomes that are in A or in B, or in both.

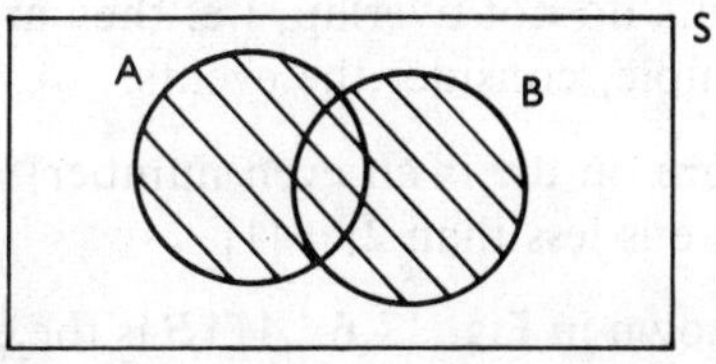

Fig. 17.3 $A \cup B$

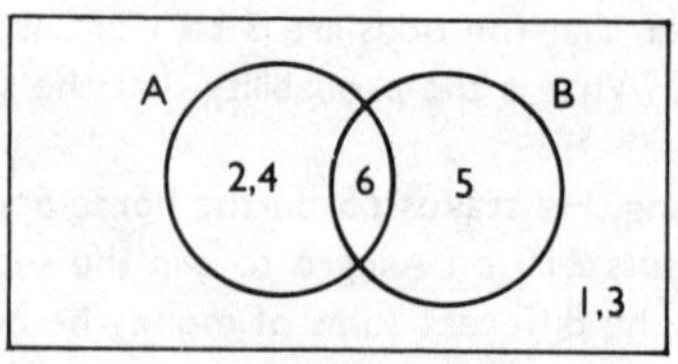

Fig. 17.4 *Venn diagram*

For example, in the experiment rolling a fair die, consider the events:

$$A = \{\text{score on die is an even number}\} = \{2, 4, 6\}$$
$$B = \{\text{score greater than } 4\} = \{5, 6\}$$

The Venn diagram to represent these events is shown in Fig. 17.4.

$$A \cup B = \{\text{score is an even number } \textbf{or} \text{ greater than } 4\} = \{2, 4, 5, 6\}$$

Assuming the outcomes are equally likely, we have:

$$P(A \cup B) = \frac{4}{6} = \frac{2}{3}$$

Intersection of events

The shaded area in Fig. 17.5 represents the intersection of events A and B. It is denoted by $A \cap B$ and contains any outcomes that are in both A and B. Using the example shown in Fig. 17.4:

$$A \cap B = \{\text{score is an even number } \textbf{and} \text{ greater than } 4\} = \{6\}$$

Assuming the outcomes are equally likely, we have:

$$P(A \cap B) = \frac{1}{6}$$

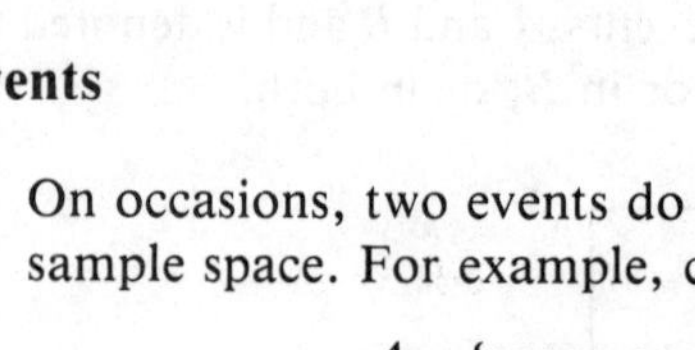

Fig. 17.5 A∩B

Mutually exclusive events

On occasions, two events do not overlap, i.e. they are disjoint subsets of the sample space. For example, consider the events:

$$A = \{\text{score on die is an even number}\} = \{2, 4, 6\}$$
$$B = \{\text{score is less than } 2\} = \{1\}$$

The Venn diagram is shown in Fig. 17.6. $A \cap B$ is the empty set as there are no outcomes common to both A and B and $P(A \cap B) = 0$. In such cases we say we

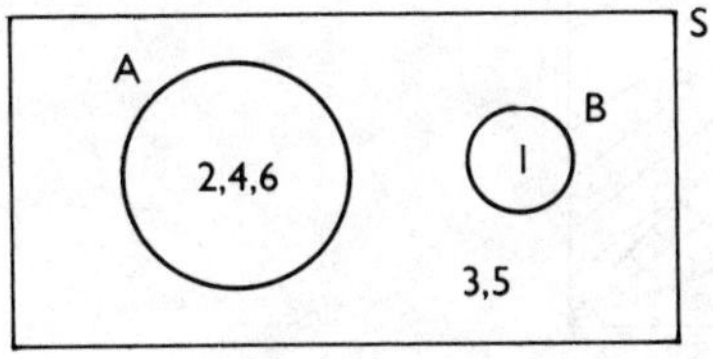

Fig. 17.6 *Mutually exclusive events*

have mutually exclusive events, i.e. if event A occurs, event B does not occur and vice-versa.

Addition law

From Fig. 17.6:

$$A \cup B = \{\text{score on die is an even number or less than } 2\}$$
$$= \{1, 2, 4, 6\}$$

$$P\{A \cup B\} = \frac{4}{6} = \frac{2}{3}$$

But we know:

$$P(A) = \frac{3}{6} = \frac{1}{2} \qquad P(B) = \frac{1}{6}$$

$$P(A) + P(B) = \frac{1}{2} + \frac{1}{6} = \frac{2}{3} = P(A \cup B)$$

This illustrates the special addition law for mutually exclusive events:

$$P(A \cup B) = P(A) + P(B)$$

It can be extended to more than two mutually exclusive events in the same way. For example,

$$P(A \cup B \cup C) = P(A) + P(B) + P(C)$$

In general, the addition law for any two events is:

$$P(A \cup B) = P(A) + P(B) - P(A \cap B)$$

For the example shown in Fig. 17.4:

$$P(A \cup B) = \frac{3}{6} + \frac{2}{6} - \frac{1}{6}$$

$$= \frac{4}{6} = \frac{2}{3}$$

This agrees with the result obtained directly from the Venn diagram.

Exhaustive events

If we have a number of events in a sample space, S, and their union is S, we say the events are exhaustive. For example, in the experiment rolling a die,

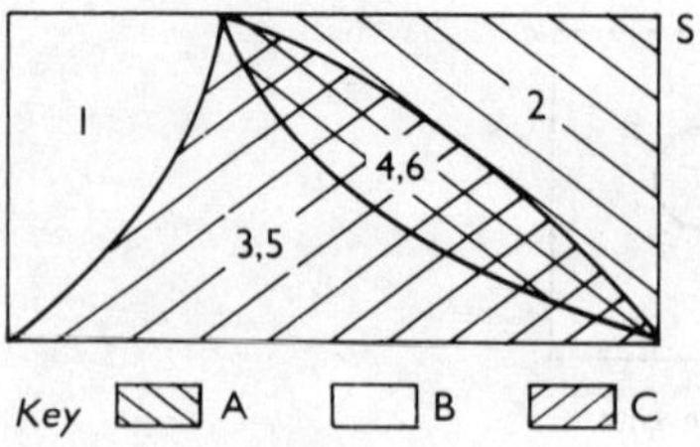

Fig. 17.7 *Exhaustive events*

consider the events:

$$A = \{\text{score on die is an even number}\} = \{2, 4, 6\}$$
$$B = \{\text{score less than 2}\} = \{1\}$$
$$C = \{\text{score is 3 or more}\} = \{3, 4, 5, 6\}$$

When we draw the Venn diagram, Fig. 17.7, we see that every outcome is in at least one of the events so $A \cup B \cup C = S$.

When we have the special case that exhaustive events are also mutually exclusive, we know that one, and only one, of them is certain to happen and the probabilities of these events must sum to one.

For example, consider the events:

$$A = \{\text{score on die is an even number}\} = \{2, 4, 6\}$$
$$B = \{\text{score less than 2}\} = \{1\}$$
$$C = \{\text{score is an odd number greater than 1}\} = \{3, 5\}$$

The Venn diagram is shown in Fig. 17.8. The events do not overlap, so using the special addition law for mutually exclusive events:

$$P(A \cup B \cup C) = P(A) + P(B) + P(C)$$

we know

$$A \cup B \cup C = S$$

Hence

$$P(A) + P(B) + P(C) = 1$$

check:

$$P(A) = \frac{3}{6},\ P(B) = \frac{1}{6},\ P(C) = \frac{2}{6} \text{ so } P(A) + P(B) + P(C) = \frac{6}{6} = 1$$

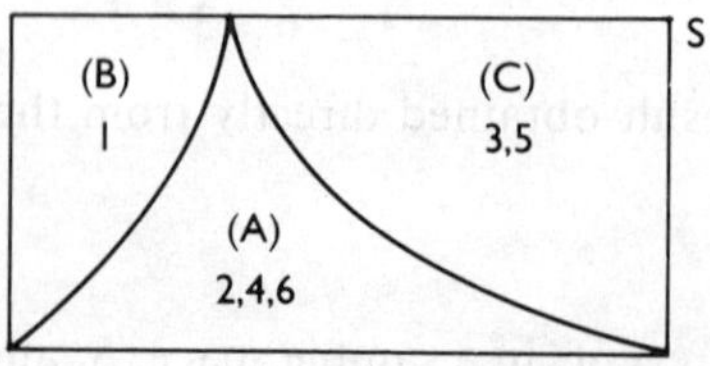

Fig. 17.8 *Mutually exclusive and exhaustive events*

Exercise 17.5

1 Draw a Venn diagram for the following experiment and events.
Experiment: Twelve identical pieces of card are numbered 1, 2, ... 12 and put in a bag. One card is selected at random and the number on it is noted.
Event A: {number on card is even}
Event B: {number on card is divisible by 3}
What outcomes are in the event $A \cup B$? Write down the values of $P(A)$, $P(B)$, $P(A \cup B)$ and $P(A \cap B)$. Check that your values satisfy the addition law.

2 One card is drawn at random from a pack of 52 cards. What is the probability that it is (a) a spade, (b) a Queen, (c) the Queen of spades, (d) a Queen or a spade?

3 Gareth can go to school by bus, cycle or on foot. The probability that he goes by bus is 0.6 and the probability that he cycles is 0.3. What is the probability that he does not go to school on foot?

4 Jaybury plc pays weekly wages to its 100 manual employees as shown.

Wage (£)	90	100	110	120
Number of employees	20	30	40	10

What is the probability that an employee selected at random has a weekly wage of (i) £100, (ii) £110, (iii) £100 or £110, (iv) more than £100, (v) less than £100?
What relationships are there between your answers
(a) to (i), (ii) and (iii);
(b) to (i), (iv), and (v)?

5 The probability that a (randomly selected) pupil at Kaybury school plays tennis is 0.8. The probability that a pupil plays hockey is 0.5 and the probability that a pupil plays both hockey and tennis is 0.4.
(a) What is the probability that a pupil plays hockey or tennis?
(b) What is the probability that a pupil plays tennis but not hockey?
(c) What is the probability that a pupil plays neither hockey nor tennis?

Independent events

Up to now, in order to work out $P(A \cap B)$, the probability that both event A and event B have occurred, we have identified the outcomes in $A \cap B$ in the sample space. If A and B are independent events, however, we can use the special multiplication law:

$$P(A \cap B) = P(A) \times P(B)$$

Event A and event B are independent if the probability of B occurring is unaffected by whether or not A has also occurred and vice versa.

Experiment: select a card at random from a pack of 52 cards

Event A: card is a spade $\quad P(A) = \frac{13}{52} = \frac{1}{4}$

Event B: card is a Queen $\quad P(B) = \frac{4}{52} = \frac{1}{13}$

Event $A \cap B$: card is a Queen and a spade, i.e. card is the Queen of spades.

Events A and B are independent because there are equal numbers of cards of each suit and each value in the pack. The probability of selecting a Queen is not influenced by the suit and the probability of obtaining a spade is not affected by the value of the card.

Applying the multiplication law:

$$P(A \cap B) = P(A) \times P(B) = \frac{1}{4} \times \frac{1}{13} = \frac{1}{52}$$

This agrees with the result we get directly knowing that there is just one Queen of spades in a pack of 52 cards.

The multiplication law can be extended similarly to more than two independent events. For example,

$$P(A \cap B \cap C) = P(A) \times P(B) \times P(C)$$

Dependent events

If events A and B are not independent, they are dependent and the probability that B occurs depends on whether or not A has occurred. We write $P(B \text{ given } A)$ to stand for the conditional probability that event B occurs, given that event A has occurred.

The multiplication law is then modified to give:

$$P(A \cap B) = P(A) \times P(B \text{ given } A)$$

or

$$P(A \cap B) = P(B) \times P(A \text{ given } B), \text{ by symmetry}$$

In Exercise 17.1 Question 3 you considered the ten cards: Ace, King, Queen, Jack of spades, Ace, King, Queen of hearts, Ace, King of diamonds and the Ace of clubs.

Experiment: select a card at random from these ten cards.

Event A: card is a spade $\quad P(A) = \frac{4}{10} = \frac{2}{5}$

Event B: card is a Queen $\quad P(B) = \frac{2}{10} = \frac{1}{5}$

Event $A \cap B$; card is the Queen of spades

Directly we can see that $P(A \cap B) = 1/10$ and $P(A) \times P(B) = 2/25$ so $P(A \cap B) \neq P(A) \times P(B)$.

Events A and B are dependent in this experiment because we have different numbers of cards in the four suits.

Event B given A: card is a Queen given that it is a spade.
To work out $P(B \text{ given } A)$ we have to look only at the spade cards. Our sample space has changed from all ten cards to the four spade cards, one of which is a Queen.

$$P(B \text{ given } A) = \frac{1}{4}$$

Event A given B: card is a spade given that it is a Queen.

Here the new sample space contains just the two queens, one of which is spade.

$$P(A \text{ given } B) = \frac{1}{2}$$

Using the general multiplication law, we obtain the correct value for the probability of selecting the Queen of spades.

$$P(A \cap B) = P(A) \times P(B \text{ given } A) = \frac{2}{5} \times \frac{1}{4} = \frac{1}{10}$$

or
$$P(A \cap B) = P(B) \times P(A \text{ given } B) = \frac{1}{5} \times \frac{1}{2} = \frac{1}{10}$$

Tree diagram

A tree diagram is a useful way of analysing a compound event into a sequence of single events. We obtain an exhaustive list, i.e. all possible events are considered. The event represented by a complete branch of the tree is mutually exclusive of the events represented by other branches.

Example 1

Sampling without replacement

Draw a tree diagram to represent the following experiment.

A bag contains 12 cards of the same size. Four cards are red and eight are blue. A card is selected at random and its colour is noted. The card is not replaced. A second card is then selected at random from those remaining in the bag and its colour noted.

The tree is shown in Fig. 17.9. We work from a point on the left of the diagram. At the start we take a card from the bag. It is either red or blue so we draw two branches labelled R and B corresponding to the two possibilities. We write in the probabilities associated with each branch. Thus $P(R) = 4/12$ and $P(B) = 8/12$ as there were 4 red and 8 blue cards in the bag.

We now consider the second card. It can be red or blue, so we draw branches representing these possibilities at the end of each of the two branches representing the colour of the first card. We write in the conditional probability associated with each branch.

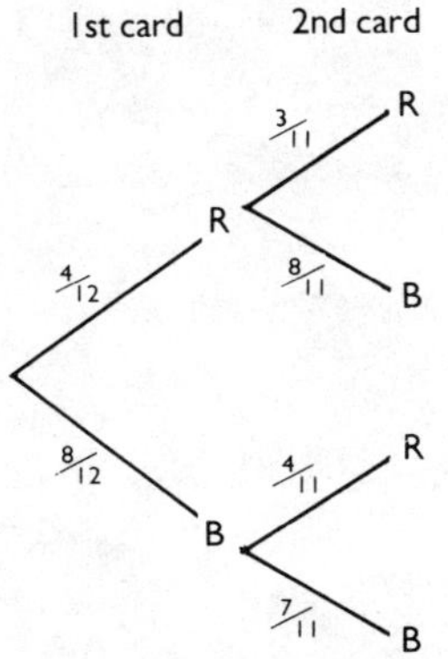

Fig. 17.9 *Tree diagram for sampling without replacement*

If the first card is red, there are three red cards and eight blue cards left in the bag.

$$P(\text{2nd card is red given 1st card is red}) = \frac{3}{11}$$

$$P(\text{2nd card is blue given 1st card is red}) = \frac{8}{11}$$

If the first card is blue, there are four red cards and seven blue cards left in the bag.

$$P(\text{2nd card is red given 1st card is blue}) = \frac{4}{11}$$

$$P(\text{2nd card is blue given 1st card is blue}) = \frac{7}{11}$$

Table 17.1 Sampling without replacement

Event	Probability
RR	$\frac{4}{12} \times \frac{3}{11} = \frac{1}{11}$
RB	$\frac{4}{12} \times \frac{8}{11} = \frac{8}{33}$
BR	$\frac{8}{12} \times \frac{4}{11} = \frac{8}{33}$
BB	$\frac{8}{12} \times \frac{7}{11} = \frac{14}{33}$
Total	1

We can list all the different events as in Table 17.1. The probabilities are worked out using the general multiplication law.

We can then pick out the probabilities that are of interest. For instance,

$$P(\text{both cards are red}) = P(RR) = \frac{1}{11}$$

$$\begin{aligned} P(\text{one red card and one blue card}) &= P(RB \text{ or } BR) \\ &= P(RB) + P(BR), \text{ since each branch is mutually exclusive} \\ &= \frac{8}{33} + \frac{8}{33} \\ &= \frac{16}{33} \end{aligned}$$

Example 2

Sampling with replacement

Draw a tree diagram to represent the following experiment.

A bag contains 12 cards of the same size. Four cards are red and eight are blue. A card is selected at random and its colour is noted. The card is replaced. A second card is then selected at random and its colour is noted.

The tree is shown in Fig. 17.10. Its form is exactly the same as for Example 1 and, for the first card, $P(R) = 4/12$ and $P(B) = 8/12$, as before. Because the first

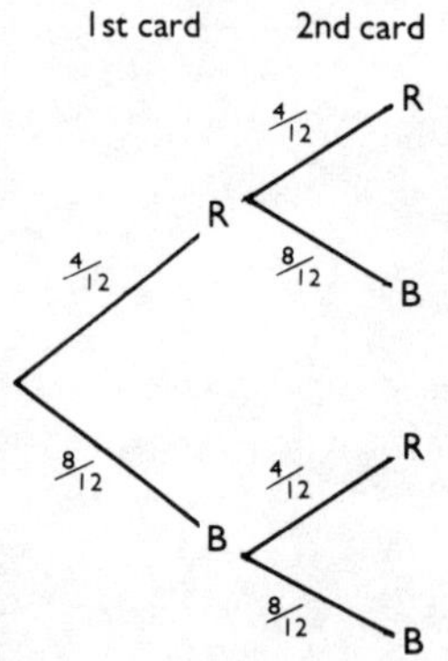

Fig. 17.10 *Tree diagram for sampling with replacement*

Table 17.2 Sampling with replacement

Event	Probability
RR	$\frac{4}{12}\times\frac{4}{12}=\frac{1}{9}$
RB	$\frac{4}{12}\times\frac{8}{12}=\frac{2}{9}$
BR	$\frac{8}{12}\times\frac{4}{12}=\frac{2}{9}$
BB	$\frac{8}{12}\times\frac{8}{12}=\frac{4}{9}$
Total	1

card was replaced before the second card was selected, however, the probability that the second card is red is also 4/12 and the probability that it is blue is 8/12, regardless of the colour of the first card. In this situation the colour of the second card is independent of the colour of the first card.

The different possible events are listed in Table 17.2. The probabilities are worked out using the multiplication law for independent events.

$$\text{P(both cards are red)} = \frac{1}{9}$$

$$\text{P(one red card and one blue card)} = \frac{2}{9} + \frac{2}{9} = \frac{4}{9}$$

Tree diagrams can have any number of stages. In some situations there may be more than two possibilities at one branching point in the diagram, so we will then need to draw more than two branches from this one point. At every stage in the diagram, the probabilities on the branches radiating from one point must sum to one. This is a useful check.

Exercise 17.6

1 A coin and a six-sided die are tossed together. Assuming they are both fair, what is the probability that (a) the die shows three; (b) the coin lands heads; (c) the die shows a three and the coin lands heads?

2 The probability that Kevin goes to a youth club on Thursday evening is 2/3. The probability that Brian goes, provided he knows that Kevin is going, is 7/8. What is the probability that both of them go the youth club on Thursday evening?

3 Alka has a bag containing three yellow sweets and four green sweets. She selects a sweet at random and eats it.

(a) What is the probability that the first sweet she eats is yellow?

(b) Draw a tree diagram to show all the different possible sequences of colours of the first two sweets she eats.

(c) What is the probability that the first two sweets she eats are both green?

(d) What is the probability that the first two sweets she eats are the same colour?

(e) What is the probability that the first two sweets she eats are different colours?

(f) How many sweets does she need to eat to be certain of eating a green one?

4 Cyrus has a bag containing three yellow sweets, four green sweets and two red sweets. He selects a sweet at random and eats it.

(a) What is the probability that the first sweet he eats is yellow?

(b) Draw a tree diagram to show all the different possible sequences of colours of the first two sweets he eats.

(c) What is the probability that the first two sweets he eats are both green?

(d) What is the probability that the first two sweets he eats are the same colour?

(e) What is the probability that the first two sweets he eats are different colours?

(f) How many sweets does he need to eat to be certain of eating a green one?

5 From a study of birth statistics it has been estimated that the probability of a baby being male is 0.51 and the probability of a baby being female is 0.49. The Smith family have one child and the Jones family have one child. What is the probability that both the children are girls?

6 A coin has been weighted so that, at any one toss, the probability of it landing heads is 0.6. The coin is tossed three times. Draw a tree diagram to show the different possible sequences of outcomes. What is the probability of obtaining (a) exactly three heads; (b) exactly one head; (c) a head on the third toss?

7 A bag contains three yellow beads, four green beads and two red beads. One bead is selected at random and its colour is noted. It is then returned to the bag. A second bead is selected similarly and its colour is also noted.

(a) Draw a tree diagram to show the different possible sequences of colours of the two beads.

(b) What is the probability that they are both green?

(c) What is the probability that the two beads are the same colour?

(d) What is the probability that the two beads are different colours?

8 A bag contains eight yellow beads, four red beads and two green beads. A bead is selected at random and its colour is noted. It is then replaced. A second bead is selected similarly and replaced. A third bead is selected at random and its colour noted.

(a) Draw a tree diagram to show all the different possible sequences of colours of the three beads.

(b) What is the probability that the three beads are all the same colour?

(c) What is the probability that each of the three beads is a different colour?

Probability distributions

When we observed a discrete variable in Chapter 7, we summarised our results in a frequency table, Table 7.10, giving the number of times each value of the variable occurred. If we can work out theoretically the probabilities of obtaining the different values of a variable, we can summarise them similarly using a probability distribution.

Refer to Table 17.1 and Fig. 17.9 (Example 1 in the last section), where we sampled two cards without replacement. Suppose we are interested in the variable 'number of blue cards selected'. We denote the values a variable can take by x, so $x = 0$, 1 or 2. We use $p(x)$ to stand for the probability that the variable takes the value x. $p(x)$ is called the **probability function**.

$$p(0) = P(0 \text{ blue cards}) = P(RR) = \frac{1}{11}$$

$$p(1) = P(1 \text{ blue card}) = P(RB) + P(BR) = \frac{16}{33}$$

$$p(2) = P(2 \text{ blue cards}) = P(BB) = \frac{14}{33}$$

Table 17.3 Probability distribution for Example 1

x	$p(x)$
0	$\frac{1}{11}$
1	$\frac{16}{33}$
2	$\frac{14}{33}$
Total	1

We list these results as in Table 17.3 to form a **probability distribution**. Note $\Sigma p(x) = 1$.

By analogy with a frequency distribution, we can illustrate a probability distribution using a bar chart, Fig. 17.11. We can also find the mean of the

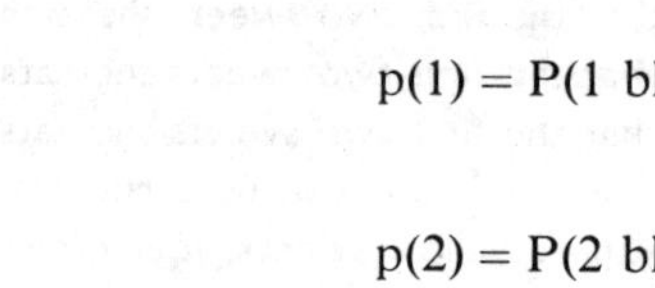

Fig. 17.11 *Bar chart*

distribution. We use the Greek letter μ (mu) to stand for the mean as it is a theoretical value and not a value that we have found from a sample of observations.

$$\text{Mean } \mu = \frac{\Sigma x\text{p}(x)}{\Sigma \text{p}(x)} = \Sigma x\text{p}(x) \text{ since } \Sigma\text{p}(x) = 1$$

$$\left(\text{Compare } \bar{x} = \frac{\Sigma fx}{\Sigma f} \text{ or } \frac{\Sigma xf}{\Sigma f}\right)$$

From Table 17.3:

$$\mu = \left(0 \times \frac{1}{11}\right) + \left(1 \times \frac{16}{33}\right) + \left(2 \times \frac{14}{33}\right) = \frac{16}{33} + \frac{28}{33} = \frac{44}{33} = 1\tfrac{1}{3}$$

We can say that, in the long run, when we select two cards without replacement from the original 12 cards, we expect to get $1\frac{1}{3}$ blue cards each time!

Binomial distribution

Some statistical experiments have the same patterns of probabilities and we may be able to find a general formula for p(x) that can be used as a model in many different situations. The binomial distribution is a particularly important probability distribution.

Consider a trial where there are just two possible outcomes. It is convenient to call these outcomes success (S) and failure (F), although this does not imply that one outcome is favourable and the other is not. Let p be the probability of success in one trial and let q be the probability of failure, so $p + q = 1$, using the rule for complementary events. When the trial is repeated, we assume that the values p and q remain the same, i.e. successive trials are independent. We want to find p(x), the probability of exactly x successes in a specified number of trials.

We can detect the pattern by using a series of tree diagrams, Figs. 17.12, 17.13 and 17.14.

Table 17.4 One trial

Number of successes (x)	Probability p(x)
0	q
1	p
Total	$q + p = 1$

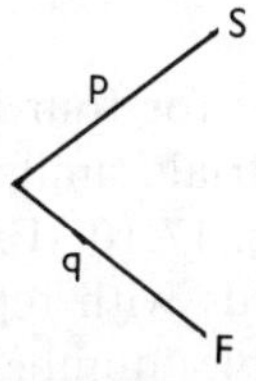

Fig. 17.12 *1 trial*

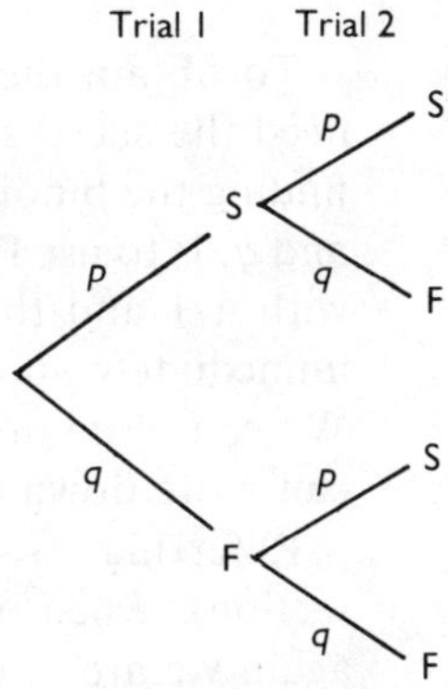

Fig. 17.13 *2 trials*

Table 17.5 Two trials

Number of successes (x)	Probability $p(x)$
0	q^2
1	$qp + pq = 2qp$
2	p^2
Total	$q^2 + 2qp + p^2 = (q+p)^2 = 1$

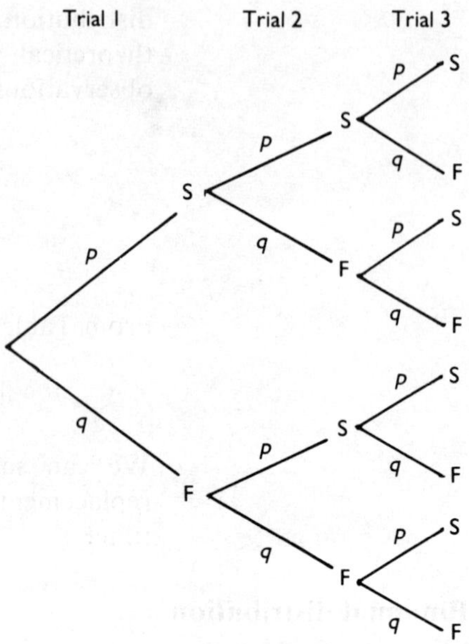

Fig. 17.14 *3 trials*

Table 17.6 Three trials

Number of successes (x)	Probability $p(x)$
0	q^3
1	$q^2p + qpq + pq^2 = 3q^2p$
2	$qp^2 + pqp + p^2q = 3qp^2$
3	p^3
Total	$q^3 + 3q^2p + 3qp^2 + p^3 = (q+p)^3 = 1$

Table 17.7 Pascal's triangle and binomial expansions

Pascal's triangle	Binomial expansion
1	$(q+p)^0 = 1$
1 1	$(q+p)^1 = q + p$
1 2 1	$(q+p)^2 = q^2 + 2qp + p^2$
1 3 3 1	$(q+p)^3 = q^3 + 3q^2p + 3qp^2 + p^3$
1 4 6 4 1	$(q+p)^4 = q^4 + 4q^3p + 6q^2p^2 + 4qp^3 + p^4$
1 5 10 10 5 1	$(q+p)^5 = q^5 + 5q^4p + 10q^3p^2 + 10q^2p^3 + 5qp^4 + p^5$

To obtain the probabilities for four trials, you will have realised that we need the successive terms in the binomial expansion of $(q+p)^4$. One way of finding the binomial coefficients, i.e. the numbers multiplying the powers of p and q, is to use Pascal's triangle, Table 17.7. Each row starts with a 1 and ends with a 1 and the intermediate coefficients are the sum of the two numbers immediately above.
We can write down the probabilities for four trials as in Table 17.8 and you can write down the results for five trials similarly.

Referring to Table 17.2 and Fig. 17.10 (Example 2 in the last but one section), when we sampled two cards with replacement, let us suppose that again we are interested in the variable 'number of blue cards selected', i.e. a success is obtaining a blue card.

Table 17.8 4 trials

Number of successes (x)	Probability $p(x)$
0	q^4
1	$4q^3p$
2	$6q^2p^2$
3	$4qp^3$
4	p^4
Total	1

Because we sampled with replacement, the probability, p, of selecting a blue card at any one trial is always $8/12 = 2/3$. It is only possible to obtain a blue card or a red card so we can use a binomial model. We have:

$$p = \frac{2}{3}$$

$$q = 1 - p = 1 - \frac{2}{3} = \frac{1}{3}$$

$$\text{number of trials} = \text{number of cards selected} = 2$$

From Table 17.5 we can work out the probabilities as shown in Table 17.9. You can confirm that the results agree with those obtained before.

Table 17.9 Probability distribution for Example 2

Number of blue cards (x)	Probability $p(x)$
0	$q^2 = \left(\frac{1}{3}\right)^2 = \frac{1}{9}$
1	$2qp = 2\left(\frac{1}{3}\right)\left(\frac{2}{3}\right) = \frac{4}{9}$
2	$p^2 = \left(\frac{2}{3}\right)^2 = \frac{4}{9}$
Total	1

Examples of trials where the binomial model can be used, provided successive trials are independent are:

Trial	*Success*	*Failure*
Tossing a coin	Heads	Tails
Birth of a child	Girl	Boy
Testing a product	Defective	Non-defective
Rolling a die	Score 6	Score not 6
Selecting a card from a pack	Diamond	Not a diamond

Exercise 17.7

1 A bag contains three yellow beads and five green beads. One bead is selected at random, its colour is noted and it is not replaced. A second bead is selected at random, its colour is noted and is not replaced. A third bead is selected at random, its colour is noted and it is not replaced. The variable of interest is 'the number of yellow beads selected'.

(a) What are the values, x, taken by this variable?

(b) By using a tree diagram, or otherwise, find the probability distribution of x.

(c) Draw a bar chart to represent the probability distribution.

(d) What is the mean number of yellow beads selected?

2 A fair coin is tossed three times. What is the probability that (a) three heads are obtained; (b) exactly one head is obtained; (c) not more than one head is obtained?

3 A seed company claims that the probability of a sweet corn seed germinating is 0.8. I sow four such seeds. What is probability that (a) just two seeds germinate; (b) more than two seeds germinate?

4 The probability function

$$p(x) = \frac{1}{3}\left(\frac{2}{3}\right)^{x-1}, x = 1, 2, 3, \ldots$$

gives the probability that a learner driver needs to take x driving tests before passing. Use this formula to find the probability that a learner needs to take more than two tests. (Hint: use P(A) = 1 − P(not A).)

5 Find, in terms of p, the mean number of successes, μ, for a general binomial distribution with (a) 1 trial, Table 17.4; (b) 2 trials, Table 17.5; (c) 3 trials, Table 17.6. What do you think is the value of μ after (d) 4 trials; (e) 5 trials; (f) n trials?

6 A coin and a six-sided die are tossed together. If a head appears, the score is recorded as the number shown on the die. If a tail appears, the score is recorded as one less than the number shown on the die. Assuming the coin and the die are fair, draw a tree diagram to show the different possible outcomes. Construct the probability distribution p(x), where x is the recorded score.

Simulation

It often takes a long time to make a detailed practical investigation of variables that are subject to random variation, such as traffic flows or lengths of supermarket queues. If we already have some information about a system or we feel justified in making certain assumptions, we may be able to simulate its long-term behaviour using random digits, see Table 13.1. We shall set up simulation models for some simple experiments. It is usual to use a computer to carry out a simulation because it is essential to consider a large number of trials.

To simulate a discrete variable we need to be able to make some assumptions about its probability distribution.

Example 1

Simulation of tossing a fair coin
Variable: number of heads, $x = 0, 1$
Probabilities: $p(0) = 0.5 \quad p(1) = 0.5$
Half the time we expect the outcome $x = 0$ (tails) and half the time we expect the outcome $x = 1$ (heads). There are ten single digits 0, 1, 2, 3, 4, 5, 6, 7, 8, 9 so if we allocate half of them, say, 0, 1, 2, 3, 4 to the outcome $x = 0$ and the other half 5, 6, 7, 8, 9 to the outcome $x = 1$, the digits will represent the outcomes in the correct proportions.

To perform the simulation we read off random digits from a table, calculator or computer. Using Table 13.1 and starting in the top left hand corner, the simulation starts as shown in Table 17.10. The simulation continues in the same way for as many trials as desired, preferably more than 100.

Table 17.10 Simulation of tossing a fair coin

Trial	Random digit	x	Outcome
1	2	0	*T*
2	1	0	*T*
3	1	0	*T*
4	7	1	*H*

Example 2

Simulation of tossing two biased coins, where $P(H) = 0.4$ for each coin. (It would be difficult to obtain two coins with this property in practice but using a simulation model we can investigate the system fully.)
Variable: number of heads, $x = 0, 1, 2$.
The probability distribution, using a binomial model, is shown in Table 17.11.

Table 17.11 Probability distribution for two biased coins

Number of heads (x)	p(x)	
0	0.6^2	$= 0.36$
1	$2 \times 0.6 \times 0.4$	$= 0.48$
2	0.4^2	$= 0.16$
Total		1.00

Table 17.12 Simulation of tossing two biased coins

Trial	Random number	x
1	21	0
2	17	0
3	11	0
4	65	1

Because the probabilities have two decimal places, we need to use two-digit random numbers for this simulation. To get each value of x to occur in the correct proportion in the long run, we assign the two-digit numbers as follows:

00, 01, 02, ..., 35 correspond to $x = 0$ (36 numbers)
36, 37, 38, ..., 83 correspond to $x = 1$ (48 numbers)
84, 85, 86, ..., 99 correspond to $x = 2$ (16 numbers)

Reading off two-digit random numbers from Table 13.1, starting in the top left hand corner, the simulation starts as shown in Table 17.12. (In practice it is best to generate a new set of random numbers for each simulation or to use a random starting point in the random number tables.)

Example 3

I have to pass through three sets of traffic lights on my way to work. Set 1 has green in my direction for 25% of the time, set 2 has green in my direction for 30% of the time and set 3 has green in my direction for 40% of the time. The lights are far enough apart for them to be considered independent. Use random numbers to simulate the colour of the lights on my journey to work for 10 days. On how many days are all three sets at green when I reach them?

We can simulate each set of lights in turn by allocating random numbers as shown in Table 17.13.

Table 17.13 Allocation of random numbers

		Probability	Random numbers
First lights	Green	0.25	00, 01, ..., 24
	Not green	0.75	25, 26, ..., 99
Second lights	Green	0.3	0, 1, 2
	Not green	0.7	3, 4, 5, 6, 7, 8, 9
Third lights	Green	0.4	0, 1, 2, 3
	Not green	0.6	4, 5, 6, 7, 8, 9

Starting from the top left hand corner of Table 13.1, we read two digits (21) for the random number simulating the first lights, one digit (1) for the random number simulating the second lights and one digit (7) for the random number simulating the third lights. Referring to Table 17.13 we see that this corresponds to the first two lights being green and the third one not green. The simulation for 10 days is shown in Table 17.14. There are two days, Day 3 and Day 7 on which all three lights are at green. You might like to continue the simulation for more days and estimate the proportion of days on which all three sets are at green.

Table 17.14 Simulation of 3 traffic lights

	First lights		Second lights		Third lights	
Day	Random number	Green	Random number	Green	Random number	Green
1	21	Yes	1	Yes	7	No
2	11	Yes	6	No	5	No
3	00	Yes	2	Yes	2	Yes
4	77	No	2	Yes	1	Yes
5	83	No	1	Yes	6	No
6	21	Yes	4	No	9	No
7	08	Yes	3	Yes	2	Yes
8	38	No	9	No	6	No
9	81	No	2	Yes	2	Yes
10	52	No	1	Yes	5	No

Exercise 17.8

1 You are to simulate the tossing of two fair coins using random number tables. Draw up the probability distribution for the number of heads when the two coins are tossed. Assign random numbers to the different values of x and use Table 13.1 or other random numbers to simulate 10 tosses.

2 Each year Keith's grandmother goes to one of four seaside resorts for a fortnight's holiday. The resorts are Abury-on-sea, Ebury-on-sea, Ibury-on-sea and Ohbury-on-sea. She selects one of them at random each year. Use random numbers to simulate her holiday destination for each of the next eight years.

3 The message 'THE ENEMY ARE ATTACKING ON THE EASTERN FRONT' is to be transmitted in Morse code. Unfortunately the signalling equipment is faulty so that the probability of a letter (or space) being received is 0.7. Use random number tables to simulate the incoming message. Can you understand the message?

4 The number of customers entering a shop in 100 five-minute periods were observed and the results are shown in the table.

Number of customers	Number of periods
0	3
1	13
2	28
3	31
4	15
5	7
6	3
Total	100

Assign random numbers to the different values of x so that each value is represented in proportion to the number of observations. Using random numbers, simulate the number of arrivals at the shop for 20 five-minute periods.

Practical exercise 17.9

1 The class requires a box of drawing pins. Each member of the class should select a drawing pin and toss it 50 times, recording each time whether the pin lands point up or point down. After each toss, work out the empirical probability of the pin landing point up. Plot a graph of the empirical probability against the number of the toss. Compare your final empirical probability with those obtained by others in the class. Do you think that the probability of a drawing pin landing point up is the same for all pins in the box? Give reasons for your answer. If your answer is yes, pool your results for the whole class and work out the empirical probability of a pin from this box landing point up.

2 Review the following Practical exercises from earlier chapters:
6.6 Questions 3 and 4, 7.7 Question 2, 8.5 Question 4, 9.4 Question 2 and 11.2 Question 3. For each experiment, find the empirical probabilities of the events you observed. Work out the corresponding theoretical probabilities assuming equally likely outcomes. Compare the two sets of probabilities using a table and/or a bar chart. Comment on your findings.

3 Use random numbers to simulate the size of population in the western region of Ruritania for each year from 1988 to 1999. You are given the following information and predictions.

Size of population in 1987 = 924 000

Expected annual number of births	Probability
1000	0.3
2000	0.4
3000	0.3

Expected annual number of deaths	Probability
1000	0.5
2000	0.5

Expected annual number of emigrants	Probability
1000	0.25
2000	0.75

Expected annual number of immigrants	Probability
1000	0.50
2000	0.40
3000	0.10

What is your estimate of the overall percentage change in the population from 1988 to 1999?

18 Demographic statistics

Office of Population Censuses and Surveys

Demography is the statistical study of human populations. A government needs to know, for example, how many people there are in each region of the country, their age distribution and their living conditions. Almost every government decision, from provision of sufficient hospitals and schools to estimating how much money can be raised by increasing the rate of income tax, relies on the availability of accurate demographic information.

The Office of Population Censuses and Surveys, OPCS, is responsible for collecting demographic statistics in England and Wales.

The statistics are gathered in two main ways. Firstly there is the Census of Population, held every ten years. This takes a 'snapshot' of the population on one date to provide what is termed a benchmark against which to monitor future changes. As detailed in the next section, it provides information on housing and employment as well as just counting the numbers of people in different districts.

Secondly there is the system of **vital registration** whereby births, marriages and deaths have to be registered. The word 'vital' in this context means pertaining to life. The General Register Office for England and Wales, out of which grew the present OPCS, was founded in 1837. Statistics of morbidity (illness), abortions, divorces etc. are also collected.

Information is first released in OPCS monitors, which are available in public reference libraries. For instance, the *Weekly Returns* of the Registrars General give the total numbers of live births, still births and deaths each week. More details, such as analyses by region and county are included every four or five weeks and analyses by cause are published quarterly. Full analyses are given in annual reference publications, each of which deal with one topic or with closely-related topics.

Estimates of international migration are derived from the International Passenger Survey which is a survey of passengers arriving at and departing from UK air and sea ports. The National Health Service Central Register provides estimates, although only approximate, of population movements within the UK. This enables an up-to-date estimate of the size and the distribution of the population in Great Britain to be maintained in the period between censuses.

Population Trends is the quarterly journal of OPCS and publishes articles of current interest. For example, Ethnic minority populations in Great Britain, The changing balance of the sexes 1851–2000 and Recent patterns of migration from and to the UK were titles of articles in *Population Trends* 46 (Winter 1986).

Census of Population

The first decennial census was taken in 1801. The information sought in the census has changed over the years and before every census the proposed questions have to be scrutinised by Parliament.

The questions asked in England and Wales in the 1981 census were:

(1) for each individual
Full name
Date of birth
Sex
Marital status
Relationship in household
Usual address
Whereabouts on census night of usual residents
Country of birth
Address one year ago
(In Wales) Ability to speak, read and write in Welsh

(2) for each individual aged 16 or over on census night
Employment activity last week
Occupation and description of work done
Name and type of business of employer
Employment status (whether employed, self-employed etc)
Address of place of work
Main means of transport used on journey to work
Higher educational, professional or vocational qualifications obtained after age 18

(3) for each household
Nature of building and whether entrance to building is shared
Number of rooms
Type of housing tenure
Whether shared or exclusive use of fixed baths, showers, inside and outside toilets
Number of cars or vans available for use by members of the household

It takes several years to process and publish in full the data obtained from one census. Planning for the next census begins five years before the census is due. The date for the census is a Sunday in late March or April (but not the Easter weekend). Well before census night, specially recruited enumerators deliver forms throughout the country to every household and to communal establishments such as hotels, hospitals and boarding schools. Each enumeration district includes between 125 and 220 households in urban areas but fewer in rural areas. The boundaries of enumeration districts correspond to the boundaries of local administrative areas. The head of the household or a joint head of household is responsible for filling in the form. In communal establishments, individuals may provide personal details on separate forms to respect confidentiality.

The enumerator collects the forms after census night and has to ensure that all questions have been answered with no obvious errors. The enumerator can deal with any queries and can call on the services of an interpreter if there are any language difficulties.

The forms are processed with the help of computers. The names and addresses of individuals are not used other than as a check that all households and persons have been enumerated. After processing, the census forms are stored for 100 years before being made available at the Public Records Office. Thus, information on named individuals is not accessible by anyone outside the census organisation until 100 years after a census.

The total population count is published almost immediately after a census. Then the forms are processed in detail, county by county. The order of processing depends partly on county size and partly on the local need for up-to-date statistics in areas where great changes have taken place recently. County reports are published as they become available followed by national reports in due course. After the 1981 census, OPCS also produced separate volumes entitled *Key Statistics for Urban Areas* in different regions and for local authorities.

OPCS has a register of census users. This enables information to be provided in the format required, i.e. paper, microfiche or magnetic tape. OPCS produces *Census Newsletters* (previously *Census Monitors*) to keep interested parties informed of all aspects of census arrangements, publications and usage.

Exercise 18.1

1 Name three publications in which OPCS provides information on demographic statistics.

2 (a) Why do you think the census forms are stored for 100 years before they can be consulted by anyone outside the Census Office?

(b) Why do you think it is necessary to conduct a Census of Population rather than a sample survey asking the same questions?

(c) Why do you think the census forms are delivered and collected by an enumerator rather than sent and returned by mail?

(d) Why do you think the census date is always chosen as a Sunday in late March or April but not Easter Sunday?

(e) If you could add one question to those asked in the 1981 census, what information would you seek and why?

(f) Why do you think a much larger number of questions was not asked in the census?

3 Look through the list of questions asked in the 1981 census. Write down three ways in which information requested could be of use to (a) government departments, (b) local authorities and (c) companies. State in each case which particular question or questions provide the useful information.

Population pyramids

A population pyramid shows the percentages of males and females in each five-year age group, Fig. 18.1. Pyramids can be used to compare the changes in

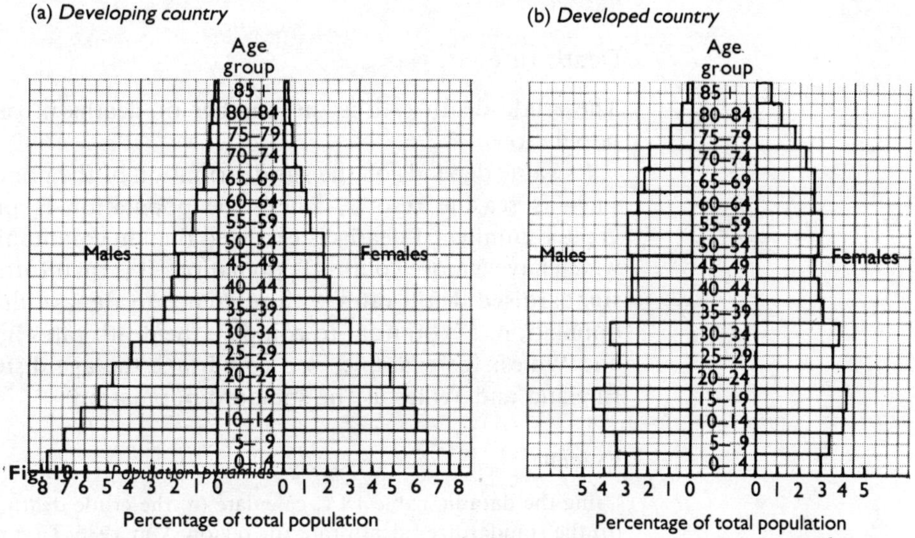

Fig. 18.1 Population pyramids

age distribution in a country over a number of years or to compare the age distributions in different countries. In general, developed countries have more slowly tapering pyramids than developing countries because people tend to live longer and infant deaths are fewer in developed countries.

Although in most countries there are more male births than female births, females tend to live longer than males so the female side of the pyramid is broader at the top. In some developed countries in recent years there has been a decline in births so the resulting pyramid does not have its widest part at the base. From Fig. 18.1(b), we can see that the greatest number of people in the developed country is in the 15–19 age group.

Demographic rates

To compare the numbers of births, marriages and deaths in one year in different countries, in different districts within a country or at different periods, it is usual to calculate demographic rates.

Birth rate

The crude birth rate is the number of live births in one year per 1000 of the population.

$$\text{crude birth rate} = \frac{\text{total number of live births in one year}}{\text{total population at mid-year}} \times 1000$$

The crude birth rate depends on the age and sex distribution within the population. It is more useful, therefore, to calculate the fertility rate, which is the number of live births in one year per 1000 women of child-bearing age, i.e. aged between 15 and 44 years.

Marriage rate

The marriage rate is the number of marriages in one year per 1000 of the population.

Death rate

The crude death rate is the number of deaths in one year per 1000 of the population.

Its value depends on the age distribution of the population. In communities, such as seaside resorts, where the population is predominantly elderly, a greater number of deaths is expected than in communities, such as new towns, which have a more youthful population. It is therefore more useful to calculate **standardised death rates** with reference to the age distribution of a standard population. If you want to compare the death rates in two regions of England and Wales, for example, you could take the age distribution in the whole of England and Wales as the standard population.

Example

Using the data in Table 18.1, calculate (a) the crude death rate for region A in 1986, (b) the standardized death rate for region A in 1986. Comment on your results given that the death rate in the standard population for 1986 was 11.12 per 1000.

Table 18.1 Deaths and population in Region A

Age group	Population at mid-year	Deaths	Standard population: Percentage in age group
0–24	150 000	400	36.7
25–44	132 000	580	26.3
45–64	100 000	2500	22.3
65 and over	42 000	4230	14.7

(a) crude death rate for region A

$$= \frac{\text{total number of deaths}}{\text{total population at mid-year}} \times 1000$$

$$= \frac{(400 + 580 + 2500 + 4230)}{(150\,000 + 132\,000 + 100\,000 + 42\,000)} \times 1000$$

$$= \frac{7710}{424\,000} \times 1000$$

$$= 18.18 \text{ per } 1000$$

It is usual to calculate demographic rates correct to two decimal places.

(b) We first calculate the death rate in each age group for region A. These are termed **age-specific death rates.**

$$\text{Age 0–24:} \quad \text{death rate per } 1000 = \frac{400}{150\,000} \times 1000 = 2.67$$

$$\text{Age 25–44:} \quad \text{death rate per } 1000 = \frac{580}{132\,000} \times 1000 = 4.39$$

Age 45–64: death rate per 1000 $= \dfrac{2500}{100\,000} \times 1000 = 25.00$

Age 65 and over: death rate per 1000 $= \dfrac{4230}{42\,000} \times 1000 = 100.71$

The standarised death rate is the weighted mean of the age-specific death rates using the percentages in each age group of the standard populations as weights.

$$\text{standardised death rate} = \frac{\Sigma\text{age-specific death rate} \times \text{weight}}{\Sigma\text{weight}}$$

$$= \frac{(2.67 \times 36.7) + (4.39 \times 26.3) + (25.00 \times 22.3) + (100.71 \times 14.7)}{100}$$

$$= \frac{97.989 + 115.457 + 557.500 + 1480.437}{100}$$

$$= \frac{2251.383}{100}$$

$= 22.51$ per 1000 to 2 dec. pl.

The standardised death rate is higher than the crude death rate for region A because of the smaller percentage of elderly people in the region as compared with the standard population.

Region A appears to be an 'unhealthy' place in which to live since its standardised death rate is more than twice the death rate in the standard population.

Life tables

Table 18.2 Life table for the UK (1981–83)

Age (x)	Males	Females
0	100 000	100 000
5	98 585	98 903
10	98 453	98 808
15	98 314	98 714
20	97 925	98 562
25	97 502	98 395
30	97 081	98 185
35	96 602	97 890
40	95 942	97 431
45	94 789	96 658
50	92 744	95 323
55	89 187	93 099
60	83 182	89 589
65	74 208	84 311
70	61 825	76 700
75	46 060	68 652
80	29 019	50 509
85	14 195	31 925

Source: *Annual Abstract of Statistics 1986*

Life tables show how many out of a specified number of births (usually 10 000, 100 000 or 1 million) survive to various ages. Numbers for males and females are tabulated separately. Comparisons can be made between countries or between different time periods in the same country.

Table 18.2 shows a life table for the UK for 1981–83. It gives the number who would survive to exact age x out of 100 000 born who were subject throughout their lives to the death rates experienced in the three-year period 1981–83. In Table 18.2 the ages are tabulated at five-year intervals but life tables are also available with annual intervals.

Life tables are of particular use to pension and life assurance companies since they can be used to work out, for example, the probability of a person, now aged x, being dead within a given number of years. Pension contributions and life assurance premiums can then be assessed according to the risks involved.

Example

Find the following probabilities, to two decimal places, assuming the survival patterns shown in Table 18.2.

(a) the probability of a newborn boy being alive at 60;
(b) the probability of a newborn girl living 85 years or more;
(c) the probability of a newborn girl being dead before 40;
(d) the probability of a 65-year-old man dying before he is 75.

(a) Out of 100 000 male births, 83 182 survive to 60.

$$\text{P(newborn boy alive at 60)} = \frac{83\,182}{100\,000} = 0.831\,82 = 0.83 \text{ to 2 dec. pl.}$$

(b) Out of 100 000 female births, 31 925 survive to age 85

$$\text{P(newborn girl alive at 85)} = \frac{31\,925}{100\,000} = 0.319\,25 = 0.32 \text{ to 2 dec. pl.}$$

(c) Out of 100 000 female births, 97 431 survive to age 40.

$$\text{number dead before 40} = 100\,000 - 97\,431 = 2569$$

$$\text{P(newborn girl dead before 40)} = \frac{2\,569}{100\,000} = 0.025\,69 = 0.03 \text{ to 2 dec. pl.}$$

(d) Out of 74 208 men alive at age 65, 46 060 survive to age 75.

$$\text{number dying between 65 and 75} = 74\,208 - 46\,060 = 28\,148$$

$$\text{P(65-year-old man dies before 75)} = \frac{28\,148}{74\,208} = 0.379\,31 = 0.38 \text{ to 2 dec. pl.}$$

Note: the denominator is 74 208 not 100 000 because the sample space has changed from all males to those who have survived to age 65.

Exercise 18.2

1 The table shows the age distribution in South Africa in 1980. Find the percentage of the total population in each age group for both males and females, giving your answers to one decimal place. Use your values to draw a population pyramid. Comment on your graph.

Age distribution in South Africa 1980

Age group	Number of males (000s)	Number of females (000s)
under 5	1 757	1 746
5– 9	1 582	1 575
10–14	1 388	1 382
15–19	1 336	1 297
20–24	1 316	1 187
25–29	1 090	956
30–34	909	800
35–39	755	680
40–44	626	577
45–49	513	488
50–54	416	401
55–59	327	340
60–64	263	290
65–69	190	221
70–74	124	160
75–79	68	93
80–84	34	59
85 +	27	52

Source: *UN Demographic Yearbook 1985*

2 Use the following data to calculate the marriage rates for 1974 and 1984 for (a) England and Wales, (b) Scotland. Comment on your results.

	Number of marriages		Population (000s): mid-year estimate	
	1974	1984	1974	1984
England & Wales	384 389	349 186	49 468	59 764
Scotland	41 174	36 253	5 217	5 146

Source: *Annual Abstract of Statistics 1986*

3 The table shows the number of deaths by age group in Exebury, (County of Wyeshire) last year. The final column shows the corresponding percentages of the population of Wyeshire in each age group.

(a) Find the crude death rate in Exebury.

(b) Copy out and complete the table.

(c) Calculate the standardised death rate for Exebury, using the County population as the standard.

	Exebury			Wyeshire
Age group	Population	Deaths	Death rate per 1000	Population
0–24	5000	140		40%
25–64	8000	120		40%
65+	4000	400		20%

4 Emburg is in the country of Ruritania. The table shows the number of deaths by age group in Emburg last year. Using Ruritania's population as the standard, calculate the standarised death rate in Emburg.

	Emburg		Ruritania
Age group	Population	Deaths	Population (millions)
0–19	5000	32	2.6
20–44	6000	18	2.8
45+	4000	132	4.6

5 The table shows the number of deaths by age group in Essbury and Teebury last year. Calculate

(a) the crude death rate for each town;

(b) the death rate for each age group in each town;

(c) the standardised death rate for each town.

(d) Comment on your results. Which place has the better survival rate?

	Essbury		Teebury		
Age group	Population	Deaths	Population	Deaths	Population
0–24	50 000	225	34 000	61	39%
25–64	77 000	730	63 000	629	48%
65+	16 000	800	28 000	1897	13%

6 Use the data shown to calculate
(a) the crude death rate for Town A;
(b) the crude death rate for Town B;
(c) the standardised death rate for Town A;
(d) the standardised death rate for Town B.
State, with reasons, which town is healthier.

	Town A		Town B		
Age group	Population	Death rate per 1000	Population	Death rate per 1000	Standard population
0–24	24%	12	22%	13	24%
25–49	46%	6	37%	6	48%
50+	30%	30	41%	28	28%

7 Assuming the survival patterns shown in Table 18.2, work out the following probabilities, correct to two decimal places:
(a) the probability of a newborn boy dying before 30;
(b) the probability of a newborn girl living 60 years or more;
(c) the probability of a 40-year-old woman dying before she is 60;
(d) the probability of a 20-year-old man living at least another 50 years.

Practical exercise 18.3

1 Refer to the most recently available copy of the Registrars' General *Weekly Return*, to be found in most reference libraries.
(a) Extract the following data:
(i) the number of live births in England and Wales in each of the last six weeks,
(ii) the number of still births in England and Wales in each of the last six weeks,
(iii) the number of deaths of all ages (excluding still births) in England and Wales in each of the last six weeks.
Are the numbers fairly constant from week to week? Does this surprise you?
(b) Find, for the district in which you live, the total number of notifications, if any, in the most recent week available, of the following infectious diseases: measles, scarlet fever, whooping cough, tuberculosis (TB). Find the corresponding data for a second district of a different type from the one in which you live, e.g. if you live in a rural district, consider an inner city district. Draw a chart to show your results and comment on any similarities and differences.
2 (Class exercise) You need to refer to a recent copy of the *UN Demographic Yearbook* which is available in public reference libraries. Find the table that gives the number of males and females by age group in each country. Each member of the class should select one country and draw its population pyramid. Display all the pyramids together and discuss any similarities and differences that you notice.
3 Refer to the OPCS *County Monitor*, giving the results of the most recent Census of Population, for the area in which you live. *County Monitors* are available in a reference library or can be purchased directly from OPCS.
Extract the following data for your county:

Total population present on census night.
Total population usually resident.
Percentage change since previous census in the population usually resident.
Density of the population.
Percentage of population under 16 years.

Percentage of population of pensionable age.
Percentage of population born outside the UK.
Percentage of population living in communal establishments.
Percentage of men in employment (full-time or part-time).
Percentage of women in employment (full-time or part-time).
Percentage of men out of employment.
Percentage of households with at least one child under five.
Percentage of households with three or more children.
Percentage of households with at least one child under 16 and only one adult.
Percentage of households with one person living alone.
Percentage of households with one pensioner living alone.
Percentage of households owner-occupied.
Percentage of households in accommodation rented from a local authority or new town.
Percentage of households with more than one person per room.
Percentage of households without sole use of a fixed bath or shower.
Percentage of household accommodation vacant.
Percentage of households with no car available.
(If in Wales) Percentage of population aged three and over speaking Welsh.

Now consider a second county and extract the corresponding data for that county. Record you results in a suitable table. Write a brief report, including charts if desired, comparing and contrasting the results from the two counties.

19 Sources of statistics

Introduction

In your studies you have had the opportunity to collect primary data. We noted in Chapter 3 that, on many occasions, data of interest may have been collected previously by other persons and you may be able to use such secondary data without needing to spend time and labour on collecting data yourself. It is advisable that you should have some knowledge of what published data are available. Official publications are particularly important as these tend to be reliable sources with explanations and definitions clearly given.

In this chapter are listed the main publications that you may need to consult. Sources of demographic statistics for Great Britain were given in Chapter 18 so they are omitted here. Many of the publications are available in a public reference library. Certain libraries throughout the country, essentially one library in each library authority area, automatically receive a copy of all major government publications from Her Majesty's Stationery Office (HMSO).

Guide to Official Statistics

If you want to know where to find statistics for the UK on some topic, let us say 'air safety', the first publication to consult is the *Guide to Official Statistics* produced by the Central Statistical Office (CSO). Look for 'air safety' in the alphabetical key word index. You will not find 'air safety' but the following topics are listed with at least one reference number against each:

air accidents
air accidents to service aircraft
air collision risk and near-misses

Turning to the section(s) indicated by the reference numbers, you will find a list of both regular and occasional sources, ranging from *Analysis of Bird Strikes to UK registered aircraft* to *World Air Transport Statistics.* Details are given for each source as to the type of information it contains, so that you can decide which is the most relevant publication to look at first.

The Central Statistical Office, set up in 1941, co-ordinates the work of the statistics divisions of the various government departments. It is responsible for bringing together, analysing and presenting some of the material collected by other government departments.

Monthly Digest of Statistics

This publication, produced by the CSO, consists of approximately 140 tables referring to economic, social and industrial statistics. Monthly or quarterly values are tabulated. There are no descriptive articles and no graphical presentation. Some figures are provisional because the information is so up-to-date that final values are not available. Units of measurement are detailed each month on the last page of the Digest. Definitions and explanatory notes are given in the *Annual Supplement* which is usually published in February.

The main section headings are National income and expenditure, Population and vital statistics, Employment, Social services, Law enforcement, Agriculture and food, Production, output and costs, Energy, Chemicals, Metals, engineering and vehicles, Textiles and other manufactures, Construction, Transport, Retailing, External trade, Overseas finance, Home finance, Prices and wages, Entertainment, Weather.

Annual Abstract of Statistics

The *Annual Abstract,* also produced by the CSO, contains approximately 350 tables in eighteen separate chapters. It uses the same definitions as the *Monthly Digest* but gives annual data for the immediate past eleven years in most cases. Its statistics come from almost all government departments so the coverage is very wide.

Employment Gazette

This is the monthly publication of the Department of Employment. The statistical section is in the centre of the journal. Monthly or quarterly values are tabulated. As well as tables, there is a commentary on the trends in the various statistics with accompanying graphs. Brief definitions are included each month. The remainder of the journal consists of news and easy-to-read feature articles, covering the wide area of Department of Employment interests.

The main headings of the statistical section are Employment, Unemployment, Vacancies, Industrial disputes, Retail prices, Household expenditure, Tourism, Other facts and figures (e.g. YTS entrants, disabled job seekers).

Regional Trends

This is an annual publication produced by the CSO. It covers about 150 economic and social topics either for the UK as a whole or for the standard regions of Great Britain. The data are mainly annual time series. The publication contains a verbal summary along with tables and some charts.

The main headings are Regional profiles, Population and vital statistics, Housing, Transport and environment, Health, Law enforcement, Education, Employment, Personal income and expenditure, Regional accounts, Industry, European Community comparisons, Regional classification. Maps showing the areas covered by Regional Health Authorities, enterprise zones, gas regions and electricity regions are also included.

Digest of Welsh Statistics

This annual publication from the Welsh Office gives more than 200 tables of economic and social statistics for the principality. The data are mainly annual.

Social Trends

This is an annual publication produced by the CSO. It includes tables and charts (not always well drawn) together with a descriptive commentary on all aspects of social statistics. Each edition usually contains a small number of articles of particular relevance to those involved in social policy. Current annual figures are given together with a selection of comparative figures for earlier years.

The main headings are Population, Households and families, Education, Employment, Income and wealth, Resources and expenditure, Health and personal social services, Housing, Transport, Communications and the environment, Leisure, Participation, Law enforcement. Definitions and terms are explained in an appendix.

Economic Trends

This is a monthly publication produced by the CSO. It consists primarily of tables over the whole range of economic statistics with good graphical presentations, although some are quite technical, and an overall summary of the latest developments in the economy. There is an occasional article of a technical nature, mainly of interest to economists. Monthly, quarterly and annual data are tabulated. The *Annual Supplement to Economic Trends* gives long series of quarterly or annual economic statistics and is particularly valuable for studying long-term trends and cyclical variations. It also includes explanatory notes and definitions.

Education Statistics for the United Kingdom

This is an annual publication that gives data from the Department of Education and Science, Welsh Office, Scottish Education Office, Department of Education for Northern Ireland and the University Grants Committee. There are explanatory notes followed by tables of data, which are annual figures, corresponding to the school or academic year.

The main headings are Population, Institutions, Finance, Teaching staff, Schools, Post-compulsory participation rates.

Local statistics

Some data for local authorities, districts, health authorities etc are contained in the publications mentioned previously. Further information is available locally in published reports, minutes or leaflets. Your local library should be able to tell you what is available in your area.

International statistics

If you require data about one particular country, you may find the Embassy or the High Commission can provide up-to-date information. The Commonwealth Institute is a useful source for all Commonwealth countries.

The United Nations is responsible for publishing data for all countries in handbooks such as the *Demographic Yearbook* and the *Statistical Yearbook*. It encourages member countries to move towards common definitions and to take population censuses at approximately the same time, but it is difficult to achieve uniformity on such a vast scale, so you must take care when making comparisons from different countries.

More detailed international figures on certain topics are published on a regular basis by the World Health Organisation, International Monetary Fund, International Labour Office, International Civil Aviation Organisation, World Tourism Organisation and the International Bank for Reconstruction and Development.

The Statistical Office of the European Communities (Eurostat) produces journals on agricultural, economic, energy and industrial topics. These are available through Her Majesty's Stationery Office (HMSO).

Non-official sources

Financial Times

This is the leading daily newspaper for economic and business information. Every day it gives details of share, stock and commodity prices and exchange rates, for example. Together with the Stock Exchange and the actuarial institutes, it is responsible for producing the leading share index numbers which are widely quoted. In some issues, there are supplements covering, for example, recent developments in UK regions, countries of the world and particular industries.

Companies and banks

Annual company reports give details of the accounts and financial standing of registered companies. These reports are sent to all shareholders. Individuals may obtain a copy of a public company's report by writing to the company's registered address. A useful list of addresses is the *Times 1000,* an annual publication listing the top 1000 companies in the UK.

The major clearing banks publish quarterly reviews mainly on financial and economic topics.

Miscellaneous

If you have a particular hobby or interest, you will probably already know which are the major publications giving relevant statistics. For instance, the Guinness series of books on *Facts and Feats* covers many sporting activities and the *Wisden Cricketers' Almanack* is unsurpassed for cricketing statistics.

The Consumers' Association publishes statistics in its *Which* guides that compare many products and services.

On-line data bases

The publications we have mentioned are all on paper. There is an inevitable delay between the collection and publication of data because of the printing process. An increasing amount of information is being held on computer data bases which can be accessed at a distance by the user through the telecommunications network. The data can be updated much more quickly than for printed publications. The CSO has a bank of data sets of economic statistics that are on sale to the public in computer-readable form. The majority of data bases, however, are organised by private bodies so there is little standardisation of accessing procedure.

Practical exercise 19.1

1 Use the *Guide to Official Statistics* to name publications that would provide data on each of the following topics:

(a) numbers of children in playgroups in England and Wales;
(b) volume and value of sales of UK pudding manufacturers;
(c) numbers of accidents on the railways in Great Britain;
(d) numbers of students on courses in further and higher education in Great Britain.

2 Refer to a recent copy of the *Monthly Digest of Statistics*. Find the section entitled Textiles and other manufactures. Look at the table relating to hosiery and other knitted items. Write a brief report on the trends and seasonal patterns shown by the data and illustrate your report with one or more charts.

3 Refer to a recent copy of *Employment Gazette*. Find the section on tourism under the heading 'Overseas travel and tourism'. There are two tables giving details of visits to the UK by overseas residents and visits abroad by UK residents.

Find, for the most recent year for which complete figures are available, the actual numbers of overseas residents that visited the UK each month and the corresponding numbers of UK residents who visited abroad. Draw a dual bar chart to show the results. Comment on what your chart shows.

4 Refer to the most recently available copy of *Regional Trends*. Find the table referring to the number of building society mortgages advanced. Draw a bar chart showing the numbers of such loans advanced in the different regions of the UK. Comment on what your chart shows.

5 Refer to a recent copy of *Social Trends*. Find the table giving details of membership of organisations for young people in the UK.

(a) For the most recent year, name the organisation that had (i) the largest number of members, (ii) the least number of members.

(b) For the earliest year, name the organisation that had (i) the largest number of members, (ii) the least number of members.

(c) Which organisation had (i) the largest increase, (ii) the largest decrease, in membership over the period covered by the tables?

(d) In percentage terms, which organisation had (i) the largest increase, (ii) the largest decrease in membership over the period?

Comment on your results.

6 Refer to a recent copy of *Education Statistics for the UK*. Find the table giving details of the numbers of schools under the following headings: Nursery, Primary, Secondary, Non-maintained, Special. Draw historigrams showing the numbers in each of these types of school for the academic years covered by the table. Comment on the notable features revealed by your data.

20 Revision exercises

Revision exercise 1

1 What is the difference between a census and a sample survey?

2 State whether the following variables, relating to a house, are qualitative or quantitative:

(a) type of roofing material, (b) area of garden, (c) number of windows.

3 State whether the following variables, relating to a garden, are continuous or discrete:

(a) number of trees, (b) area of flower beds, (c) total length of paths.

4 At a DIY store there are eight different brands of white emulsion paint for sale at the following prices:

Brand	A	B	C	D	E	F	G	H
Price	£8.59	£8.01	£8.59	£7.75	£8.73	£8.32	£8.91	£8.80

If the brands are ranked in order of price, so that Brand G has rank one, what is the rank of Brand F?

5 The diagram shows the percentage of the UK workforce who are members of a trade union.

(a) State two ways in which the diagram is misleading.

(b) Draw, on graph paper, a diagram which correctly represents this information.

Trade union membership

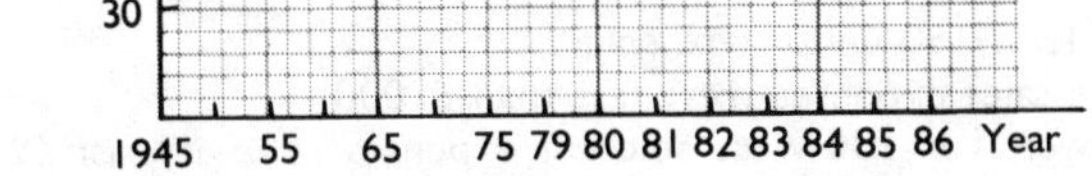

Lorry loads

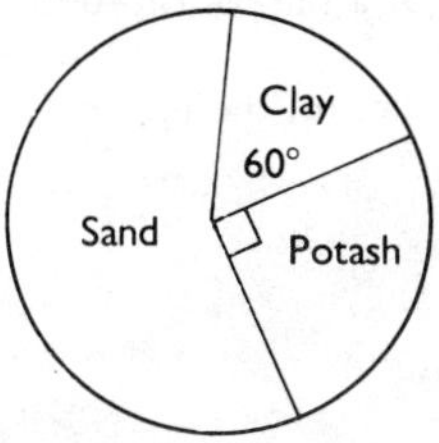

6 Deabury factory uses three raw materials which are delivered by lorry. The numbers of loads of each type are shown in the pie chart. There are 120 lorry loads delivered each month. How many of these loads are (a) potash, (b) clay, (c) sand?

7 A car hire firm has a fleet of 40 cars. For a period of one month, a record is kept, for each car, of the number of faults that required attention by mechanics before the car could be hired out again. The tally chart shows the results.

Number of faults per car	Tally of cars
0	III
1	~~IIII~~ III
2	~~IIII~~ ~~IIII~~ ~~IIII~~ I
3	~~IIII~~ II
4	III
5	III

(a) Draw a frequency bar chart to show the data.
(b) What is the modal number of faults?
(c) What is the total number of faults that required attention?
(d) What is the mean number of faults per car?
(e) What percentage of cars had no faults?

8 A tin contains 10 chocolate biscuits and 29 plain biscuits. A biscuit is taken at random from the tin.
(a) What is the probability that it is a chocolate biscuit?
(b) What are the odds against it being a chocolate biscuit?

9 A house was sold for £50 000 in 1980. The same house was sold for £95 000 in 1986.
(a) Taking 1980 as base, calculate a house price index for 1986.
(b) By what percentage did the price of the house increase from 1980 to 1986?

10 A company sells the same product in 50 areas. The sales vary from area to area and so do the expenses, as shown in the table.

Number of areas

Sales (units)	Sales expenses (£) Less than 1000	1000–1999	2000–2999	3000–3999
Less than 50	7	—	—	—
50– 99	9	2	1	—
100–149	3	9	5	—
150–199	—	3	5	—
200–249	—	—	2	—
250–299	—	—	—	4

Use the table to find out in how many areas
(a) the sales were between 100 and 149 and the expenses were between £1000 and £1999;
(b) at least 150 units were sold;
(c) the sales expenses were less than £1000;
(d) fewer than 100 were sold but expenses were at least £2000?

11 The cumulative frequency graph shows the distribution by height of a sample of 4000 women.

Use the graph to estimate (a) the median height, (b) the lower quartile, (c) the upper quartile and (d) the semi-interquartile range.

Why might this graph be of use to a clothing manufacturer?

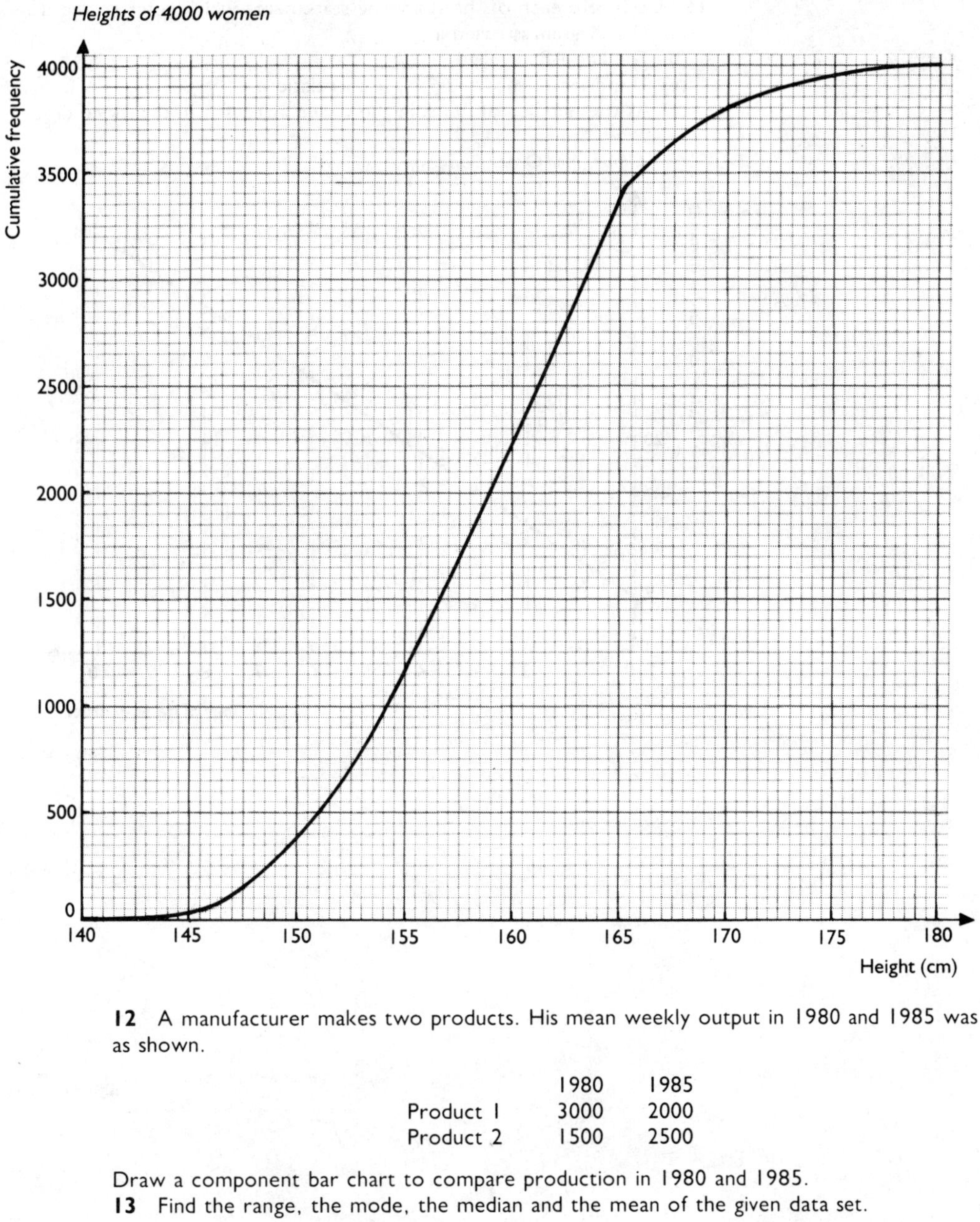

12 A manufacturer makes two products. His mean weekly output in 1980 and 1985 was as shown.

	1980	1985
Product 1	3000	2000
Product 2	1500	2500

Draw a component bar chart to compare production in 1980 and 1985.

13 Find the range, the mode, the median and the mean of the given data set.

14 56 83 56 22 67 75 43 64

14 A market research company is commissioned to carry out a sample survey for a sweet manufacturer to discover the response to a new product. Give a reason why (a) the electoral register, (b) the telephone directory, may not be a suitable sample frame for this survey.

15 Complete each of the following statements which refer to the diagram shown.

(a) The diagram is called a ....

(b) The line AB is called ....

(c) The diagram shows .... correlation.

(d) As the number of items in the order increases, the packing time ....

Effbury Mail Order Company

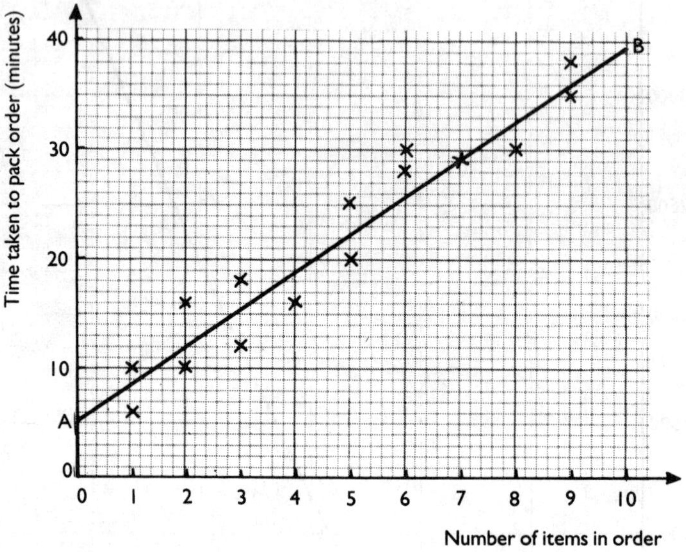

Revision exercise 2

1 The meteorological data given in the table refer to two towns, one in the northern hemisphere and one in the southern hemisphere. The data have been collected over a period of more than 50 years.

Town A

Month	Temperature °C Highest recorded	Mean daily max	Mean daily min	Lowest recorded	Mean monthly rainfall (mm)
J	48	30	16	7	20
F	46	30	17	7	18
M	44	27	15	7	25
A	37	23	13	4	46
M	32	19	10	3	69
J	24	16	8	1	76
J	23	15	7	0	66
A	29	17	8	0	66
S	33	19	9	1	53
O	39	23	11	2	43
N	45	26	13	5	28
D	46	28	15	6	25

Town B

Month	Temperature °C Highest recorded	Mean daily max	Mean daily min	Lowest recorded	Mean monthly rainfall (mm)
J	26	18	13	0	33
F	26	17	13	3	46
M	28	19	16	7	74
A	32	24	19	11	137
M	33	28	23	16	292
J	34	29	26	19	394
J	34	31	26	22	381
A	36	31	26	22	367
S	34	29	25	18	257
O	34	27	23	13	114
N	30	23	18	7	43
D	28	20	15	5	31

Anwer the following questions:

(a) In which month was the highest temperature recorded in Town A?
(b) In which month was the lowest temperature recorded in Town B?
(c) Which month in Town A is the wettest month?
(d) Which month is wettest in Town B?
(e) What is the rainfall in the wettest month as a percentage of the rainfall in the driest month for (i) Town A, (ii) Town B?
(f) What is the difference between the highest temperature ever recorded and the lowest ever recorded for (i) Town A, (ii) Town B?
(g) What is the largest difference in one month between the mean daily maximum temperature and the mean daily minimum temperature for (i) Town A, (ii) Town B?
(h) What is the smallest difference in one month between the mean daily maximum temperature and the mean daily minimum temperature for (i) Town A, (ii) Town B?
(j) Is Town A in the northern or the southern hemisphere?

2 The following data set refers to the profits of a manufacturing company.

Year	1969	70	71	72	73	74	75	76	77	78
Profit (£000s)	42	63	47	58	67	43	65	50	60	70

Year	79	80	81	82	83	84	85	86	87
Profit (£000s)	45	67	50	63	72	46	70	53	65

(a) Plot a historigram of the data.
(b) Identify the appropriate length of moving average to use to remove the cyclical variations.
(c) Find these moving averages and plot them on your graph. Do you think there is a linear trend?

3 Calculate the mean and the standard deviation of the following data set:

9 6 18 12 13 10 7 13

The numbers 5 and 17 are now included in the data set. Write down the value of the mean of the new data set. Is the standard deviation of the new data set greater than or less than before?

4 A manufacturer of chemicals keeps drums of a particular solvent in store before repacking the contents in smaller cans for sale. During storage, evaporation takes place and testing of a random sample of drums that had been in store for varying times showed the evaporation losses as displayed in the figure.

Evaporation loss in storage

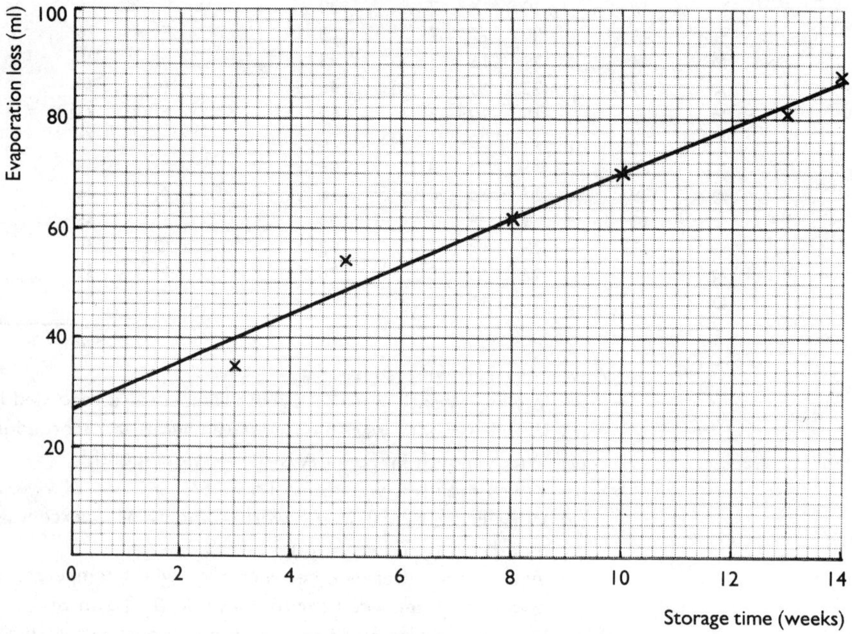

A line of best fit has been drawn through the points in the diagram. Use the line to estimate the evaporation loss of a drum that has been in storage for (i) 6 weeks, (ii) 12 weeks. Would you use this line to estimate the evaporation loss after 26 weeks? Give reasons for your answer.

5 A red die and a blue die are tossed together and their scores are noted. The scores are then multiplied together.

(a) Complete the table to show all possible products.

	Red die					
Score	1	2	3	4	5	6
Blue die 1	1	2				
2		4				
3				12		18
4						
5						
6	6					36

(b) How many outcomes result in a product equal to 12?

(c) What is the probability that the product is equal to 12?

(d) What is the probability that the product is divisible by 6?
(e) What is the probability that the product is divisible by 5?
(f) What is the probability that the product is divisible by 6 or 5?
(g) What is the probability that the product is divisible by 6 and 5?

6 A random sample of the output of a machine producing components was tested. The results indicated that the lengths of the components have a normal distribution with mean 46 cm and standard deviation 2 cm.

Sketch the shape of this distribution and, on the horizontal axis, mark (a) the position and value of the mean, (b) the approximate position of 40 cm and 52 cm.

In a further testing of components from this machine, one component was recorded as having a length of 64 cm. What action would you take?

7 The values of a price index number, with a fixed base of 1980, are shown for 1980 to 1987.

Year	1980	1981	1982	1983	1984	1985	1986	1987
Index	100	108	116	119	120	120	126	129

(a) Recalculate the values of the index number with 1984 as the fixed base.
(b) Recalculate the values of the index number using the chain-base method.

8 In a survey of 150 households in a block of flats, each household was asked, 'How many children, under the age of 16, reside in your flat?' The results are shown in the frequency table.

Number of children	Number of households
0	31
1	61
2	46
3	10
4	2
Total	150

Draw a cumulative frequency step diagram of the data. Use your diagram to find (a) the median number of children per household, (b) the second decile, D_2 and the eighth decile, D_8.

9 In a textile factory, the machines have been installed over a number of years. The workers on the older machines are dissatisfied because they feel they have to deal with more breakdowns than those workers on the new machines. For one week the management monitored the number of breakdowns on a random sample of eight machines. The results are shown in the table.

Machine	Age of machine (years)	Number of breakdowns
A	16	20
B	9	15
C	1	4
D	2	3
E	10	7
F	8	10
G	5	3
H	4	5

Calculate Spearman's rank correlation coefficient for this data set and interpret your result.

10 At Geebury school, five classes took the same English examination. The mean marks in each class are as shown.

Class	1	2	3	4	5
Number of pupils	30	29	31	28	29
Mean mark	75	72	64	62	50

Find the mean mark of all the pupils.

11 Angela was born in Teebury District Hospital. She was weighed at birth, correct to the nearest 10 g, and this weight, 3000 g, was entered by the midwife on the hospital record card. Because it is thought that mothers prefer to know birthweights in imperial units, the midwife uses a conversion chart to change the weight into pounds and ounces. This chart assumes 1 kg = 2.2 lb and the result is rounded to the nearest ounce (1 lb = 16 ounces). The Community Health Department is informed of the birthweight in pounds and ounces and it then uses a computer program to convert the weight back to grams. The program assumes 1 lb = 454 g and rounds the result to the nearest 5 g. This value is then printed on the child's health card that is sent to the local health visitor.

(a) What is Angela's weight as printed on the card sent to the health visitor?

(b) What is (i) the least amount, (ii) the greatest amount by which this weight may differ from Angela's actual birthweight?

12 Kevin surveyed the pupils in his year at school to discover where they had been for their main family holiday, if any, last year. He included himself in the survey. He displayed his results in a pictogram as shown.

(a) How many pupils stayed at home?

(b) Where was the most popular destination?

(c) How many pupils went to Greece?

(d) How many pupils are in Kevin's year at school?

Holiday destinations

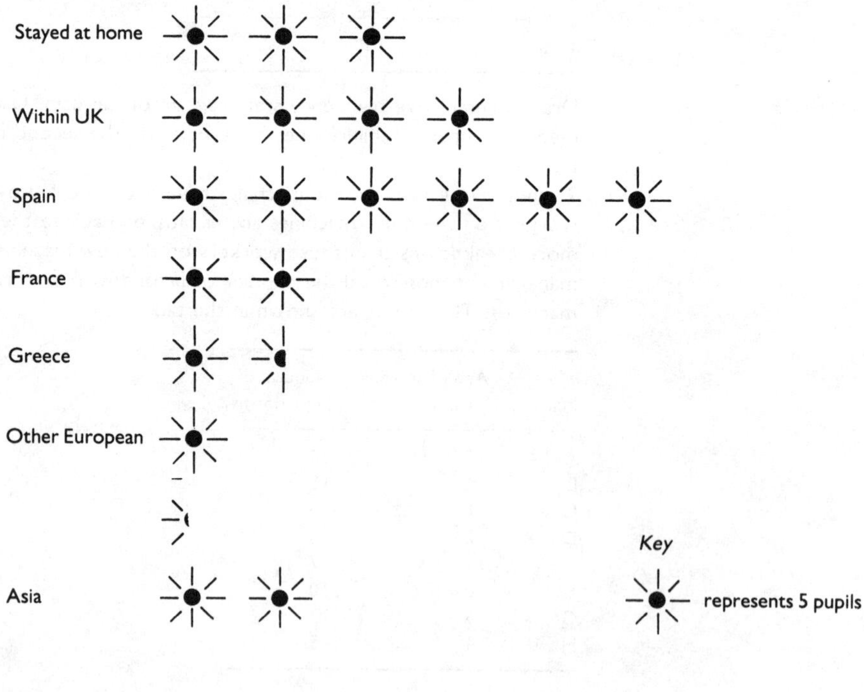

13 The lengths of time that a machine was stopped for routine maintenance during one month were noted. The times were recorded correct to the nearest minute and are shown in the table.

Stoppage time (mins)	Frequency
Less than 5	0
5– 9	12
10–14	16
15–19	23
20–24	10
25–29	10
30–34	7
35–39	2
Total	80

(a) What are the class boundaries of the modal class?

(b) Draw a histogram to show the data. (Suggested scale: 2 cm to represent five minutes on the horizontal axis, 2 cm to represent five machines on the vertical axis.)

14 Gemma always has a can of drink with her packed lunch. At the start of last week she noticed there were five cans of cola, three cans of lemonade and two cans of orangeade in the cupboard. She selected one of them at random before she went to school each day.

(a) What is the probability that she had lemonade on Monday?

(b) In fact, she had a cola on Monday. What is the probability that she had cola on Tuesday?

(c) She had cola on Monday and Tuesday. What is the probability that she had the same flavour of drink on Wednesday and Thursday?

15 To test opinion about the proposed construction of a ring road round Ohbury, a planning officer selects 50 Ohbury numbers from the telephone directory. He rings each number and asks the person answering the telephone, 'Do you agree that the construction of a ring road round Ohbury is to be welcomed?'

Give two reasons why this procedure is unlikely to produce reliable results.

Revision exercise 3

1 Use (a) component bar charts, (b) pie charts, to represent the following data sets. Comment on the particular features highlighted by the different presentations.

Marital status of adults in Cuebury

	Males (%)	Females (%)
Married	65	64
Single	21	15
Widowed	5	12
Divorced	6	5
Separated	3	4

2 The two-digit random numbers shown in the table were produced on Ian's calculator. Draw a stem-and-leaf diagram for the data set.

Random numbers

42	39	86	41	14	32	14	75	23	31
71	16	81	20	93	13	89	83	68	76
47	69	03	75	17	64	89	20	01	32
86	40	19	38	21	37	18	47	99	37
27	09	00	52	59	55	78	01	29	11

On the basis of this sample, do you think that Ian's calculator is a reliable producer of random numbers? Give reasons for your answer.

3 The heights of 500 men were measured to the nearest centimetre and are shown in the table.

Height (cm)	Number of men
160–164	3
165–169	12
170–174	48
175–179	122
180–184	158
185–189	117
190–194	34
195–199	6
Total	500

(a) Construct a cumulative frequency distribution.

(b) Draw an ogive (cumulative frequency curve) for the distribution. (Suggested scale: 2 cm for a height of 5 cm, 2 cm for 50 men.)

(c) Use your graph to estimate the median and the quartiles.

(d) Given that the shortest man measured 161 cm and the tallest was 198 cm, draw a box-and-whisker plot for this data set.

(e) Comment on your results.

4 A drinks company packages a fizzy drink in bottles, labelled 1 litre, and cans, labelled 330 ml. A random sample of 100 bottles was taken from the bottling line and the actual contents were measured correct to the nearest millilitre. The results are shown in the table overleaf.

Volume (ml)	Number of bottles
940– 949	1
950– 959	0
960– 969	3
970– 979	4
980– 989	12
990– 999	19
1000–1009	24
1010–1019	17
1020–1029	12
1030–1039	8

(a) Find the mean volume of fizzy drink per bottle and the standard deviation.

(b) A random sample of 100 cans was examined and the mean volume of the contents was 329.9 ml with a standard deviation of 8.6 ml. Calculate the coefficient of variation for the contents of (i) the bottles, (ii) the cans.

(c) Write a paragraph explaining the results to the manager of the company.

5 In 1987 Wyeshire County Council reviewed its provision of secondary education for children in the Zedbury district. As part of the review the council wanted to estimate the number of forms of entry needed in 1993, assuming 30 pupils per class. The following information was available:

The number of children in the appropriate age group resident in Zedbury at the start of 1987 was 2220, correct to the nearest 20.

Based on past trends, the number of these children likely to leave the district before 1993 was estimated to be 400 correct to the nearest 10.

The number of children in this age group coming to live in Zedbury by 1993 was estimated to be 230, correct to within 10%.

Use the given information to estimate

(a) the largest number of forms of entry needed in 1993,

(b) the smallest number of forms of entry needed in 1993.

6 In order to evaluate the effectiveness of its teachers, Yewbury college asks students to fill in a questionnaire, anonymously, at the end of every course. The majority of students are from overseas and English is not their first language. The students are asked to allocate the course teacher to one of five categories:

Top 10%, Above average, Average, Below average, Lowest 10%

as compared with other teachers within the college. This allocation has to be done under various headings, amongst which are:

(a) Appropriateness of material to level of course and students,

(b) Beginning and ending classes on time,

(c) Receptiveness to teacher-student interactions.

Give three criticisms of the above procedure, explaining clearly why it fails to produce reliable data.

7 In the town of Kaybury there are four environmental health officers, each of whom is responsible for a different geographical area. As part of their work, the officers had to survey the state of repair of 10% of the town's pre-1920 houses. A sample frame was available. The chief officer suggested that random sampling should be used but one of his juniors said that the stratified sampling, with houses stratified by geographical area would be better.

Give one advantage and one disadvantage of (i) random sampling, (ii) stratified sampling, for this survey.

The numbers of pre-1920 houses in each area are shown in the table.

Area	Numbers of houses (pre-1920)
A	1020
B	1480
C	570
D	1130

It was decided that stratified sampling would be used. How many houses were surveyed in each of the areas?

8 Find the mean (absolute) deviation (a) from the mean, (b) from the median, for the following data set.

9 3 9 11 13 5 10

9 In an Economics examination, the mean mark of all candidates is 65 with standard deviation 10. What is the standardised score of a student whose mark is 81?

All the marks were linearly transformed to a scale with mean 55 and standard deviation 14. What is the new mark of a student who scored 60 on the old scale?

10 Students taking a Physics course are assessed on both their practical and their written work. Seven students obtained the following marks. The practical marks are out of 30 and the written marks are out of 40.

Student	A	B	C	D	E	F	G
Practical mark (x)	11	13	14	17	18	21	26
Written mark (y)	20	23	25	28	30	34	38

(a) Display the marks on a scatter diagram.
(b) Find $\bar{x}$ and $\bar{y}$. Plot the point $(\bar{x}, \bar{y})$ on your diagram and draw in the line of best fit 'by eye'.
(c) If the equation of the line is $y = mx + c$, estimate m and c.
(d) Estimate the written mark of a student who scored 20 for the practical work.

11 The table shows the quarterly sales of a clothing manufacturer from 1985 to 1987.

Sales (£000s)

	Quarter			
Year	1	2	3	4
1985	52	104	34	113
1986	67	108	42	120
1987	83	120	57	135

(a) Plot the data on a line graph.
(b) Comment on the main features of the data.
(c) Calculate moving averages over an appropriate period to remove seasonal variations.
(d) Plot the moving averages on your graph and draw in the line of best fit through these points.
(e) Estimate the average seasonal variation in each of the four quarters.

12 A manufacturing company uses three raw materials in a production process. The prices of these raw materials in 1980 and 1985 are shown in the table, together with the mean monthly quantity used.

Raw material	Price (£) per tonne 1980	1985	Mean monthly quantity used (tonnes)
A	15	25	100
B	20	30	200
C	48	60	200

(a) For each raw material, calculate the price relative for 1985 with base year 1980. From 1980 to 1985 which raw material showed (i) the greatest actual price increase, (ii) the greatest percentage price increase?

(b) Using the given quantities as weights, find a weighted mean of price relatives index number for 1985 (1980 = 100). Comment on the result.

(c) Find the geometric mean of the price relatives. Why is a geometric mean sometimes used when constructing a composite index number?

13 The data in the table show the numbers of deaths occurring last year in Aybury and Bebury.

	Aybury		Bebury		
Age group	Population (000s)	Deaths	Population (000s)	Deaths	Standard population
Under 20	20	60	8	40	25%
20–44	15	80	10	50	30%
45–64	8	180	10	60	25%
65 and over	10	400	15	350	20%

Calculate

(a) the crude death rate for Aybury;
(b) the crude death rate for Bebury;
(c) the death rate of each age group in Aybury;
(d) the death rate for each age group in Bebury;
(e) the standardised death rate for Aybury;
(f) the standardised death rate for Bebury.

Comment on your results.

14 From a life table it is known that the probability of a man aged 30 living to at least 65 is 0.76. An insurance salesman sells life policies to four men, all aged 30. What is the probability that in 35 year's time

(a) all four will be alive,
(b) exactly two will be alive,
(c) at least one will be alive?

15 A company manufactures a product that sells for £40. The monthly sales are variable but, from past records, the probability distribution of sales is as shown in the table.

Monthly sales (units)	Probability
400	0.4
500	0.3
600	0.3

The company has fixed costs of £7000 per month but the cost of making the product varies according to the probability distribution shown.

Variable monthly cost per unit (£)	Probability
15	0.3
20	0.5
25	0.2

Use random numbers to simulate the sales and total costs for a period of 12 months and work out the resulting annual contribution to the profit of the company.

Index